KAREN BROWN'S

German

Country Inns & Itineraries

KAREN BROWN'S

German
Country Inns & Itineraries

Written by

CLARE BROWN JUNE BROWN KAREN BROWN

Sketches by Barbara Tapp
Cover Painting by Jann Pollard

Travel Press
Karen Brown's Country Inn Series

Travel Press editors: Karen Brown, June Brown, Clare Brown, Susanne Lau Alloway,
Iris Sandilands; Technical support: William H. Brown III; Aide-de-camp: William H. Brown

Illustrations: Barbara Tapp; Cover painting: Jann Pollard
Maps: Susanne Lau Alloway, Greenleaf Design & Graphics

Written in cooperation with Town & Country-Hillsdale Travel, San Mateo, CA 94401

Distributed USA & Canada: The Globe Pequot Press
Box 833, Old Saybrook, CT 06475-0833, tel: 203-395-0440, fax: 203-395-0312

Distributed Europe: Springfield Books Ltd., tel: (0484) 864 955, fax: (0484) 865 443
Norman Road., Denby Dale, Huddersfield HD8 8TH, W. Yorkshire, England,
A catalog record for this book is available from the British Library

Distributed Australia: Little Hills Press Pty. Ltd., tel: (02) 437-6995, fax: (02) 438-5762
1st Floor, Regent House, 37-43 Alexander St, Crows Nest NSW 2065, Australia

Distributed New Zealand: Tandem Press Ltd., tel: (0064) 9 480-1452, fax: (0064) 9 480 1455
P.O. Box 34-272, Birkenhead, Auckland 10, New Zealand

Library of Congress Cataloging-in-Publication Data

Brown, Clare
Karen Brown's German country inns & itineraries / written by Clare
Brown; June Brown & Karen Brown : sketches by Barbara Tapp ; cover
painting by Jann Pollard. -- 4th ed.
    p. cm. -- (Karen Brown's country inns series)
 Includes index.
 ISBN 0-930328-22-1 : $14.95
      1,   Hotels, Germany--Guidebooks.   2. Germany--Guidebooks.
I. Brown, June, 1949- . II. Brown, Karen. III. Title.
IV. Title: German country inns and itineraries. V. Series.
TX907.5.G3B76 1994
647.944301--dc20

93-29545
CIP

Dedicated with Love
to
Our Children

Alexandra, Richard, Emily, Christopher, William
Clare, Simon, Georgia, Alexander, Jonothan and Claire

KAREN BROWN TITLES

California Country Inns & Itineraries

English Country Bed & Breakfasts

English, Welsh & Scottish Country Hotels & Itineraries

French Country Bed & Breakfasts

French Country Inns & Itineraries

German Country Inns & Itineraries

Irish Country Inns & Itineraries

Italian Country Bed & Breakfasts

Italian Country Inns & Itineraries

Spanish Country Inns & Paradors

Swiss Country Inns & Chalets

Contents

Introduction

"ROMANTIK" is Germany's major promotional theme. The term translates as "romantic"—denoting the genius and passion of Germany's architects, artists, musicians and writers, and implying the richness and beauty of her landscape. But Germany is far more than just a beautiful romantic country of music and mountains. Germany is a prosperous country, her prosperity resulting from hard work, efficiency and prudence—characteristics displayed both in business and home life. This combination of a well-organized, tidy, clean, efficient country that also offers such romantic beauty creates a happy destination brimming with wonderful tourist possibilities to suit all tastes—whether it would be cruising down the Rhine on a luxurious ship or hiking in Bavaria with a sandwich and bottle of wine tucked in a knapsack on your back. But no matter where you travel there are certain experiences you will bring home in your packet of memories which are typically "German"—regardless of the region explored: down comforters fluffed high on the beds of every inn; linens hanging from shuttered windows airing in the freshness of the cool morning air; breakfast buffets heaped with a tempting assortment of breads, salami, cheeses and jams; pretty barmaids carrying heavy steins of icy beer to laughing customers sitting at tables under the chestnut trees; hearty meals of good "home cooking" always served in all-too-generous portions; chambermaids scrubbing floors until they glisten; wood stacked so neatly, so perfectly, that one wonders if any logs less than perfect were discarded. You will also bring home the memory of the graciousness of the Germany people. "Gruss Gott" is a greeting that replaces "Guten Tag" or "Morgen" in regions bordering Austria, but regardless of the phrase or region, Germans are wonderful hosts and extend a warm welcome.

ABOUT THIS BOOK

This book is divided into four sections. The first section, *Introduction*, gives a general overview of Germany. The second section, *Itineraries*, outlines itineraries throughout Germany to help you plan where to go and what to see. The third section, *Hotel Descriptions*, is our recommended list of places to stay, appearing alphabetically by town. This list provides a wide selection of hotels throughout Germany in all price ranges with a description, an illustration and pertinent information provided on each one. The fourth section, *Maps*, pinpoints each of the recommended hotels.

BEER

Germany's national drink, beer, is served at beer halls and taverns, particularly in the southern part of the country. Munich is the capital of beer drinking and a visit would not be complete without taking in the Hofbrauhaus beer hall and in summer, visiting a German beer garden such as the one in the Englischer Garten. Brewed across the nation, the beers vary from light (helles) to dark (dunkles). From bottled beer served in glasses to foaming steins filled straight from the barrel, beer is consumed in copious quantities.

BOATS and RIVER CRUISES

Köln-Düsseldorfer German Rhine Line (known as KD for short) operates cruises and ferry service on the Rhine, Moselle and Elbe Rivers. These excursions vary in duration from several hours to a week. No reservation is needed for day-ferry boat services—you buy your ticket from the pier before departure. The most popular day trips are: along the Rhine's most handsome stretch between Cologne and Mainz, the half day trip through the Rhine gorge between Koblenz and Mainz, along the Moselle river between Koblenz and Cochem and the Elbe trip between Dresden and Hamburg. Schedules can be easily obtained while in Europe. Cruises can be booked in advance through the KD Cruise Line, 170 Hamilton Avenue, White Plains, NY 10601, tel: 914-948-3600, or KD Cruise Line, 323 Geary Street, San Francisco, CA 94102, tel: 415-392-8817. Note: In addition to its long-time popular cruises on the Rhine and Moselle, in 1994 the KD Line added cruises between Nuremberg and Budapest and Nuremberg and Vienna.

BUSES

In conjunction with the German Railroad, buses make the trip along the "Romantic Road" between Füssen and Würzburg. Principal stops include Rothenburg ob der Tauber and Dinkelsbühl. Additional service connects Mannheim, Heidelberg and Rothenburg. If you have a German Flexipass or a Eurailpass, the price of the bus ticket is included and you do not need to pay a supplement. The buses operate on a seasonal basis. The schedules are published in the Thomas Cook European Timetable—a reference guide used by most travel agents or one you can special order through your book store.

CURRENCY

The unit of currency in Germany is the Deutsche Mark, abbreviated to DM. One DM is equivalent to 100 Pfennigs. Banking hours vary, but banks are usually open weekdays from 9:00 am to 12:00 pm and again from 2:00 pm to 3:00 pm. Currency exchange offices are located at airports and railway stations in large cities. As a convenience to their guests and clients, hotels and department stores will also often convert foreign currency to Deutsche Marks.

DRIVING

CAR RENTALS: All major car rental companies are represented throughout Germany at airports and in the city areas. There is a definite price advantage to reserving and pre-paying for a car rental. Remember you will have to pay taxes and insurance locally. Also, depending on the policies and locations of a particular company, there are often surcharges for returning a car to a place other than the originating rental location. Automatic transmission is usually available only in larger, more expensive models.

DRIVER'S LICENSE: Your local driver's license, which of course must be current, is accepted in Germany. Some people prefer to travel with an International Driver's License, although this is not mandatory. The minimum driving age is 18.

DRUNK DRIVING: It is a very serious offense to drive when you have been drinking. Anyone with an alcohol blood level of 0.8 % (less than two beers) is considered "under the influence." Very important—please be aware that in the eastern part of Germany, absolutely any alcohol at all in the blood is considered a serious offense (in other words, absolutely *NO* drinking and driving in eastern Germany).

GASOLINE: Gasoline is very expensive so budget this as part of your trip if you are driving. Many of the large service stations will accept payment on your credit card.

ROADS: The German highway network consists of autobahns (similar to our freeways and marked with blue signs) and secondary roads (also excellent highways). Traffic moves fast on the autobahns where, unless signposted, there is no speed limit. On the secondary highways, and on all autobahns in what was formerly East Germany, the speed limit is 100 kilometers (62 miles) per hour. The speed limit within city and town limits is usually 50 kilometers (31 miles) per hour. There are a few toll roads. These are usually over secondary mountain passes and are not always open.

SEATBELTS: It is mandatory and strictly enforced in Germany that all passengers wear seatbelts. Children under twelve must not sit in the front seat.

ELECTRICITY

The voltage is 240. Most hotels have American-style razor points for 110 volts. If you want to take your favorite hairdryer, make certain it has dual voltage and purchase a kit of various sized and shaped electrical plugs.

ENGLISH

Many Germans speak some English. In large cities, airports, major hotels and most tourist destinations you will have no problem communicating in English, but in eastern Germany, small towns, cafes, rural railway stations and the like, you may find that very little English is spoken.

FESTIVALS AND FOLKLORE

With claim to such legends as "Snow White" and "The Pied Piper of Hamelin" and with a colorful history, the Germans can find numerous occasions for festivals and celebrations honoring everything from children saving a town from destruction to the completion of the grape harvest. Since these are staged over the course of the year, it would be difficult to experience them all when on a limited holiday but it might prove rewarding to plan your travel dates to coincide with a particular festival. (During special festivals, be aware that hotel rates frequently inflate to prices above what we show as the standard double.) Some of the possibilities are the following:

BAD DURKHEIM: 2nd and 3rd Sundays in September—Germany's largest wine and sausage festival

BAD HARZBURG: April 30—"Walpurgisfeier," the night the witches come to life for one night of merry celebration

BAD TOLZ: November 6—"Leonhardiritt," a filled-with-fun parade to honor the patron saint of animals.

DINKELSBÜHL: 3rd Monday in July—"Kinderzeche," a re-enactment of the children saving the town during the Thirty Years' War.

HAMELIN: Sundays in July and August—a re-enactment of the Pied Piper spiriting away the town's children.

HEIDELBERG: 1st Saturday in June, July and September—the castle is illuminated and fireworks are fired over the river.

KOBLENZ-BRAUBACH: 2nd Saturday in August—"The Rhine in Flames," the Rhine Valley between the towns of Koblenz and Braubach is lit by bonfires and floodlights.

MUNICH: late September and early October—"Oktoberfest," world's biggest beer festival.

ROTHENBURG: one Sunday a month in summer—"Maistertruk," a re-enactment of the drinking feat that saved the town from destruction during the Thirty Years' War.

ULM: Mondays in July—"Fischerstechen," jousting on boats.

FOOD

Food in Germany is plentiful and delicious and enjoyment of different regional dishes is a pleasure not to be resisted. To visit Germany and not experience the ambiance of a beer hall or relax at a sidewalk cafe and savor a "kuchen mit schlag" (pastry with whipped cream) would be to miss a truly German experience.

Breakfast or "Frühstuck" usually consists of a copious assortment of delicious rolls, wurst or sausages, patés, cheeses, homemade jams, country butter and often cereals, yoghurt or fresh cream. Lunch or "Mittagessen" is the main meal in Germany. Served customarily from noon to 2:00 pm, it generally consists of soup, meat and vegetables. However, when traveling, you might opt to save valuable afternoon time by stopping at a pub or beer hall for a simpler fare of hot sausage, sauerkraut and homefried potatoes accompanied by a glass of cold beer, or enjoying a wurst sold by street vendors. Afternoon coffee or "Kaffee" is popular, especially on weekends, and is served approximately from 4:00 to 5:00 pm. Pastries and cakes are served "mit schlag," a thick helping of cream that makes any regional specialty a delight (albeit a caloric one). Dinner or "Abendessen" is usually enjoyed between 6:00 pm and 9:00 pm. When served at home it is usually a lighter meal but in restaurants you will find the same type of meals as at midday.

South of Frankfurt the menus highlight a variety of sausages, pork, salads, potatoes, dumplings or noodles; while in the north, fresh seafoods, vegetables, meat and ham dominate the selections. There are eating places available for any budget, from inexpensive sausage stands to plush elegant restaurants.

Portions are usually generous. Most countryside inns cultivate small gardens that provide their delicious salads and vegetables. Jams are often homemade, breads usually fresh from the oven. The hotel owners are frequently the chefs, and, if not, closely supervise the preparation of food. Except in tourist centers, the menus are printed only in German so take your dictionary to dinner with you.

GEOGRAPHY

Germany is a very large country when compared to her neighbors the Netherlands, Belgium, Luxembourg, Switzerland, Austria and Czechoslovakia, yet small in size when compared to America. There is great geographic diversity: sand dunes of northern islands, heathered moorlands, thick forests where the Brothers Grimm found Sleeping Beauty, the Rhine Gorge flanked with castles, the picturesque Romantic Road, the Bavarian plateau, the towering Alps.

HISTORY

Germany has always been a country of shifting frontiers. Since Roman times the country was continually subdivided in an ever-changing mosaic of "units" of different degrees of political importance. These "units" comprised states, kingdoms, Hanseatic cities, free towns, principalities and ecclesiastical fiefs. Held together by leagues, reichs, confederations and empires, German history fills vast volumes of European history. In 1871 Germany became a united country and this unity lasted until 1945 when the country was occupied by Britain, France, America and Russia (the Allies) at the conclusion of World War II. In 1949 the British, French and American sectors were linked as the German Federal Republic—West Germany. The Russian sector developed into the German Democratic Republic (East Germany). In November 1989, the "Wall" came crashing down, astounding and inspiring the entire world. It took only until the fall of 1990 until Germany was officially again a single nation with plans to move the capitol once again to Berlin.

This nation has been home to some of the world's most influential leaders: Charlemagne, Frederick Barbarossa, Otto the Great, Martin Luther, Frederick the Great, Bismarck and Adolph Hitler. Although there has been an impressive list of German leaders who have shaped world history, it is Ludwig II, King of Bavaria, who is most often remembered by tourists. Ruling Bavaria between 1864 and 1886, Ludwig II is fondly known as Mad King Ludwig. A notable patron of art and music, he idolized and subsidized the composer Richard Wagner. Lonely, eccentric, cut off from the mainstream of world politics and obsessed by the glories of the past, Ludwig sought solace in a fanciful building scheme—his Bavarian castles of Neuschwanstein, Herrenchiemsee and Linderhof. His building extravaganzas brought Bavaria to the brink of bankruptcy and, before he could begin on further palaces, he was declared unfit to rule by reason of insanity. Within a week of his deposition, Ludwig drowned in Lake Starnberg (under circumstances always shaded with mystery). Your travels will be enriched if you do some reading before your departure to comprehend and associate all that you will see.

HOLIDAY ROUTES

Germany has a network of holiday routes that allow visitors to follow special interest, scenic and historical routes. All are signposted and indicated on most maps. A sampling of the more popular routes are:

BURGENSTRASSE—The Castle Highway between Mannheim and Nürnberg.

DEUTSCHE ALPENSTRASSE—The German Alpine Way between Berchtesgaden and Lindau.

DEUTSCHE MARCHENSTRASSE—The German Fairytale Route between Hanau and Bremen.

DEUTSCHE WEINSTRASSE—the German Wine Road between Schweigen and Bockenheim.

MOSELWEINSTRASSE—The Moselle River Wine Route between Trier and Koblenz.

ROMANTISCHE STRASSE—The Romantic Road between Würzburg and Füssen.

SCHWARZWALD HOCHSTRASSE—The Black Forest High Road between Baden-Baden and Freudenstadt.

HOTELS

HOTEL—BASIS FOR SELECTION: This guide does not try to appeal to everyone's taste in choice of accommodation. Our selection of places to stay is definitely prejudiced: each hotel included is one we have seen and liked. It might be a splendid 12th-century castle crowning a mountain top or a simple vintner's house with 5 rooms perched on the banks of the Moselle. But there is a common denominator—they all have charm. Therefore, if you too prefer to travel spending your nights in romantic wine houses, appealing little chalets, dramatic castles, thatched cottages, and 14th-century post stations, we are kindred souls, you can follow the paths we have suggested and each night will be an adventure.

For some of you, cost will not be a factor if the hotel is outstanding. For others, budget will guide your choices. The appeal of a simple little inn with rustic wooden furniture will beckon some, while the glamour of ornate ballrooms dressed with crystal chandeliers and gilded mirrors will appeal to others. What we have tried to do is to indicate what each hotel has to offer, and describe the setting, so that you can make the choice to suit your own preferences. We feel if you know what to expect, you will not be disappointed, so we have tried to be candid in our appraisals. Also, some hotels are ideal for children while others are definitely adult oriented. We have indicated these special situations under the hotel's description.

HOTELS—CREDIT CARDS: Whether or not a hotel accepts payment by credit card is indicated in the *Hotel Description* section using the terms: none accepted, AX-American Express, MC-MasterCard, VS-Visa, or simply, all major.

HOTELS—HOW TO ECONOMIZE: For those of you who want to squeeze the most value out of each night's stay, we have several suggestions:

AVOID SPECIAL EVENTS: Avoid special holidays and festivals when the prices can soar. Many hotels have special rates (above the ones we quote) during prime time.

OFF SEASON TRAVEL: Travel off season—in the off season the rates are sometimes lower (except for the ski resorts where winter prices sometimes exceed those in summer).

HUB TRAVEL: Stay out in the countryside instead of in the cities. We cannot stress enough how much more value you receive when you avoid the cities—especially the tourist centers. Of course stay right in the heart of town if you are not watching your budget, but if you are trying to squeeze the greatest value from your Deutsche Mark, choose hotels in the countryside and take side trips to visit the pricey tourist centers.

MEAL PLAN: Ask about rates with meals included—if staying for three days or longer, many hotels offer a special rate including meals: MAP (Modified American Plan) means two meals a day are included, AP (American Plan) means three meals a day are included.

ROOM WITHOUT PRIVATE BATH: Ask for a room without a private bathroom—some hotels have very nice rooms, usually with a washbasin in the room, but with the bathroom "down the hall."

WEEKLY RATE: Ask if there is a weekly rate—frequently hotels will offer a price break for guests staying a week or more. If traveling with children, ask if there is a special family suite at a lesser price than separate rooms.

HOTELS—RATES: Rates given in the *Hotel Description* section are those quoted to us by the hotel for the 1994 high season. The rates given are for two people sharing a room, including tax, service and breakfast. (Breakfast in Germany is usually a hearty buffet featuring cheeses, cold cuts, cereals, fruit and an assortment of breads, but in some hotels, breakfast can be a continental affair consisting of only tea or coffee and rolls.) Some hotels have suites at higher prices. Also, throughout Germany, during festivals, conferences, or special market fairs, the rates increase. Please consider the rates we give as a guideline and always check prices and terms when making a reservation. Hotels do not guarantee their rates and prices are always subject to increase. Rates are quoted in Deutsche Marks.

HOTELS—RESERVATIONS: People frequently ask, "Do I need a hotel reservation?" The answer really depends on how flexible you want to be, how tight your time schedule is, in which season you are traveling, and how disappointed you would be if your first choice is unavailable. Reservations should always be made in advance for the major tourist cities during the peak season of June through September, and also during certain special events such as Oktoberfest in Munich or the Passion Play in Oberammergau. Space in the countryside is a little easier, but if you have your heart set on some special little inn, to avoid disappointment make a reservation. Be aware though that reservations are confining. Most hotels will want a deposit to hold your room and frequently refunds are difficult should you change your plans—especially at the last minute. Suggestions for various ways to book hotels are as follows:

FAX: If you have access to a fax machine, this is probably the most efficient way to reach a hotel. With a fax there is less of a chance for a misunderstanding because you have your response in "black and white." The majority of hotels in Germany now have fax numbers that are listed in the back of the book under each hotel listing. Be specific as to your arrival and departure dates (spelling out the month), number in your party, and what type of room you want. And, of course, be sure to include your fax number for their response. You can photocopy and use the request letter written in German and English (following the Map Section) for your fax. The system is the same as dialing a telephone number: Dial 011, next the country code 49, then the city code (dropping the 0 in front of the city code), then the fax number. Should for any reason, you need to fax a hotel while *WITHIN* Germany, you need to include the 0 before the city code.

GAST IM SCHLOSS: You will notice that many of the castle-like hotels listed in the *Hotel Description* section at the back of this guide have the notation "Gast im Schloss," which translates into English to "Guest in a Castle." This indicates that the hotel belongs to an affiliation of historical castle hotels that have individual style and charm. Most of these places to stay are in proper castles, although some are in charming old mills or romantic manor houses—the common denominator is that they must be in an old structure of historical charm. All of the Gast im Schloss hotels can be booked directly through the head office in Germany. When you call or fax, you can book several hotels at one time. To make a reservation for any of the Gast im Schloss hotels, contact:

Gast im Schloss, Postfach 120620, 68057 Mannheim, Germany
Telephone: (0621) 12.66. 213, Fax: (0621) 12.66.212

LETTER: If you start early, you can write directly to the hotels and request exactly what you need. Clearly state the following: number of people in your party; how many rooms you desire; whether you want a private bathroom; date of arrival and date of departure; ask rate per night and if a deposit is needed. When you receive a reply, send the deposit requested and ask for a receipt. NOTE: When corresponding with Germany, be sure to spell out the month. Do not use numbers since in Europe they reverse the format used in the United States—such as 6/9 means September 6, not June 9. Allow four weeks for an answer. Although most hotels can understand a letter written in English, you will find at back of the Map Section, a letter written in German with an English translation. Photocopy it and use it for your actual request letters (and/or faxes).

ROMANTIK HOTELS: You will notice many hotels in this guide are prefaced by the name "Romantik." This designates the hotel as belonging to an affiliation of inn keepers who have a similar standard of hospitality and charm. To become a member, the hotels must have many of the qualities that we also look for in a hotel—a romantic ambiance, owner managed, historical building, warmth of welcome, and a good kitchen. Reservations can be made directly to the hotel, or through your travel agent, or, if in the United States, through Euro-Connection (telephone 800-645-3876). If you have at least 14 days prior to your arrival, another option is to book directly with the Romantik Hotels' head office in Germany (there is no booking fee). Their address is:

Romantik Hotels, Postfach 1144, 63786 Karlstein, Germany
Telephone: (06188) 95.020, Fax: (06188) 60.07

TELEPHONE: If you call direct, the cost is minimal and you can have your answer immediately. If space is not available, you can then choose an alternate. Ask your local operator when to call for the lowest rates. Also consider what time it is in Germany when you call (even the most gracious of owners are sometimes a bit grouchy when awakened at 3 am). Basically, the system from the United States is to dial 011 (the international code), 49 (Germany's code), then the city number (dropping the 0 in front of the city code), then the telephone number. If you are calling *WITHIN* Germany, do not drop the 0 before the city code. Most of the hotels have someone who speaks English. The best chance for finding the owner or manager who speaks English is to call when it is late afternoon in Germany.

TRAVEL AGENT: A travel agent can be of great assistance—particularly if your own time is limited. A knowledgeable agent can handle all of the details of your holiday and "tie" them together for you in a neat package including hotel reservations, airline tickets, boat tickets, train reservations, ferry schedules, theater tickets, etc. For your airline tickets there will be no service fee, but most travel agencies make a charge for their other services. The best advice is to talk with your local agent. Be frank about how much you want to spend and ask exactly what he or she can do for you and what the charges will be. If your travel agent is not be familiar with all the small places in this guide (many are so tiny that they appear in no other major publications), you can loan him or her your book—it is written as a guide for travel agents as well as for individual travelers.

UNITED STATES REPRESENTATIVE: Some hotels have a United States representative through whom reservations can be made. Many of these representatives have a toll free telephone number for your convenience. This is an extremely convenient and efficient way to secure a reservation. However you might find it less expensive to make the reservation yourself since sometimes a representative makes a charge for his service, reserves only the more expensive rooms, or quotes a higher price to protect himself against currency fluctuations and administrative costs. Furthermore, usually only the larger or more expensive hotels can afford the luxury of a representative in the United

States. Nevertheless, if you understand that it might cost you more, contacting the hotel representative is an easy, very convenient way to make a reservation. If a hotel has a representative, the name and telephone number for the representative are listed as the last line in the hotel's description.

INFORMATION

Within Germany, a big, blue "I" denotes the location of the tourist information booths in all major towns, train stations, airports and tourist centers. Before you go, information can be obtained from the German National Tourist Offices.

German National Tourist Office, 122 East 42nd Street, 52nd Floor
New York, NY 10168, U.S.A., tel: (212) 661-7200, fax: (212) 661-7174

German National Tourist Office, 11766 Wilshire Blvd., Suite 750
Los Angeles, CA 90025, U.S.A., tel: (310) 575-9799, fax: (310) 575-1565

German National Tourist Office, Nightingale House, 65 Curzon Street
London W1Y7PE, England, tel: (071) 495-3990, fax: (071) 495-6129

German National Tourist Office, 175 Bloor Street, North Tower, 6th Floor
Toronto, Ontario M4W3R8, Canada, tel: (416) 968-1570, fax: (416) 968-1986

German National Tourist Office, Lufthansa House, 143 Macquarie Street, 9th Floor
Sydney 2000, Australia, tel: (021) 367-3890, fax: (021) 367-3895

ITINERARIES

The second section of this guide outlines itineraries throughout Germany. You should be able to find an itinerary, or section of an itinerary, to fit your exact time frame and suit your own particular interests. You can custom tailor your own vacation by combining segments of itineraries or using two "back to back."

The itineraries do not indicate a specific number of nights at each destination. We cannot, however, help adding our recommendation: *DO NOT RUSH*. Learn to travel as the Europeans do. Allow sufficient time to settle into a hotel properly and absorb the special ambiance each has to offer. Use your imagination. If part of an itinerary seems especially appealing, choose one of the hotels as a hub; settle in and go out each day to explore the countryside. If the recommended hotel (or hotels) in the town we suggest as an overnight stop are not available (or do not appeal to you), look at the itinerary map at the front of the itinerary where alternate towns with recommended hotel places to stay are marked with a star.

MAPS

ITINERARY MAPS: At the beginning of each itinerary a map shows the itinerary's routing, places of interest along the way, and alternate towns with recommended hotels. These itinerary maps are artist drawings, not to exact scale, and should be considered as no more than an overview. To supplement our routings, you will need a set of detailed maps that will indicate all of the highway numbers, autobahns, alternative little roads, autobahn access points and exact kilometers. Our suggestion is to purchase a comprehensive set of city maps and regional maps before your departure, and with a highlight pen mark your own "personalized" itinerary and pinpoint your city hotels.

HOTEL LOCATION MAPS: At the back of the book is a key map of the whole of German plus four regional maps showing each recommended hotel's location. In order to find which of the four regional maps highlights the town where your hotel is located, the pertinent map number is located on the *top line* of each hotel's description. There are so many towns on these regional maps that it might be difficult to find the one you are looking for. To make it easier for you to locate your hotel, on the *bottom line* (or next to the bottom line) of the hotel's description, we give some clues (example: Lübeck: 66 km NE of Hamburg, 92 km SE of Kiel).

SUGGESTED MAPS: If you live in a metropolitan area you should have no problem buying maps in a travel-oriented bookstore. If not, your local bookstore should be able to place a special order. There are many excellent maps on the market, but be sure to buy one with an index. Our personal preference for Germany are the Rand McNally Hallwag maps (there are Rand McNally stores in many major cities so Hallwag maps are readily available). Depending upon your itinerary, you need either the Hallwag map of "Southern Germany" or their map of "Northern Germany"—or both. If you are going into the northeastern region (previously called "Eastern Germany") you will need to purchase the Hallwag map that covers the whole of Germany. Each Hallwag map comes with a small index booklet to help you find the towns you are seeking. Almost every town in our guide can be found on these maps.

RESPONSIBILITY

Our goal in this guide is to outline itineraries in regions that we consider of prime interest to our readers and to recommend hotels that we think are outstanding. All of the hotels featured have been visited and selected solely on their merits. Our judgments are made on the charm of the hotel, its setting, cleanliness, and above all the warmth of welcome. No hotel ever pays to be included. However, no matter how careful we are, sometimes we misjudge a hotel's merits, or the ownership changes, or unfortunately sometimes hotels just do not maintain their standards. If you find a hotel is not as we have indicated, please let us know, and accept our sincere apologies. We are sorry when hotels have changed and are no longer as we describe them. The rates given are those quoted to us by the hotel. Please use these figures as a guideline and be certain to ask at the time of booking what the rates are and what they include. As a source of information for our American readers, we list various hotel representatives in the back of the guide. We receive no compensation for mentioning these hotel booking services. We are in no way affiliated with any of the hotel representatives and cannot be responsible for any reservations made through them nor money sent as deposits or prepayments.

SHOPPING

Most shops are open Monday through Friday from 9:00 am to 6:00 pm and Saturday until noon or 2:00 pm. Many small shops close for an hour or two in the middle of the day when the shopkeeper goes home for lunch. In resort areas, some of the shops are open seven days a week.

You will discover the same consistently high standard of products throughout Germany as a group of well-known manufacturers distribute their products nationwide. Price variations are minimal. The department stores are large and display a magnificent assortment of items. In the cities some of Germany's larger department store chains to watch for are Kaufhof, Hertie, Karstadt and Horten, as they usually have an excellent souvenir department and competitive prices. Some favorite items to take home are:

CAMERAS: German cameras are magnificent: Leica is perhaps the most famous name.

CARS: Since Germany is the home of Volkswagen, Porsche, Mercedes and BMW, many travelers consider purchasing a car while in Europe, driving it while on vacation (thus saving car rental costs) and then shipping it home. If you are considering this option, be sure to do thorough research and advance planning before leaving home.

CHINA: Meissen, Nymphenberg and Rosenthal china is exquisite and expensive.

CLOCKS: From the region of the Black Forest come the charming traditional cuckoo clocks and the handsome desk clocks.

DIRNDLS: From the region of Bavaria, dirndls are charming pinafores usually of provincial print material worn with a white blouse and apron. All sizes are available from adorable tiny dresses for little girls to matching costumes for mommy and grandmother. In addition to all sizes, the dresses come in all fabrics and designs from gay daytime cotton models to fabulous pure silk high-fashion designer creations.

KNITWEAR: Hand-knitted sweaters, jackets and heavy wool knee socks are typical of the southern Alpine regions of Germany.

LEATHER GOODS: German leather goods are especially beautiful. The skirts, jackets and luggage are expensive, but absolutely gorgeous. A trip to southern Germany would not be complete without bringing home a pair of "Lederhosen," the sturdy leather shorts for all the men and little boys in the family, and perhaps a jaunty leather Alpine hat.

POTTERY: Beer steins make a useful souvenir from a German vacation. From Goebel come the whimsical Hummel figurines of Bavarian children in lederhosen and dirndls.

TOYS: Wooden toys for babies and small children are easy to tuck into the unoccupied spaces of your suitcase and fun to bring home as gifts. Especially appealing to children of all ages are the Stieff animals with the yellow button in their ear, available throughout Germany. It is possible to visit the factory in Giengen where these famous stuffed animals are made and find some bargains in their seconds shop.

WOOD: From Bavaria come tinkling music boxes and religious carvings. Nativity scenes and wooden Christmas tree ornaments make wonderful gifts.

SALES TAX: If you buy goods and have the store ship them out of the country you will not be charged Germany's 15% Value Added Tax. If you plan to carry your purchases home with you, you can be reimbursed tax paid by one of two methods: The first is to show all your receipts and merchandise at the Tax Check Service at the airport as you depart the country and they will reimburse you immediately less a small commission. The more time-consuming process involves asking for a tax refund form at the time of purchase or saving all receipts and getting forms from the customs office. When you leave the country or cross a border, be sure to have these forms stamped by the Germany customs official. If you are leaving by train, you must get off the train at the border and have the customs inspector stamp the form. Keep your purchases together because the customs agent will probably want to see what you have bought. After your trip, mail the forms back to the stores from which you made your purchases and they will reimburse the tax you paid in Deutsche Marks to your home address.

TELEPHONES

Calls made from your hotel room can be exceedingly expensive due to a surcharge system. The easiest and least expensive method to call the U.S.A., is to use one of the readily available telephone calling cards that are issued by AT&T, MCI, and Sprint. With these credit cards, you dial a local number from the hotel, and then your long distance call is charged to your credit card. Contact whatever telephone service you use, and ask how to set up a charge card.

TRAINS

From the high-speed ICE Train to the local trains that stop in every little village, Germany has a rail system that is easy to use, operates on time and embraces over 30,000 kilometers of track, enabling the tourist to criss-cross the nation with ease. Trains arrive and depart with clockwork-like precision. The cars are marked on the outside with their destination, first and second class, and within each there are seating areas for smoking and no smoking. Most trains of substantial size have a dining car, while those that do not often have a vendor who sells snacks and drinks from a cart.

In each train station there is usually an information desk where someone speaks English to assist you with schedules. Other services at large stations include currency exchange, accommodation information, shops and restaurants. Baggage carts are free.

For trains within Germany you can buy point to point tickets, a German Flexipass or use a Eurailpass. We highly recommend the Flexipass that permits unlimited rail travel in all of reunited Germany for five, ten, or fifteen days within the period of one month. Travel does not have to be on consecutive days. The super-high-speed ICE Trains that link many of the major cities in Germany (such as Hamburg to Munich, Hamburg to Frankfurt, and Berlin to Munich) are covered under the Flexipass, but reservations are necessary. The Flexipass also allows free travel on buses along the "Romantic Road" and reductions on river steamers on the Rhine and Moselle rivers. Your travel agent can purchase these tickets for you or you can contact their agent in the United States: DER Tours, 9575 West Higgins Road, Suite 505, Rosemont, IL 60018, telephone 708-692-4209. For Eurailpasses, or Flexipasses you can fax 800-782-2424. For point to point reservations and general information you can fax 800-282-7474. Note: In addition to being the agent in the United States for the German Flexipass and train tickets, DER offers many short tours that would fit in beautifully with many of the itineraries in this book. As an example, if instead of doing the "Romantic Road" on your own, you could take a DER package that includes hotels and bus transportation.

WEATHER

Rainfall occurs at all times of year. Autumn is mild and long, spring chilly and late, winter often snowy and cold, and summer can vary from cloudless and balmy through hot and muggy to cold and wet. Bring a woolly sweater, a fold-up umbrella, and a raincoat that can be taken off as the day warms, and you will be all set to enjoy Germany rain or shine, cold or warm.

WINES

Eleven different German wine-growing regions stretch from Bonn south to Lake Constance. Most of the wine is white wine. Each region produces a wine that is similar in taste to other wines of that region yet differs from wines produced in other parts of Germany. The wine regions often have a signposted route that combines sights and wineries in such a way that you work up a proper thirst. You can sample wines by the glass in taverns—weinstube and weinhaus. Restaurants offer house wines served in pottery jugs, and bottles can be selected from the wine list. But the most appealing way to celebrate German wines is to attend one of the more than 500 wine festivals that take place in the wine regions from July to late October—the German Tourist Office can give you details about festivals and tours.

When looking at German wine lists, selecting an appropriate bottle often seems a daunting task. If you can see the wine labels your job is made much easier. The label tells you the district, producer, type of grape used and the year it was bottled. In addition, look for labels with yellow borders or backgrounds to denote dry wine, and those with lime green to denote semi-dry wine. Sometimes the labels are not color-coded and the word "trocken" indicates dry and "halbtrocken" semi-dry. Labels grade the wine into "tafelwein"—tablewine, "qualitatswein"—quality wine and "qualitatswein mit pradikt"—quality wine with special attributes. Some of the wine regions also have special glasses "just for their wine" such as the amber-colored wine glass of the Rhine and the green-colored wine glass of the Moselle.

Germany by Rail, Boat and Bus

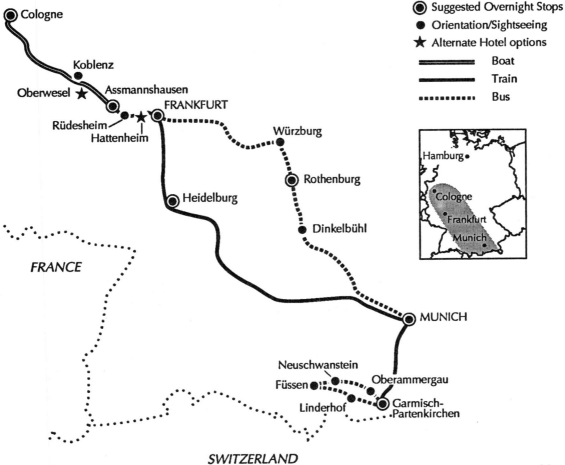

Suggested Overnight Stops
Orientation/Sightseeing
Alternate Hotel options
Boat
Train
Bus

Cologne

Koblenz

Oberwesel

Assmannshausen

Rüdesheim

Hattenheim

FRANKFURT

Würzburg

Rothenburg

Heidelburg

Dinkelbühl

FRANCE

MUNICH

Neuschwanstein

Füssen

Oberammergau

Linderhof

Garmisch-Partenkirchen

SWITZERLAND

Hamburg

Cologne

Frankfurt

Munich

23

Germany by Rail, Boat and Bus

Sit back, relax and enjoy traveling through Germany by rail, boat and bus. This itinerary was designed to link some of Germany's loveliest destinations in such a way that the transportation becomes part of the sightseeing experience. How much more enjoyable to savor the Rhine from the deck of a boat, or sit on a train or bus enjoying the scenery knowing that no one has to concentrate on the road. Frequently the lasting impressions you have of a holiday are of the people you have met and there is no better opportunity to get to know Germans and visitors from around the world than by traveling with them. The German Flexipass is the most convenient ticket for this itinerary. If you are also traveling elsewhere in Europe, consider the Eurailpass. Either card will relieve you of the frustration of purchasing point-to-point train tickets plus entitle you to free bus transportation on the Romantic Road or Castle Road buses and reductions in the cost of river steamers. The key to carefree travel is to pack lightly and limit yourself to one small suitcase. While all German stations provide luggage carts, more often than not there are long flights of steps to negotiate.

In the following itinerary approximate train and boat times have been included. Please note that these are given as a reference to show how the itinerary fits together. Schedules are constantly changing, so these times must be verified. Also boat, bus and some train services are seasonal, so be very meticulous in making your plans. All the latest times of trains, boats and buses used in this itinerary can be checked in a Thomas Cook European Timetable (ask your bookstore to special order one for you). To book a Eurailpass or Flexipass, contact your travel agent or DER Tours, 9575 West Higgins Road, Suite 505, Rosemont, IL 60018, tel: 708-692-4209, fax 800-782-2424.

Below are a few helpful words to know when traveling by public transportation:

ABFAHRT: Time of departure

BAHNHOF: Train station

BAHNSTEIG: Platform number at the train station

GLEIS: Track number

NACH: Traveling to

SCHIFFAHRT: Boat dock

With these few terms you should be in business.

ORIGINATING CITY   COLOGNE

Cologne is a delightful starting point for any vacation. A beguiling blending of old with new, a town just perfect for walking, and a populace that welcomes visitors combine to make this city a favorite. This prosperous town and port were a prime target of Allied bombers during World War II. Looking at the reconstructed city today, it is hard to realize that over 90 percent of the city was flattened.

The Dom (Cologne's Cathedral) occupies a square that is the heart of the city. Beloved by all, the cathedral's twin steeples and delicate twin spires are the city's landmark. The building is as beautiful inside as out. Next door to the cathedral, the Roman Museum is a must: its fabulous mosaic floor dates from the 2nd Century and its mock-ups of rooms in Roman houses are an easy, interesting way to get a feel for life in Roman times. The main shopping street, the Hohenstrasse, runs south from the cathedral and connects into the other main shopping street, the Schildergasse, which turns west towards the Neumarkt Square. All the major museums and churches are within easy walking distance of these two streets. Spend your day sightseeing and leave the evening free to explore the quaint old town that fronts the River Rhine. Here, set on narrow streets, you will find slender, gaily painted houses filled with bars and restaurants.

Before taking the early morning train, it is convenient to overnight in Cologne. In the back of the guide are listed three hotel recommendations, each quite different in facilities and ambiance. The Haus Lyskirchen, located just a few minutes' walk from center of the town near the River Rhine, is very simple, yet quiet and sedate. The hotel blends stark modern with country decor in a way that is not jarring. Another simple hotel with a colorful facade is the Stapelhauschen das Kleine, located on the colorful Fish Market Square (Fischmarkt). If you prefer a deluxe hotel, stay instead at the Dom Hotel. Although large and expensive, the Dom Hotel has a superb location in the center of town (if this is your choice, request a room with a view of the cathedral).

DESTINATION I   ASSMANNSHAUSSEN

The scenic boat trip down the Rhine has been a favorite of travelers for many years. These cruises are sold by your travel agent or can be purchased directly through KD Cruise Line, 170 Hamilton Avenue, White Plains, NY 10601, tel: 914-948-3600. If you have the pleasure of unlimited time, consider a leisurely cruise all the way from Amsterdam to Basel. However, in our estimation, the highlight of the trip is the short segment between Koblenz and Assmannshausen. This scenic portion is frequently portrayed on enticing travel posters and is the image that usually comes to mind when thinking of a Rhine cruise. Here the valley is at its narrowest, with steep banks enclosing the river in walls of green and once mighty castles looming on hilltops. To squeeze the most enjoyment from your journey, we suggest the following:

10:13 am depart Cologne by train
11:31 am arrive Koblenz

By taking a later train from Cologne, you can make a "tighter" connection in Koblenz, but it is fun to enjoy lunch in Koblenz, stroll around the old town, and allow ample time get to the dock to buy your ticket. Most of Koblenz was badly damaged in World War II, however many of the characterful old buildings have been restored.

2:00 pm depart Koblenz by boat
6:50 pm arrive Assmannshausen

Your modern boat is equipped for all weather: if it looks as though the day will be warm and clear, you can find a seat on the open deck; if it is cool and raining, you can watch the river churn by from the snug comfort of one of the heated lounges. Fabled for its beauty, the Rhine presents one vista after another. Majestic castles present themselves to be photographed, steep vinyard-covered banks glide by, and picturesque villages huddle along the river edge. As the boat slows to navigate the narrowest part of the gorge, the fabled Lorelei rock rises before you. Legend has it that the beautiful Lorelei, sitting atop her rock combing her golden tresses, so entranced the sailors with her singing that the rules of navigation were forgotten and their ships were dashed onto the rocks.

Many legends are told about this section of the Rhine, such as the story of the Sterrenberg and Liebenstein castles perched side by side high above the river bank. These castles supposedly belonged to two brothers whose hatred of each other was so intense that they built a high wall between their two adjacent forts. Another tale is of the seven maidens of Oberwesel castle. These pretty young damsels were so hard-hearted towards their suitors that the river capsized their boat and turned them into seven rocks.

Arriving at Assmannshausen, our recom-mended place to stay is the Hotel Krone, just a few-minute's walk from the pier. Upon request, the hotel will send someone to the pier to meet you and help you with your luggage. The hotel's vine-covered terrace and restaurant provide excellent food and a perfect position for watching all the parade of boats as they pass by.

Assmannshausen

The location of the Hotel Krone is superb, the dining room very attractive, the wisteria-covered terrace a romantic oasis, and the bedrooms (all recently refurbished) are decorator perfect. Note: Sometimes, when the river is low, boats cannot dock in Assmannshausen and stop instead at the nearby town of Rüdesheim. If so, you will need to take a taxi to your hotel.

DESTINATION II   HEIDELBERG

Allow some time this morning to explore the quaint old streets of Assmannshausen, then go to the train station to continue your journey. You will need to hip hop off and on trains today en route to Heidelberg.

10:54 pm depart Assmannshausen by train
11:31 pm arrive Wiesbaden

11:39 pm leave Wiesbaden by train
12:19 pm arrive Frankfurt Hauptbahnhof

 1:47 pm leave Frankfurt Hauptbahnhof by train
 2:42 pm arrive Heidelberg

Germany by Rail, Boat and Bus

Paralleling the river, the train passes through the vineyards of the Rheingau, then on to the spa town of Wiesbaden. From there it is a quick commuter ride on to Frankfurt's main train station where you might plan to eat a bite of lunch at Frankfurt's main train station called the Hauptbahnhof. It is quite a scene—a perfect place to people watch before turning south to Heidelberg. The tourist information office is just outside the Heidelberg train station, so pick up information pamphlets before taking a taxi to your hotel. In the *Hotel Description* section we describe two hotels, the Romantik Hotel Zum Ritter St Georg and the Zur Backmulde. If you are looking for a place to stay that offers charm combined with great value, the newly remodeled Zur Backmulde can't be beat.

History has been kind to Heidelberg: unlike so many less fortunate German cities, it has been spared the ravages of recent wars. Surprisingly though, it was the romantic operetta "The Student Prince" that put Heidelberg on the tourist map. The streets of its old town are a maze of cozy restaurants and lively student taverns. Above the town looms the famous ruins of its picture-postcard-perfect castle: you can walk up to the castle, but it is easier and more fun to take the mountain railway from the Kornmarkt. The castle is now mostly a ruin, but still great fun to explore, and offers spectacular views of the town and the river from the terrace. The very best views of the castle and the town are from the Philosophers' Walk on the northern bank of the Neckar river. Cross the Alte Brucke or Old Bridge spanning the Neckar—the Philosophers' Walk is clearly indicated by signs.

Boat lovers will enjoy a boat trip along the Neckar river. Operating only in summer, these go round trip from Heidelberg to Neckargemund.

DESTINATION III GARMISCH-PARTENKIRCHEN

There is excellent train service between Heidelberg and Munich. Trains leave every hour, but since you will be making a direct connection in Munich, one of the best connections is as follows:

12:07 pm depart Heidelberg by train
5:11 pm arrive Munich, Hauptbahnhof (main station)

5:33 pm depart Munich, Hauptbahnhof (main station) by train
6:59 pm arrive Garmisch-Partenkirchen

Lakes and mountains come into view as the train approaches Garmisch-Partenkirchen, considered one town yet in actuality two: Partenkirchen on one side of the railway track and Garmisch on the other. Garmisch is beautiful. No matter what time of year you come, the high Alpine peaks ringing the town provide a spectacularly beautiful setting and opportunities for skiing in the winter or hiking in the summer.

We list three hotels in Garmisch-Partenkirchen. All are excellent. One of our favorites is Posthotel Partenkirchen, centrally located in the heart of the oldest part of town. Its pink stucco facade has a deeply overhanging roof and in summer, red geraniums spilling from window boxes. With a trio of antique-clad dining rooms and an array of lovely guest rooms, Posthotel Partenkirchen provides a wonderful base for explorations of this especially picturesque area of Germany.

Although the less energetic can admire the view from a cable car window, Garmisch-Partenkirchen is a walker's paradise. Germans love to walk and you can join them on the well-marked trails, one of the loveliest of which is through the Partnachklamm Valley. Follow the road to the right of the Olympic ski stadium and take the Graseckbahn cable car to the Forsthaus Graseck. From here a trail leads to the narrow Partnachklamm gorge. You walk along a rocky ledge with a guardrail between you and the tumbling river, sometimes passing through rock tunnels and behind cascading waterfalls. You get a little wet and the gorge is chilly even in summer, but the experience is breathtaking. As you leave the gorge you pay a modest toll and find yourself back on the road leading to the Olympic ski stadium.

Not surprisingly, the finest view in Germany is from atop its highest mountain, the Zugspitze—remember to take warm sweaters for this excursion. The Zugspitze cog

30   *Germany by Rail, Boat and Bus*

railway departs from the Zugspitzebahnhof, next to the main railway, almost every hour on the hour. The train ascends through the valley and brings you out at the Hotel Scheefernerhaus below the summit of the Zugspitze. The train trip takes about an hour so try to plan your arrival to coincide with lunch at this scenic spot—a cable car departs about every half hour and whisks you the last 3 kilometers up the mountain. Enjoy the view, soak up the high Alpine sunshine and return to the valley on the other cable car for the ten-minute descent to the Eibsee Lake. From Eibsee you take a bus or taxi back into town.

King Ludwig II of Bavaria's dream was to ring his kingdom with five fanciful castles. Only three (Herrenchiemsee, Neuschwanstein, and Linderhof) were partially completed

Linderhof

before his death at age 40 in 1886. Raised in isolation at Hohenschwangau, Ludwig began his reign with great promise at the young age of 18. Before long though, his interest in politics diminished and, in a vain pursuit of happiness, he embarked on his monumental building spree of fairytale castles. The expense of the program and Ludwig's erratic behavior alarmed the government, who feared (probably justifiably) that Ludwig might bankrupt the country with his wildly extravagant projects. So they declared Ludwig unfit to rule by reason of insanity. Four days later Ludwig was found drowned under mysterious circumstances—supposedly suicide, but the world still wonders, "who done it?" But today the tourist benefits, as all of Ludwig's palaces are now museums. Of the three, Neuschwanstein is a must. On Mondays and Wednesdays a coach tour, leaving from Garmisch, incorporates a visit to Neuschwanstein and the adjacent Hohenschwangau Castle with a drive through the nearby towns of Füssen and Oberammergau.

Many travelers will immediately recognize Neuschwanstein, located high above the valley atop a rocky ledge, as being the inspiration for Walt Disney's Sleeping Beauty's Castle at Disneyland and Disneyworld. You begin to appreciate the effort that went into building this castle as you walk up the steep path to the fortress high above. The only way to decrease a half-hour uphill hike to a ten-minute one is to take a shuttle bus or horse-drawn wagon part-way to the castle.

In summer you may have to wait in long lines to tour the castle's fanciful interior, for this is understandably one of Germany's most popular sightseeing attractions. Designed by a theater set designer and an eccentric king, the interior is a romantic flight of fancy whose rooms afford spectacular views of Alpine lakes and snowy peaks. Ludwig greatly admired Richard Wagner and scenes from his operas are found throughout the decor.

At the end of the castle tour, if you are not too tired, walk up the Pollat Gorge to the Marienbrucke that spans the ravine above the castle: you will be rewarded with a spectacular view of the castle.

From the road at the foot of the castle, it is a short walk to King Ludwig's childhood home, Hohenschwangau Castle. Though the interior is somewhat heavy, it has a homey quality to it. It was here that Ludwig met his adored Wagner, and it was here that the young king lived while he kept a watchful eye on the building progress at Neuschwanstein.

Note: If your visit to Garmisch does not coincide with the coach tour, you can still visit the castle using the local bus to Füssen that leaves from the bus station at 8:00 am and drops you at the castle at 9:30 am. The early arrival means that you avoid the crowds. Upon arrival, visit the castle and take an afternoon bus into Füssen. The return bus to Garmisch leaves Fussen in the early evening.

Linderhof, the smallest of the three castles, is an afternoon bus tour from Garmisch. The ornate, low-lying building contains an opulent French rococo interior. But it is the formal Italian baroque gardens with their pools and cascades, formal flower beds and clipped box hedges that are most pleasing. The tour also includes Oberammergau, a village of traditional-style painted houses, home of the world-famous Passion Play, performed by the villagers every decade in the years ending with zero. The Passion Play was first performed in 1634 and has been performed consistently ever since. The town is loyal to the vow they made to God that if he protected their town from the Plague, they in turn would stage a religious play in thanksgiving. Every ten years the town bustles with activity as everyone in the village is involved in one way or another with the production. Oberammergau is also famous for its lovely wood carvings—a tradition that keeps the villagers busy between plays.

Ludwig's third castle, Herrenchiemsee, was modeled on the French palace of Versailles. Lying beyond this itinerary, it is found on an island in the middle of the Chiemsee.

Ringed by the Karwendel mountains, Mittenwald is a short train ride from Garmisch. From the railway station it is a delightful walk around this small town, known not only as a holiday resort, but also as a violin makers' village. Mittenwald violins are famous throughout the world and the Geigenbau (violin) Museum is well worth a visit.

When it is time to return to Munich, there are trains that leave at least once an hour. Below is just a suggestion—allowing time for a leisurely breakfast in Garmisch-Partenkirchen and arriving in Munich for lunch.

10:27 am depart Garmisch-Partenkirchen by train
11:51 am arrive Munich Hauptbahnhof (main station)

As you travel to Munich, the beautiful countryside whisks by and you soon find yourself at Munich's Hauptbahnhof. Before you leave the train station, visit the tourist office where you will be gladly supplied with maps and information. In the *Hotel Description* section we have a selection of places to stay in various price categories.

Munich has something to offer everyone, so be generous with your time in Germany's most popular city. You must visit the Marienplatz. Plan on being there at 11 am, 12 noon, or 5 pm (also at 9 pm in summer) for the glockenspiel performance. As the clock on the town hall chimes, little enameled copper figures emerge from arches around the clock and perform a jousting tournament. The cameras click; the crowds disperse. This whimsical show is fun, but Munich has many other attractions: fine buildings of all periods, renowned shopping streets, numerous magnificent museums filled with priceless treasures, music, theater, beer gardens under massive chestnut trees where quarts of beer and enormous pretzels are merrily served and consumed, beer halls like the Hofbrauhaus (Munich's largest), and the Viktualienmarkt filled with sausage stands, fruits and flowers. But Munich's greatest attraction is the Oktoberfest, sixteen days of merriment that ends on the first Sunday in October. What began as a wedding celebration in 1810 when Prince Ludwig married, has grown to be the world's largest folk festival. For further sightseeing suggestions please see Bavarian Highlights itinerary.

DESTINATION V ROTHENBURG OB DER TAUBER

You need to make reservations at least 3 days in advance for the bus trip on the Romantic Road. Reservations can be made at:

Deutsche Touring GMBH
Am Roemerhof 17
60486 Frankfurt am Main, Germany
tel: (069) 23.07.35 or 79.03.256, fax: (069) 70.47.14.

When you request a reservation, indicate date, where you want to go, and number of seats needed. The bus departs Munich's main train station (Hauptbahnhof) at bus stop 21 on Arnulfstrasse.

> 9:00 am depart Munich Hauptbahnhof by "Romantic Road" bus
> 3:00 pm arrive Rothenberg ob der Tauber.

If you have a Eurailpass or German Flexipass, the bus is free and you pay only a small fee for the transportation of your bag. The Romantic Road bus driver is accompanied by a charming hostess who gives a multi-lingual commentary on the places of interest you pass en route.

The further north the bus travels, the more picturesque the scenery and the towns. Passing through Donauworth and Harburg, the bus then stops briefly to pick up and drop off passengers in Nordlingen and Wallerstein and arrives in Dinkelsbühl in time for lunch.

You will find Dinkelsbühl a delightful small town of medieval gabled houses and cobbled streets encircled by a formidable wall. The long lunch stop gives you plenty of time for food, shopping and sightseeing. Many towns in this area were defeated and destroyed during the Thirty Years' War: Dinkelsbühl was conquered but saved from destruction by the children who pleaded with the conquering Swedes to spare their town. Every July the town commemorates the bravery of its children with the "Kinderzeche" (children's festival). Amble about—down narrow cobblestoned streets, by picture-perfect little houses with their steep-peaked roofs and window boxes overflowing with flowers, and under painted oriel windows protruding from old houses' upper stories.

The bus continues down lovely country roads and through rolling countryside that becomes more beautiful as the day progresses. Saving the very best for last, you enter through the old city gates into Rothenburg ob der Tauber, truly one of Europe's most enchanting towns. Walking down the cobblestoned streets of Rothenburg is rather like taking a stroll through an open-air museum: there is history in every stone.

Rothenburg ob der Tauber

Rothenburg's old houses, towers and gateways that have withstood the ravages of the centuries are there for you to explore. Tourists throng the streets but somehow the town has the ability to absorb them, and not let their numbers spoil its special magic. Being such a popular tourist destination, Rothenburg has a rich choice of places to stay. Hotel space is usually at a premium, so it is definitely advisable to book a room in advance. In the *Hotel Description* section, we recommend a selection of four excellent places to stay in various price ranges.

Rothenburg has narrowly escaped destruction on several occasions. During the Thirty Years' War, General Tilly's army laid siege to the town and, despite spirited resistance, breached the walls. Tilly demanded that the town be destroyed and its councilors put to death. He assembled the town councilors to pass sentence on the town and was offered a drink from the town's ceremonial tankard filled with three and a half liters of the best Franconian wine. After having drunk and passed the cup among his subordinates, Tilly then, with a touch of humor, offered to spare the town and the lives of the councilors if one of its representatives could empty the tankard in one go. Nusch, a former mayor, who seems to have been good at drinking, agreed to try. He succeeded and saved the town. Apparently he slept for three days after the feat. Five times a day in the marketplace the doors on either side of the clock open and the figures of Tilly and Nusch re-enact the historic drinking feat.

In 1945 the Allies ordered Rothenburg destroyed as part of the war reprisals. An American General, remembering the picture of Rothenburg that hung on his mother's wall, tried to spare the town. His efforts were successful and although Rothenburg was somewhat damaged, the town remained intact. Rothenburg is a town to be explored on foot—buy a guide that includes a walking tour and set out to explore the town. Be sure to include a section of the city walls: climb the stairs to the walkway and follow the covered ramparts that almost encircle the town. The town itself is the most enchanting of sightseeing excursions, but should you want to include a bit of proper sightseeing (particularly if you have some adolescents in tow whose delights gravitate toward the gruesome), make a stop at the Mittelalterliches Kriminalmuseum (Museum of Medieval Justice). Here you will find displayed various instruments of torture and execution.

Rothenburg has many lovely shops and boutiques, one of the most enchanting of which is Kathe Wohlfahrt's Christkindlmarkt. Claiming to offer the world's largest selection of Christmas items, a tiny storefront near the market square opens up to a vast fairyland of decorated Christmas trees and animated Stieff animals.

DESTINATION VI   FRANKFURT

From Rothenburg, it is a pleasant bus journey back to Frankfurt. If you prefer to include more sightseeing en route, you can make plans to get off the bus in Würzburg and overnight there before taking a bus or train the next day to Frankfurt.

    4:30 pm depart Rothenburg ob der Tauber by bus
    8:15 pm arrive Frankfurt, Hauptbahnhof (main train station)

From there are fast trains to cities throughout Germany. However, if you can extend your holiday, we have several suggested itineraries that begin in Frankfurt. Browse through the book and see what appeals to you.

Germany by Rail, Boat and Bus

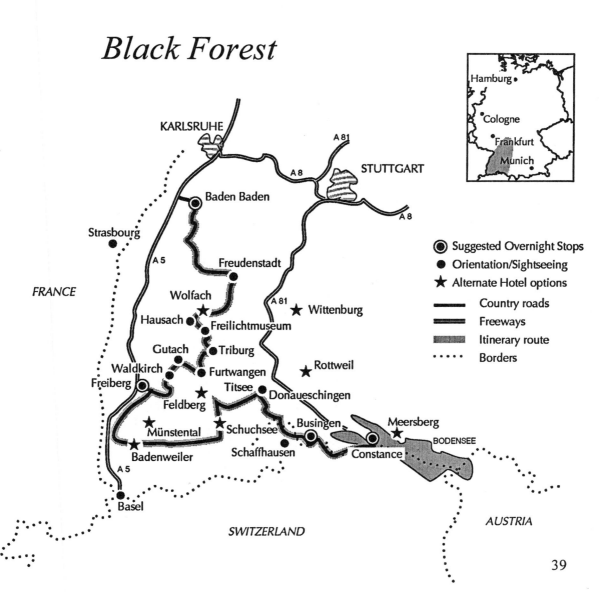

Black Forest

KARLSRUHE

A 81

STUTTGART

A 8

A 8

Strasbourg

Baden Baden

FRANCE

A 5

Freudenstadt

Wolfach

A 81

Wittenburg

Hausach

Freilichtmuseum

Gutach

Triburg

Rottweil

Waldkirch

Furtwangen

Freiberg

Titsee

Donaueschingen

Feldberg

Meersberg

Münstental

Schuchsee

Busingen

Badenweiler

Schaffhausen

BODENSEE

A 5

Constance

Basel

SWITZERLAND

AUSTRIA

Hamburg

Cologne

Frankfurt

Munich

◉ Suggested Overnight Stops
● Orientation/Sightseeing
★ Alternate Hotel options
── Country roads
═══ Freeways
▨ Itinerary route
•••• Borders

39

Black Forest

The Black Forest is a delightful mix of dense forests, gentle mountains, spectacular crevasses, wild rivers and quiet valleys. In both summer and winter, sports are popular—especially hiking, with 22,000 kilometers of hiking trails in the region. The Black Forest is gorgeous in spring through autumn when the weathered, country farmhouses are set against a landscape of various shades of lush green. In winter too, when quietly blanketed in snow, this is an area of great beauty. This itinerary follows the peaks and forests of the region.

The people show a strong pride in the cultural tradition of the Black Forest, folk costumes are still worn on Sundays, holidays and at weddings. The dress of the Gutachtal is the best known, featuring billowing black skirts and the Gutach straw hat—a costume that has become a symbol of the region. Unmarried women wear hats adorned with red pom poms, while married women wear more conservative black. Medieval market squares and patrician houses add grandeur and character to the towns and weathered great farmhouses dress the landscape..

People come to the Black Forest to rest and use its thermal spas and resorts, and, with health a main focus, fresh food accompanied by fine wines is demanded. Culinary specialties include: trout—fresh from streams, ham—smoked dark and flavorful, fruit brandies—most popular of which is a cherry liqueur known as kirschwasser, internationally recognized wines, and, of course, the ever-delicious Schwarzwalder torte mit schlag (Black Forest torte with cream).

If time and energy allow, try hiking without a backpack, a program whereby you set out each morning for a hike of 20 to 28 kilometers with only a thoughtfully packed lunch to carry, and when you arrive at your next hotel, your luggage will be waiting in your room. There are three packaged routes that are priced to include lodging and two meals. Each routing—"On the Track of the Stag," "Following the Path of the Clock Carriers," and "Around Feldberg"—takes approximately one week with five to seven hours of hiking scheduled for each day. Destination III on this itinerary, the Parkhotel Wehrle in Triberg, is involved in this program.

Constance, on the border of Switzerland and just a short drive from Austria, is a convenient starting point for this itinerary. This itinerary not only ties in very well for the traveler coming from Switzerland or Austria, but also connects beautifully with the "Bavarian Highlights" itinerary in this guide. A hint that this city was once a Roman fortress is hidden in its name—"Constance" derives from a Roman, Constantius Chlorus. In Roman times Constance had over 80,000 residents. Today Constance is still a large city whose surrounding vineyards produce some of Germany's finest wines.

Meersburg

Constance is located on der Bodensee. On a warm day, take the boat ride across the lake from Constance to Meersburg. This medieval town is certainly one of the loveliest old towns in Europe. Here you find the Alte Schloss: dating from the 7th Century, this is the oldest inhabited castle in Germany. You will also see in Meersburg the baroque style

Neue Schloss (or new castle) which is really not so new as it was built in the middle of the 18th Century.

There is a highly recommended side excursion by boat to the tiny island of Mainau. For garden lovers especially, this will be a real treat. The entire island has been transformed by the owner, a Swedish count, into a tropical paradise. The fragrant gardens bloom from March to October, but are at their peak of glory in May when tulips dominate the gardens and in October when over 20,000 dahlias color the island.

DESTINATION I   BUSINGEN

Travel a short distance by car from Constance, winding back and forth along the German-Swiss border to the small and popular village of Stein am Rhein.

Stein am Rhein

Colorful frescoes, intricate painted facades, stained glass windows, bright flower boxes and ornate wrought-iron signs dress the main square of this small riverside town. The

Roter Ochsen, a charming tavern-restaurant, is set on the square and since 1446 has tempted many to linger over a cold, refreshing beer. Allow time to visit the 450-year-old Rathaus (Town Hall) and the 11th-century Benedictine Abbey of St George that harbors a fine small museum, carved woodworkings and paintings.

From Stein am Rhein the road winds along the Untersee and the Rhine river, a graceful scene of green hills capped by monasteries, castles, citadels and charming villages (Diessenhofen, Gailingen, Obergailingen, Rheinklingen). Continue on to Busingen, a small enclave of German soil, encircled completely by Switzerland. Here you will discover a timbered mill that dates back to 1674. There is nothing more charming than a timbered, heavy beamed mill converted to an inn. The back of the Alte Rheinmuhle hugs the edge of the Rhine and from the first floor dining room an entire wall of windows exposes a blissful river scene. The hotel has earned an outstanding reputation for its cuisine and extensive wine cellar. The bedrooms are decorated in a country theme and some are furnished with antiques. Request, if possible, a room overlooking the Rhine. How romantic it is to enjoy a gourmet dinner in an enchanting restaurant, then to be lulled to sleep by the river flowing beneath your window.

DESTINATION II   FREIBURG

Although in Switzerland, Schaffhausen lies only 4 kilometers west of Busingen and merits a detour. Constructed upon the site where the busy Rhine river boat traffic was interrupted for portage around the nearby huge waterfall (the Rheinfall), Schaffhausen grew into a very important medieval city. It was granted a city charter in 1045, joined the Swiss Confederation in 1501, constructed its first hydro-electric works in 1866, and now supports a population of over 40,000. Schaffhausen is an elegant, medieval city that sits dramatically above the impressive Rheinfall. The old city is a complex of little winding pedestrian streets and passages studded by sidewalk cafes. It is fun to wander on Vorstadt, a main street where smart shops nestle into the first floors of old houses whose facades are ornately sculpted and painted. Shadowing the city and river is Munot Fortress, a circular keep constructed between 1564 and 1585. Uninhabited today, a watchman however continues to ring the old bell each evening, a signal to the revelers of other centuries that the town gate and public houses were soon to close.

A few minutes' drive west of Schaffhausen is the boat station where you board a small skiff that travels out to the base of a single rock that rises in mid-fall. You climb out of the small boat and clamber up the spray-soaked staircase to stand almost inside the cascade. Described by Goethe as "the source of the ocean," at 70 feet this is Europe's mightiest waterfall.

From Schaffhausen travel north in the direction of Donaueshingen and then west in the direction of Freiburg and the Black Forest. At Hinterzarten the road descends and winds down into a valley bounded by forest. The road cuts through narrow, high stone canyon walls: the drive is beautiful. The next village you come to is Falkensteig followed almost immediately by the town of Buchenbach where the densely forested valley opens up again with snow-capped mountains visible in the distance. En route to Freiburg you will pass the few houses that constitute the village of Burg and then the old barns set on the river's edge at Zeiten. The road then cuts through a wide valley where residential homes spread out on rolling low hillsides.

With a gorgeous setting at the base of the mountains, Freiburg is a delightful city. The tree-covered hills actually come right down within a block or two of the center of town. Full of character, the old section, founded in 1120, is laden with numerous quaint buildings, and the main square boasts a dramatically beautiful cathedral whose tall spires crest all vistas. Freiburg provides wonderful shopping and a lovely inn: on the church square, at the center of the old city, is Oberkirchs Weinstuben, a cozy wine tavern-hotel combination. This inn is located in two buildings. The principal building sits on the Munsterplatz in the shadow of Freiburg's striking cathedral, the other just a short cobblestoned block away. The Weinstuben serves a satisfying lunch or dinner in a very congenial, cozy atmosphere. Beamed ceilings, wooden tables, white linen and contented chatter set the mood for the stuben, a popular choice for dining. The 26 rooms, found either directly above the weinstube or in the neighboring building, are all comfortable and very attractive in a traditional decor. It is somewhat difficult to maneuver by auto through the pedestrian dominated area, especially during the Saturday market, but the hotel provides a map and directions for parking.

DESTINATION III   TRIBERG

Note: The route suggested from Freiburg to Titisee is a scenic circle trip through the southern region of the Black Forest. Depending on your time frame, you can include this journey or head directly north from Freiburg to the country market town of St Margen.

From Freiburg head south in the direction of Basel. This route travels at the base of orchards and vineyards through small villages, with a destination of Badenweiler only 30 kilometers away. Staufen is particularly pretty with a colorful market place, interesting Rathaus and castle ruins. Badenweiler is a sleepy German village near the Swiss border and is one of Germany's oldest spa towns with a history that dates back 2,000 years. The Romans discovered that the waters of Germany had remarkable curative powers and thus was born the German spa. Ever since, "taking the waters" in Germany, by drinking them or bathing in them, has proven a popular formula for those bent on healing, soothing, relaxing or beautifying the body. And because music, art and sports have long been considered as important to the restorative process as their medicinal waters, muds and herbs, the spas have become the meccas for those seeking a vacation that will provide for all the senses. Badenweiler is one of Germany's 250 registered spas, and the comfort of its visitors is the town's primary concern: all streets are closed to traffic after one each afternoon to provide for quiet and calm. This fascinating town has a Kurhaus, or concert hall, that boasts performances three times a day, seminars and tea in the afternoon. The concerts are held either indoors or in a lovely outdoor setting amongst flowers. An old bath house dates back 100 years, but a newly constructed bath house is set in a building of glass and metal with an all-encompassing exposure to the surrounding greenery. Take time to find a wonderful inn, the Romantik Hotel Sonne, and its owner, Herr Fischer. If time permits, linger here, as this hotel boasts as much tradition as the town and Herr Fischer is an exceptional host and maintains the excellence of service that previous generations of his family have established.

An excursion just 20 kilometers south will take you to Burgeln Castle. Set on an extension of the Blauen, it provides an impressive view of the surrounding countryside as far as the Swiss Alps.

From Badenweiler continue east in the direction of Schonau im Schwarzwald. You come first to the town of Schwieghof, located at the base of the mountains, then the road winds and loops up through small farming villages. After Neuenweg the road reaches the top of the summit where vistas open to rolling hills settled below. The drive then curves down, banked on one side by rocky cliffs and on the other side by green slopes. Hiking trails beckon in every direction. Wembach is a pretty village of weathered farmhouses and wooden stables with ski lifts dotting the edge of town.

A few kilometers further and you arrive at the town of T.-Gschwend. From here you can either continue north through the resort towns of Todtnau, Feldberg (nice view from the town's chairlift), on to Titisee, or detour a little longer by winding south in the direction of Todtmoos. Geschwend is a pretty village edged by farmhouses and topped by the steeple of its church. A lovely old lumber mill maintains a picturesque setting on the water's edge. Prag is a sweet hamlet tucked into the valley and cut by a rushing stream.

Todtmoos is a resort town whose setting is softened in winter by layers of snow. Ski lifts sit right on the edge of town. Soon after Todtmoos is the elegant spa town of Hochenschwand where you follow the Scharza river north in the direction of Schluchsee. Schluchsee is a lovely large lake, its shores unspoilt by development. At the town of Aha heavy forests line the road as it climbs up and then winds down to another lake and quiet valley. Titisee is a pretty little village on the banks of the lake with the same name, where the timberline comes right down to the water's edge, hiding a number of chalets nestled along the shores.

From Titisee travel a few kilometers north to the junction of the main road then head west in the direction of Freiburg for a few kilometers before veering north again to the country market town of St Margen. Set on a high plateau, the town boasts a baroque church. A few kilometers further on, is the resort town of St Peter whose abbey towers dominate the skyline. From St Peter the road twists and winds along the river and reaches a crest at Kandel. If you want to stretch your legs, note that it is about a fifteen-minute walk along the road to the pavilion for a view of the entire region. The panorama displays the Vosges mountains in France to the Rhine plain and the towers of St Peter's Abbey and the Feldberg and Belchen heights in the Black Forest.

The road curls down from Kandel to the charming town of Glotteral. Just outside Glotteral take the main road north in the direction of Freudenstadt. Waldkirch is a larger town with a pretty setting and a market place adorned by some 18th-century houses. Beyond the town of Gutach you come to Bleibach where you turn in the direction of Furtwangen. Before leaving Bleibach, allow yourself to be tempted to stop for a meal at the Hotel Stollen. Set on a corner of the main street, this charming timbered building has an excellent restaurant where even a simple request of soup and salad can prove to be a gourmet's delight, graciously served and beautifully presented. From Bleibach the road curves once more back along the base of the Black Forest through the villages of Simonwald and Obersimonwald, then climbs to Gutenbach and on to Furtwangen.

Not long after leaving Furtwangen you arrive at Schonwald, a small town whose history deserves mention. This is where the cuckoo clock was born. Schonwald was the home of Franz Anton Ketterer who at the beginning of the 18th Century thought of combining a clock with bellows. He incorporated a timepiece with a cuckoo carved in wood whose tiny bellows marked the hours with the notes of a cuckoo call. Records show that clocks were manufactured in the Black Forest as early as 1630, but when cuckoo clocks were invented, they became the rage.

The original cuckoo clocks were constructed entirely out of wood, from their inner works to wheels, while the more expensive specimens had glass bells that struck the hours. The dials with the traditional Roman numerals were painted and decorated with all sorts of colorful designs—flower wreaths, angels and peasant scenes. With winter snows and cold keeping families indoors, it was not unusual to find all members of the peasant households working on the clocks. Even now clock-making is a considerable industry for the region, and, although factories exist, the production of cuckoo clocks is still frequently a home business with the whole family working on the intricately carved boxes and painted dials.

Triberg, located in the heart of the Black Forest just a few kilometers beyond Schonwald, is an ideal spot to stay. The town has one main street comprised of clock shop after clock shop whose selection, variety and competitive prices will amaze you. Catering to tourists, they are all equipped to accept major credit cards and see that your clocks are shipped safely to the destination of your choice. At the town's edge is a romantic waterfall and local Black Forest Museum whose walls are covered in a display of clocks, crafts, regional costumes and a mineral exhibit. Tour buses will come and go from Triberg in the course of a day but overnighting here affords you the luxury of an evening to think about and select a clock.

The Parkhotel Wehrle, located in an ivy-covered yellow stone building, occupies a corner position on the main street. For those of you who are fortunate enough to have the Wehrle as a base for your travels, you will experience the professional care and welcome of the Blum-Wehrle family, the warmth of their hotel and the excellence of their restaurant. If you are looking for an antique ambiance, ask for one of the rooms in the original house (the annex by the swimming pool is a modern building).

The Parkhotel Wehrle, in conjunction with other regional hotels, has organized walking vacations where your luggage is sent ahead to the next hotel. Walking is an enticing way to see the region. The hotel can provide you with details on the program.

DESTINATION IV   BADEN-BADEN

From Triberg continue on route 33 in the direction of Offenburg. The countryside is very lush, dotted by farmhouses typical of the region. Approximately a half-hour's drive from Triberg brings you to a complex of farmhouses, clustered together as architectural examples of what the farm life was like in the "olden days." Located near the town of Gutach, this marvelous outdoor museum with the fancy name of Bogtsbauernhof Schwarzwaelder Freilichtmuseum is well worth a visit.

After leaving the museum, just before the town of Haussach, follow signs to Freudenstadt then travel a valley cut by the scenic Gutach river. At Wolfach pass through the town's gates, follow the attractive main street, cross the Gutach and then turn right following signs again to Freudenstadt. The road winds back into the hills, following the river. Along the way you will see many wonderful Black Forest farmhouses. Next you come to the picturesque town of Shiltach with its wooden gabled houses. From Schiltach the road climbs and the "Schwarzwald Hochstrasse" (or High Road of the Black Forest) officially begins. The route takes you through the town of Alpirsbach, a fairly large town whose Romanesque cloister and timbered facades still dominate its older section. The road then twists up through the trees to the fairly modern town of Lossburg and then on to Freudenstadt. Destroyed by fire in 1945, Freudenstadt is a modern resort town whose large castle square is interesting in that it was laid out in the 16th Century for a castle that was never built.

Enjoy the heavily forested highroad of the Black Forest as it loops down to one of Europe's most elegant and renowned spa towns, Baden-Baden.

Spring comes early and the parks and gardens are a mass of blossoms, summer is long and sunny, autumn colors the foliage on the Lichtentaler Allee in russet hues, and winter is mild and beautiful with the surrounding mountains dusted in powdery snow. With its temperate climate, medicinal springs and gorgeous setting, Baden-Baden has been popular since Roman times. It possesses one of the world's finest botanical gardens: set along the banks of the lovely River Oos. Manicured gardens, attractive white wrought-iron lounge chairs set out to take of

Baden Baden

the sun, cobbled pedestrian streets, exclusive boutiques, antique shops, parks, fountains and an abundance of colorful flowers stage a delightfully romantic setting in this beautiful city. Open to the Rhine Plains, but protected from harsh winds by the surrounding hills, Baden-Baden enjoys a unique climate and her loyal patrons return year after year, swearing to the curative powers of the climate and the waters.

The open English-type gardens and parkland afford serene paths that loop around the Kurhaus, Trinkhalle and Casino. During the warmer months, concerts are held at the Kurhaus, the focal point of social activity and entertainment. An exclusive meeting place, the Casino, built in the middle of the 19th Century, is furnished in the elegant style of the French Renaissance.

Closed to traffic, Baden Baden's Old Town, nestled below the collegiate church, is a wonderful place for shopping. The stores display their elegant wares artistically, ever competing with the smells from the nearby pastry shops that summon you to an afternoon tea break. Baden-Baden is also a sportsman's paradise—golf, riding, tennis, fishing and hiking are all available in the vicinity. Race week is held each year in August when Baden-Baden becomes a sophisticated meeting place for the wealthy "horsey set." One of the town's traditional attractions is the Merkur mountain railway. Built in 1913, it reopened after repairs in the spring of 1979 and you can now travel up the incline and enjoy sweeping vistas from the observation tower at its summit.

Baden-Baden is a delightful, romantic city and would serve as an excellent base, especially if you would like to rest and take advantage of the spa facilities. Our suggested place to stay in Baden-Baden is the family-run, very friendly Romantik Hotel "Der Kleine Prinz."

Black Forest

Exploring the Rhine and Moselle

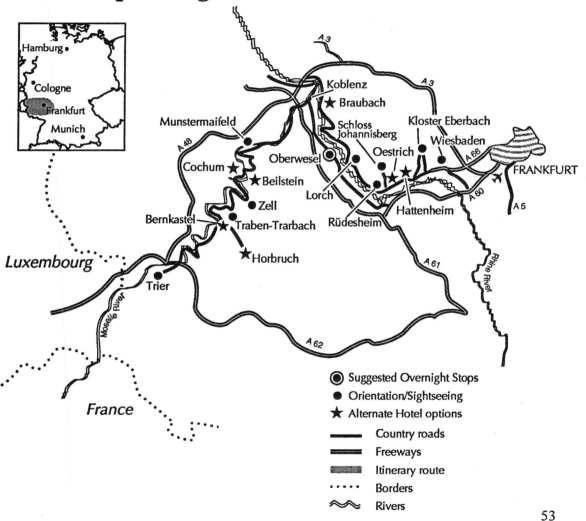

Hamburg
Cologne
Frankfurt
Munich

Koblenz
★ Braubach
Munstermaifeld
Schloss Johannisberg
Kloster Eberbach
Wiesbaden
Cochum ★
Oberwesel
Oestrich
FRANKFURT
★ Beilstein
Lorch
Zell
Hattenheim
Bernkastel
★ Traben-Trarbach
Rüdesheim
★ Horbruch

Luxembourg

Trier

France

◉ Suggested Overnight Stops
● Orientation/Sightseeing
★ Alternate Hotel options
━━ Country roads
═══ Freeways
▨ Itinerary route
····· Borders
〰〰 Rivers

Exploring the Rhine and Moselle

This itinerary covers two of Germany's most magical destinations—the Rhine and the Moselle wine regions. Powerful and broad, the River Rhine rushes towards the sea. High above the river, castles guard the heights or lie on islands amidst the churning flow. The river narrows to swirl past the legendary Lorelei rock whose muse dashed unwary sailors and their boats onto jagged rocks. A procession of famous villages and towns hug the river's banks. At Koblenz "Father Rhine" is joined by his loveliest daughter, the Moselle river. The Moselle's path is gentler, looping lazily back and forth as it passes tiny ribbon villages of half-timbered houses. Steep vineyards line her banks while castles stand guard from the hilltops above.

The beauty of these rivers is enough to fill a rich chapter in your vacation, but if this is not sufficient to tempt you, be reminded that this itinerary offers the opportunity to alternate excursions with sampling the fine wines of the Rheingau, Mittelrhein and Moselle wine regions.

ORIGINATING CITY   FRANKFURT

Frankfurt is a convenient starting point to begin an itinerary. The Frankfurt/Main airport is the destination of planes from all over the world. Centuries of flourishing commerce have brought this city great prosperity: its commercial importance led to it being a target for wave after wave of Allied bombers during World War II. Those responsible for reconstruction after the war, chose to rebuild Frankfurt as a modern city. Fortunately a few historic gems have been restored: Goethe House, where Johann Wolfgang von Goethe was born in 1749, is open as a museum showing how a well-to-do family lived in the 18th Century, and nearby you find the Romerberg—a square of old restored gabled buildings. Today, Frankfurt's prosperity lives on in streets of elegant shops, attractive restaurants, its vast entertainment calendar and its large conventions or fairs. As in days of old, it is here that the roads converge, but nowadays it is the trains, planes and autobahns that whisk you to all parts of Germany. If you want to spend your first night in the city, the Westend Hotel is an excellent choice.

DESTINATION I   OBERWESEL

Follow the autobahn 66 west from Frankfurt through Wiesbaden. In a few kilometers the autobahn ends and continues as road 42: this main road and the busy inter-city railway trace the river's bank. The first part of today's itinerary loops back and forth from this main artery, exploring the gently sloping vineyard-covered hillsides that line the bank of the Rhine River. Known as the "Rheingau," this small wine area is especially famous for its Riesling wines.

A short drive brings you to the wine town of Eltville where in medieval times the archbishops of Mainz had their summer palaces. Here you leave the busy river road and climb through the vineyards to Kiedrich. Drive into the little village and visit its pretty pink church with its elaborate interior before continuing up the hill to Kloster Eberbach. Set in a snug little hollow at the upper reaches of the vineyards, this former Cistercian monastery enjoyed 700 years of prosperity thanks to the production of wine. The Cistercian monks led an austere, silent life of prayer and hard work, allotting only a few hours a night for sleep on hard, narrow wooden pallets. Stroll through the quiet cloisters and cool halls with their graceful fan-vaulted ceilings to the refectory that now houses an impressive collection of enormous old wine presses. The severe architecture, plain plaster walls and lack of embellishments mirror the austere lifestyle led by the monks.

Leaving the monastery grounds, turn to the right and follow the country road as it dips down through the vineyards back to the river at Hattenheim. Drive through the old town center to the adjacent village of Oestrich. Turn left down one of the winding village streets and you emerge back on the busy Rhineside road for the short drive to Winkel.

Turn right in Winkel and follow the road up through the vineyards to the bright yellow castle on the hill, the Schloss Johannisberg. This famous castle is the emblem of wines produced in this area and its name, "Johannisberg," is synonymous with the production of Riesling wine. From April to December you can enjoy a meal at their country-style restaurant (closed Tuesdays) and visit the wine-shop. On a fine day the castle terrace affords a panoramic view across the vineyards to the river below. Note: The palace cellars contain century-old wines of fabulous value. You can arrange for a private tour of the cellars and wine tasting (on weekdays only) by writing to Schloss Johannisberg, 65366 Geisenheim-Johannisberg, Germany, telephone (06722) 7.00.90, fax: (06722) 70.09.33.

Returning to the river road, it is a short distance to the most famous wine town of this area, Rüdesheim. Park you car by the river, bypass the many tourist shops selling gaudy souvenirs and head for the town's most picturesque street, Drosselgrasse. Here, on what is reputed to be the jolliest street in the world, one wine tavern props up another. Even if you do not partake of the wine, it is fun to wander along this festive street. A short stroll along the river brings you to the more serious side of wine production, the wine museum in Bromserburg Castle. This splendid museum is filled with artifacts pertaining to the production of wine from the earliest days.

Leaving Rüdesheim, the river road winds below steeply terraced vineyards as the river Rhine forsakes its gently sloping banks and turns north into a rocky gorge. Passing below the ruins of Ehrenfels Castle, the Mauseturm (Mouse Tower) comes into view on an island near the opposite bank. Legend has it that Archbishop Hatto II was a cruel master who paid a terrible price for his sins: he was driven into the mouse tower by mice who then proceeded to eat him alive.

The river valley narrows as you near the town of Assmannshausen and the first of the famous castles that overlook the river comes into view on the opposite bank—Rheinstein Castle. Take time to drive into Assmannshausen, and explore its poky narrow streets full of charming little old houses. The wisteria-covered terrace of the Hotel Krone provides you with a refreshment stop and fine views of the passing river life.

As you drive north along the riverbank, as fast as one castle disappears from view, another comes into sight perched high above the rocky river valley. The Rheingau wine region ends in the little town of Lorch, where you take the small chugging car ferry that fights the strong river currents and slowly transports you across the river to Rheindiebach. As you enter the Mittelrhein wine district, you see the Rheingau's verdant vineyards gently sloping to the river replaced by steep river terraces occupying every southern facing slope, where the grapes can soak up the warm summer sun. Between the vineyards, the high river banks are thickly wooded.

It is just a few minutes' drive from the ferry to Bacharach. Park your car by the river and walk into the town to discover that the plain riverfront facade conceals a picturesque village of half-timbered medieval houses around a market square. As you leave

Bacharach, a much photographed castle, the Pfalz, comes into view marooned on an island amidst the swirling flow.

As you drive into Oberwesel, pause at the foot of the castle road and visit the reddish-pink church, the Liebfrauenkirche. Gothic in style, the church is noted for its many beautiful altarpieces, the oldest built in 1506. Although there are several recommended places you can choose to overnight along this area of the Rhine (marked by stars on the itinerary map), a highly recommended choice is the Auf Schonburg castle, perched high above Oberwesel.

Auf Schonburg Castle
Oberwesel

Turn left by the church and follow the winding road upwards to the castle. Cross the wooden bridge spanning the gully that isolates the Auf Schonburg on its rocky bluff. Park your car beneath the castle walls and climb the well-worn cobbles that wind you through the castle to the hotel at the summit. The facade is out of a fairytale—towers, turrets, battlements and a dear little black and white building tucked against the outer castle wall. The interior is a joy—little bedrooms nestled in a circular tower or tucked neatly into nooks in the old buildings, romantic old beds and furnishings. (Incidentally some of the castle's most romantic rooms do not have Rhine river views.) Wonderful food is served in cozy dining rooms with service that could not be kinder. And the view!

Exploring the Rhine and Moselle

From the hotel a magnificent landscape spreads before you as the hillside drops steeply to the village and the swiftly flowing river. Let the enchantment of your castle hotel tempt you to stay for several days, giving you time to explore the castles that you have seen from a distance, time for a leisurely river "cruise" and time to visit the secluded little villages high above the river valley.

A thousand years ago your hotel, the Auf Schonburg, was built as a Roman fortress. It played its part in the centuries of European history until it was almost destroyed by the French in 1689. For over 200 years it lay in ruins until a wealthy New York banker, whose family emigrated from these parts, bought the property and spent 35 years and two million gold marks on restoring the castle as a summer home. In 1951 his son sold the castle back to the town, which then converted a portion of it into a youth hostel. Several years later Hans Hüttl, an enterprising local vintner, converted another portion into this exquisite hotel.

DESTINATION II   THE MOSELLE WINE REGION

As you bid your castle on the Rhine farewell, glance to the river where it swirls and eddies amongst the rocks on the opposite bank. Legend has it that these rocks are the seven maidens of Oberwesel Castle who were so cold-hearted towards their suitors that the river overturned their boat and turned them into stone.

Around the first river bend, the fabled Lorelei rock comes into view. The currents around the rock, which juts out sharply into the river, are so dangerous that the legend arose of an enchantress sitting high on top of the rock combing her golden tresses and so entrancing the sailors with her singing that the rules of navigation were forgotten and their boats were dashed onto the rocks.

The Rhine landscape is splendid when viewed from the river but even finer views await you from the ramparts of the castle, Burg Rheinfels, located high above St Goar. Below flows the mighty Rhine dotted with chugging barges and on the opposite bank are the whimsically named Burg Mauz (Mouse Castle) and the adjacent larger Burg Katz (Cat Castle). In the Burg Rheinfels museum, a model shows that what is now largely a ruin, was once a mighty fortress.

Keeping the river close company, about a 45-minute drive brings you to the outskirts of Koblenz where you bid the Rhine farewell, and by following signposts for Trier, navigate through town to the banks of the Moselle River.

The pageant of the river bank marches steadily on, but how different the Moselle is to the Rhine. The Moselle is narrower, moving more slowly—gracefully looping back and forth. The road too is narrower, with thankfully less traffic and no busy adjacent railway track. The Moselle's steep banks are uniformly covered with vines—for this is wine country. Every little ribbon village, with the terraced vineyards rising steeply behind it, is involved in the production of wine. The villages are often no more than a cluster of houses, yet they all have their own famous brand of wine.

High above the river, castles guard the heights. The loveliest and best preserved castle, the Burg Eltz, is most easily reached by taking one of the many bridges to the river's northern bank and following the riverside road to the tiny hamlet of Hatzenport. Turn right in the village for the short drive to Munstermaifeld and on to Wierschem, following signposts for your destination, the Burg Eltz. You will soon see an area designated for parking. Leave your car here (no cars allowed at the castle) and follow the well-marked path to Burg Eltz. Your trail winds through a beautiful forest where benches are strategically placed should you need to rest or just pause to see the view. You might think you are on the wrong path because you walk for about fifteen minutes before catching your first glimpse of the majestic turreted castle in a clearing of the woods. Tour the rooms furnished in Gothic style and admire the collections of armor and weapons.

Retrace your path back to your car, then drive down the hill to the Moselle river and follow the road that hugs the northern bank for the short drive into Cochem. Park your car and explore the pedestrian center of this small town. Turn a blind eye to the rather tacky souvenir shops and let yourself be tempted inside a coffee shop for some mouthwatering pastries and a cup of coffee. Thus fortified, wander through the narrow streets and follow the well-signposted walk to the castle, Reichsburg Cochem, sitting atop a hill above the town. The trek is worth it, for while the valley is beautiful when viewed from below, the view from above is spectacular.

Beilstein on the Moselle River

As you leave Cochem, the prettiest stretch of the Moselle opens up before you as the loops of the river almost double back on themselves. Cross the river at Cochem and follow the river to Beilstein. The village is perfect—a tiny cobbled square crowded by centuries-old houses. Walk up the quiet cobbled streets to the church and return to the square to sample wine in the cool deep cellars of the Haus Lipmann. Or, if the weather is warm, settle on the hotel's terrace to watch the little ferry as it shuttles cars back and forth across the river while long river barges chug slowly by.

Luckily, in this enticing region of the Moselle, there are many charming places to stay. In Beilstein, the Haus Lipmann (mentioned above for its wine cellar) makes an excellent choice for accommodation, especially if you want to be so close to the Moselle that you can watch the river activity from your cozy room. In Bernkastel-Kues we suggest two hotels, the Doctor Weinstuben and the Hotel Zur Post. In the delightful old town of Cochem, the Alte Thorschenke is an absolute jewel of architecture.

Cochem on the Moselle River

Instead of staying in a village right along the Moselle river, another suggestion is to overnight in an old mill, nestled in the hills above the Moselle. If this appeals to you, continue on from Beilstein. Several more long looping bends brings you to the twin villages of Traben-Trarbach. Leave the river behind and take the small road in the center of Trarbach that winds you upwards out of the river valley to Longkamp. Turn left in the center of Longkamp following signs for the road 327 to Koblenz. Turn left on 327 towards Koblenz, then it is only a few kilometers to the Rhaunen exit. You will find the Historische Bergmuhle a short drive from the junction, about half a mile beyond the pastoral village of Horbruch. It is a little complicated getting to the hotel—a detailed map will certainly aid you, but the effort is worthwhile for the Historische Bergmuhle is one of those rare "perfect hideaways"—an idyllic old mill, the wheel still turning lazily beyond the dining room window.

Plan on spending several days along the Moselle river valley, taking daytrips to explore the many colorful towns hugging the banks of the Moselle. You must not miss Trier. Founded by the Roman Emperor Augustus in 15 BC, Trier had the largest fortified gateway in the Roman Empire, the Porta Nigra. Still intact, it stands guard over the city nearly twenty centuries later. This gate is like a giant wedding cake of three and a half tiers standing nearly a hundred feet high. The tourist office by the Porta Nigra will supply you with a city map showing you the route to the Roman amphitheater and a map of the walk through the vineyards. The amphitheater was built above the town to provide up to 20,000 people with gladiatorial entertainment. After the Roman Empire fell, the site was used as a quarry, and now soft grassy mounds have taken the place of the stone seats, and from behind the amphitheater, the Weinlehrpfad (an educational wine path) leads you up through the vineyards.

Another of the picture-perfect villages not to be by-passed is Bernkastel-Kues. As you enter the town, look for a small sign directing you to the Berg Landshut, an impressive ruined castle above the town. From the castle grounds, the vineyards tumble steeply to the river below and the view is spectacular.

Bernkastel-Kues is two towns: Bernkastel on one side, Kues lying just across the bridge on the other side of the river. In this wine valley, Bernkastel stands out as being the most attractive larger town. Park your car by the river and walk down to the boat dock where you will find posted the schedule for the ferries. Figure out an excursion that will integrate into your time frame, buy your tickets, then while waiting for your departure, go back to explore Bernkastel-Kues. You will fall in love with this quaint wine village where colorful, 400-year-old, half-timbered houses are grouped around a flower-filled marketplace and beautiful medieval houses extend for several blocks.

Bernkastel-Kues

When it is time to leave the idyllic wine region of the Moselle, it is only a short drive to Germany's borders with Luxembourg, France and Belgium. Of course you can return to Frankfurt to tie in with another itinerary.

Exploring the Rhine and Moselle

The Romantic Road and the Neckar Valley

Hamburg

Cologne

Frankfurt

Munich

FRANKFURT

A3

A5

Würzberg

A3

Miltenberg

Iphofen

Amorbach

Tauberbischofscheim

A7

Erbach

Weilkersheim

Rothenburg

Heidelberg

A81

RIVER NECKAR

A6

Badfriedrichshall

Heinsheim

Crailsheim

Feuchtwanger

A6

Heilbronn

Dinkelsbühl

Schwäbisch-Hall

◉ Suggested Overnight Stops

● Orientation/Sightseeing

★ Alternate Hotel options

━━━━━ Freeway

━━━━━ Country road

• • • • • • Border

▓▓▓▓▓ Itinerary route

The Romantic Road and The Neckar Valley

The Romantic Road (or Romantische Strasse) is one of Germany's most famous tourist routes—a road that travels between the towns of Würzburg in Franconia and Füssen in the Bavarian Alps. Every bend along the way between Würzburg and Rothenburg ob der Tauber is spectacular. However, the beauty of the scenery begins to wane a little after leaving Rothenburg, so this itinerary deviates from the traditional route. Rather than traveling the entire 340 kilometer stretch of the Romantic Road, this itinerary assumes Frankfurt as your arrival city, samples the northern highlights of Germany's most traveled route and then detours west at Rothenberg to incorporate the enchanting city of Schwäbisch Hall and the picturesque university city of Heidelberg. However, the beautiful southern portion of the Romantic Road has not been forgotten—it is incorporated into the Bavarian Highlights itinerary.

Rothenburg ob der Tauber

The Romantic Road and The Neckar Valley

ORIGINATING CITY   FRANKFURT

If you arrive at Frankfurt airport on an international flight, you might be pleased to note that within fifteen minutes' drive you can check into the very polished, sophisticated, and well-run Hotel Gravenbruch-Kempinski. This large hotel offers several dining rooms, a swimming pool and a nearby forest with paths for walking. It is an ideal stop to overcome any symptoms of jet-lag. However, if you prefer to be located right in the city of Frankfurt, in our opinion, there is no better choice for a small hotel than the Hotel Westend. We consider this hotel a real "find" as it combines quiet elegance with a welcoming and home-like ambiance. Twenty rooms insure an intimate feeling and personalized service.

DESTINATION I   AMORBACH

If you are eager to experience the flavor of the German countryside, it is just a few hours' drive south of the Frankfurt airport to the village of Miltenberg. Located on the left bend of the Main river, this village is wonderful to explore and a perfect stopping point to stretch your legs. One of the first things you'll notice is a turreted bridge and the fading ruins of a castle on the hillside. The village is a charming mix of cobblestoned streets and sloping slate and tile roofs. It is a quick and rewarding hike up from the market place to the castle ruins for a splendid view overlooking this picturesque village. On Haupstrasse, a street reserved for pedestrians, you will enjoy a number of quaint shops and might choose to sit a while and sample your first "bier und wurst." Miltenberg has an inn, Hotel Zum Riesen, but for one of Germany's most enchanting inns and a guaranteed night of quiet, continue on to the farming village of Amorbach and Der Schafhof.

A short drive from the center of the village, nestled on a hillside dotted with grazing sheep, you will find your hotel, Der Schafhof. Built in 1721, it originally belonged to the estate of the Amorbach Benedictine Abbey. Now the flag bearing the crest of the Winkler family from the Oberhessen district, who held the position of titled millers, is proudly raised in front. Dr Winkler is an attorney in Oftenbath, but still finds time to manage Der Schafhof—still an operating farm with sheep, some goats, hens and ducks. The family provide excellent accommodations and cuisine. The decor is consistently beautiful, with a theme of natural dyes and colors of rich browns, soft creams and whites—enriched by the country feeling of weathered beams. Anyone would feel fortunate for just one night here and envious of those with an extended stay.

DESTINATION II   ROTHENBURG OB DER TAUBER

Tauberbischhofsheim is an appealing small medieval town that you will want to visit en route to Würzburg. With unspoilt countryside surrounding it, Tauberbischhofsheim has a local history museum housed in the former palace of the Prince Electors of Mainz and a number of interesting churches. Also, the town has recently become a popular center for fencing enthusiasts. As described back in the 12th Century by the well-traveled diplomat, Gottfriedvon Viterbo, Würzburg is "lovely, like a rose set in deep-green foliage—sculpted into the valley like an earthly paradise." This beautiful baroque town is crested by the Marienberg citadel and has at its feet, spanning the river Main, the old bridge lined by statues of saints. Adding to the beauty of the region, vineyards slope down to surround this old university town. Masterpieces of European structure are the Cathedral of St Kilian and the Residenz (the former palace of the prince-bishops). The historic Ratskeller, once the town hall, is now open to the public—a maze of rooms including a witch's hole and large Bierstube. The Marienberg Fortress houses the Mainfrankisches Museum and displays some wonderful treasures including thumbnail sketches by Tiepolo and incredibly beautiful wood carvings by Riemenschneider. Würzburg is graced with many art treasures and a lovely location on the banks of the looping Main river.

Würzburg

Würzburg tempts visitors with its grand wine, beer and local "Meefischli" (Main fish). Head south from Würzburg along a country road (19) to Bad Mergentheim on the River Tauber. The old order of the Teutonic Knights left Prussia to reside here in a castle in 1525 and remained until they were disbanded in 1809. The magnificent Renaissance palace now houses a museum on the Teutonic Order as well as a local-history museum. Bad Mergentheim's history as a world renowned health spa dates back to 1826 when a shepherd uncovered an old, long-buried mineral spring.

From Bad Mergentheim, the romantic road winds its way along the most scenic stretch of the Tauber valley. The serenity of the lush, ever-changing landscapes in the next few kilometers epitomizes the meaning of the title given to this idyllic stretch of countryside—the romantic road.

The village of Weikersheim is set on the left bank of the Tauber only a few kilometers from Bad Mergentheim. The palace of Weikersheim was the former residence and ancestral seat of the Princes of Hohenlohe. The well-preserved interior furnishings of the palace reflect Renaissance, baroque and rococo styles and the baroque gardens are among the finest in Germany. A short distance farther, pretty half-timbered houses line the market square of Rottingen. This wine center also boasts a castle steeped in legend, Brattenstein Castle.

Your road follows the Tauber as it weaves south, passing under the clock tower building in Schaffersheim, through the pretty village of Klingen (dominated by its high church steeple), then it winds on to Creglingen with its wealth of romantic vistas and charming houses. People come to Creglingen from all over the world to see the isolated Herrgottskirche that was built about 2 kilometers from this medieval city in 1389. Its altar piece, "Ascension of Mary," dates from 1510 and is a masterful example of the wood carver Tilman Riemenschneider's work and talent. This lovely church stood hidden and forgotten from 1530 to 1832 and miraculously escaped the destruction of World War II.

The road now follows the gentle Tauber as it winds through a narrow lush valley. Quaint villages fill the gaps along the road and the river meanders in their shadow. Footpaths stretch out for many kilometers paralleling this incredibly scenic drive and tempt one to abandon the car and continue the journey by bike or on foot. Along the way you will pass through Tauberzell (a small farming village with a cluster of timbered houses), Tauberscheckenbach (a neighboring, equally attractive hamlet), and Bettwar (with an especially picturesque setting). From Bettwar you can see the medieval "fairytale" town of Rothenburg ob der Tauber in the near distance.

Rothenburg is an unspoiled gem of the Middle Ages. The outlines of today's existing structure of fortified towers and walls remain intact and date from 1274 when Emperor Rudolf I of Hapsburg proclaimed Rothenburg a free imperial city. It then obtained a charter and the right to self-government, thus becoming responsible solely to the emperor. Remarkably well-preserved from the 14th and 15th Centuries, Rothenburg is truly a treasure for all to visit and experience. Its beautiful gates, towers and massive walls stage a stunning silhouette. Stroll the narrow cobbled streets of this little township. Horse drawn carts add to the character of the streets and the clomping of hoofs on cobblestone lends a bit of nostalgia to the activity and bustle. Intricate wrought iron hallmarks and gorgeous displays of flowers decorate many of the facades of the medieval and Renaissance houses. Wander and enjoy the fascination and intriguing personality of each street and alleyway, but be sure to watch the time so that you will not miss the clock chimes in the dramatic town hall.

You will definitely also want to include in your exploring the vast cathedral and other notable structures such as the Poenlein, St Mark's Tower, the White Tower, Gerlach's Forge, the Franciscan Church and the Dominican Convent. Three kilometers of stone wall with forty towers and gates encircle Rothenburg and you can walk along the ramparts for almost the entire distance. From the municipal gardens on the promontory where Rothenburg was founded, there is a magnificent panoramic view of the town and the surrounding valley. All of Rothenburg has been declared a national monument and its buildings are protected by law. The history of Rothenburg is recreated in pageants and festivals numerous times during the year.

Stay in Rothenburg for as long as your travel arrangements allow: a day is not enough to absorb the history and magic of this delightful medieval town. One must also take the luxury of an afternoon break to sample the town's specialty, Schneeballen (snowballs), a dessert that is a layer of thin strips of pastry rolled up, deep fried and then dusted with confectioner's sugar, its final appearance being that of a snowball: it is utterly delicious.

There are many excellent hotels choices for Rothenburg. Study the listings in the *Hotel Description* section and pick out the one that seems to best fit your taste and budget.

It is disappointing to compare the character of Rothenburg to almost any other medieval town in Europe. Few can challenge its dramatic structures and atmosphere. But don't make the mistake of ending your vacation after your visit to Rothenburg as there are still destinations on this itinerary to pique and satisfy your interests.

The Romantic Road travels south from Rothenburg—shaded by groves of pine trees as it winds through numerous small farming villages. The drive exposes a slice of rural lifestyle as it edges close to farmhouses and open barns. The farmland is rich and green and the orange tile roofs of the village houses provide a lovely contrast. En route is Feuchtwangen, a small town whose market square is referred to as "Franconia's festival hall." Of interest are the Romanesque cloisters, the collegiate church, the Wolgemut altar, St John's Church, historic burgher houses, craft workshops and a local-history museum. The town also has one of the region's most delightful inns—the Romantik Hotel Greifen Post, managed by the Lorentz family. You might choose to use this hotel as your base or simply sample the bounties of its restaurant.

South of Feuchtwangen is the historic old town of Dinkelsbühl, well-preserved behind a wall with twenty towers and gateways, which has one main street of picturesque old burgher houses and tourist shops. Its major attraction, however, is the "Kinderzeche" (children's festival), held each year in mid-July to commemorate the town's salvation by the village's brave children in the Thirty Years' War. Consider a short detour south to see Dinkelsbühl.

Your next stop is Schwäbisch Hall, a town removed from the ever popular Romantische Strasse by only a short drive through gentle farmland and sleepy villages. Schwäbisch Hall profits from the fact that it is not very heavily visited by tourists and therefore has retained much of its original atmosphere, character and charm. Set on two sides of the river, the town boasts picturesque covered bridges, lovely cathedrals and old timbered houses (leaning so precariously, they threaten to tumble into their own shadows). It is a lovely town to explore. The outskirts of Schwäbisch Hall are not too pretty—some industrial plants mar the landscape—but the heart of this old town is delightful and offers a reasonable hotel for the night, the Romantik Hotel Goldener Adler, located right on the main square.

Romantik Hotel Goldener Adler
Schwäbisch Hall's marketplatz

DESTINATION IV   HEIDELBERG

From Schwäbisch Hall head west in the direction of Heilbronn, an industrial community that is also the largest wine producer in the valley. From Heilbronn continue north along the path of the Neckar river valley. The route travels through fruit orchards languishing in the shadow of sloping vineyards and hillsides dotted with impressive castles. You will drive past Bad Friedrichshall, a small town with old salt mines and spas. Your next interesting sightseeing excursion will be to visit the fortress of Guttenberg Castle, a bird of prey conservation center and one of Europe's largest falconries. Its gamekeeper gives demonstrations with falcons and vultures every day at 11:00 am and 3:00 pm.

Perched on the hillside, Hornberg Castle appears as the Neckar follows the bends of the valley. Shortly beyond, the ivy-covered ruins of the 9th-century fortress of Eberbach can be seen. A final highlight before reaching tonight's destination is the "Gem of the Neckar," the towering Hirschhorn Castle. Fortified by its keep and sentry wall, this castle has been converted to accommodate overnight guests. Although it is not included in this guide as an overnight stop, you can enjoy lovely views of the Neckar river valley from its open air terrace restaurant.

Heidelberg

The Neckar river next rounds a bend to expose the enchanting city of Heidelberg. In rich rust tones, Heidelberg's crowning castle, set against a backdrop of contrasting green, creates a spectacular sprawling skyline with its octagonal towers, belfries and gates. A visit to the castle affords a sweeping view of the valley over the pitches and angles of Heidelberg's distinctive old rooftops and buildings.

Heidelberg
Romantik Hotel Zur Ritter Sankt George

Heidelberg is a city whose mood is set by its dominating castle, old university and the lovely River Neckar that meanders through its center. This is a city of romance. Goethe fell in love here and the musical career of Schumann, a master of the romantic period, began here. The setting of Heidelberg was the inspiration for "The Student Prince," an opera by Sigmund Romberg that depicts student life as jovial and merry. This wonderful old university town has one main street that is the center of activity and captures most of Heidelberg's atmosphere. The cobbled pedestrian street of Hauptstrasse is bordered on each side with a melange of student taverns, lovely shops and assorted coffeehouses. Explore the town: visit the Rathaus, view the stunning cathedral, see the students' punishment cell at the university and walk the few blocks to the picturesque Alte Brucke (Old Bridge). Then cross the river and enjoy a stroll along Philosophers' Way (Philosophenweg), a path skirting the river—beautiful by day as well as by night when lit by soft lights.

In Heidelburg, if you want to stay in a landmark hotel, the 16th-century Romantik Hotel Zum Ritter Sankt Georg's intricate and stately facade is easy to recognize on the cobbled pedestrian street of Hauptstrasse. However, just steps from the main street, is the recently renovated Zur Backmulde. The decor in the guest rooms is excellent and the hotel, in our opinion, is the best buy in town.

Enjoy the sightseeing and the shopping in the old world city of Heidelberg. Then when it is time to continue your journey, you have many convenient options: you can easily take the expressway south to the Black Forest or north to the Rhine and Moselle, or if your holidays must end, it is only a short drive to either the Frankfurt or Stuttgart airports.

The Romantic Road and The Neckar Valley

Bavarian Highlights

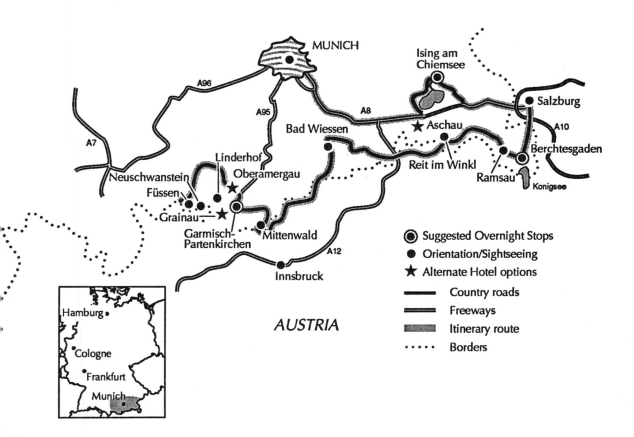

MUNICH

Ising am Chiemsee

Salzburg

A96

A95

A8

A10

A7

Bad Wiessen

Aschau

Berchtesgaden

Linderhof

Neuschwanstein

Oberamergau

Reit im Winkl

Füssen

Ramsau

Grainau

Konigsee

Garmisch-
Partenkirchen

Mittenwald

A12

Innsbruck

AUSTRIA

⊚ Suggested Overnight Stops

● Orientation/Sightseeing

★ Alternate Hotel options

── Country roads

══ Freeways

▒ Itinerary route

····· Borders

Hamburg

Cologne

Frankfurt

Munich

Bavarian Highlights

It is no wonder that Bavaria is a favorite destination for so many travelers. This small region in the southeastern corner of Germany proudly maintains the reputation of having the friendliest people, the most breathtaking mountains, the quaintest villages, the prettiest lakes and the handsomest castles in Germany.

Neuschwanstein-Mad King Ludwig's Castle

Summertime paints Bavaria's valleys and hillsides with edelweiss, alpine roses and orchids. Winter gently softens the landscape in a carpet of white snow and turns Bavaria into a sportsman's paradise. This is a region where traditional costume is worn with pride. This itinerary traces a route that begins in Munich, Germany's "secret capital city," dips briefly into Austria to visit Salzburg, winds through Bavarian hamlets, visits the resort towns of Garmisch-Partenkirchen and Oberammergau, highlights Ludwig II's fairytale castles and concludes in the splendid Oberallgau region.

ORIGINATING CITY   MUNICH

Bavaria is an enchanting region and Munich, the "gateway to Bavaria," stars as one of Europe's most beautiful cities. Munich, a wonderful crusty old beer-drinking, music-loving city, rivals Paris and London with its excellent shopping and traditional architecture. The heart of the city is magical to explore on foot, and a logical place to start is at the main train station. From there, go directly towards the Stachus. This square is officially called the Karlsplatz, after Elector Karl Theodor, but the townspeople had such a high regard for Foderl Stachus, that they named the square after him in 1730.

Leaving the Stachus, wander under Karlstor Gate into the pedestrian zone of the old city that is laced with fountains, fruit stands, ballad singers and lay preachers. Off to the left, notice the Renaissance facade of St Michael's and behind it the Cathedral, "Frauenkirche," both a landmark and symbol of the city. Marienplatz is just a short distance farther. This is a dramatically beautiful square and serves as the heart of the shopping district and the historical core of the city. When the clock on the town hall strikes 11 am, 12 noon, or 5 pm, little figures emerge from around the clock to perform a jousting tournament. Awaiting the hour is a perfect excuse to sit at one of the little cafes in the square for some refreshment before continuing on with your sightseeing. Since the main business district of Munich has been converted to a pedestrian mall, window shopping is a pleasure. Peek into some of the beautiful shops then take a short walk over to Munich's oldest parish church, Alter Peter, with its impressive 11th-century interior. Climb its tower for a panoramic view which on a clear day extends to the Alps.

Clock in the Rathaus Munich's Marienplatz

Just short walk from the Alter Peter church is the Viktualienmarkt, a permanent market that flavors the city with glimpses of the past. Meander through the Burgasse to Alter Hof, the first Residence of the city. Then straight on to Maxi-Joseph-Platz where you will discover the National Theater and Residence, and catch a glimpse of the

Bavarian Highlights

Maximilianeum at the end of Maxmilianstrasse. Continue along the Residenzstrasse with a glance into the lovely inner courtyards of the Residence and on to Odeonsplatz, then circle back to the station via Brienner Strasse, Maximiliansplatz and the Stachus.

Although removed from the heart of the city, a few other sights deserve mention. The Deutsche Museum (the German Museum), is often referred to as "Germany's Smithsonian" and is known for its diverse collection of scientific and technological displays. The BMW Museum is interesting to car buffs as well as to those who understand the importance of the business to the financial welfare and history of Munich.

The Alte Pinakothek museum has an incredible display of works by 14th-to 18th-century masters such as Raphael, Michelangelo, Van Dyck, Rembrandt, Breughel, Goya and Titian. The Neue Pinakothek, whose collection is limited to 19th-century artists, is a relatively new structure replacing the original 19th-century building that was destroyed in the World War II. The Haus der Kunst, located on the edge of the English Garden, has a continually changing art collection. If time and weather permit, walk the length of the gardens to the student district of Schwabing.

Fall of course translates as the "Oktoberfest" and many from all over the world congregate in Munich to participate in the festivities. This happy, noisy celebration of the sausage and the hops begins in September and concludes on the first Sunday in October. The festival confines itself to a meadow in the southwestern part of Munich called the Theresienwiese. Whatever the season, enjoy Munich for its opera, theater, shopping, beauty, character and history.

On Munich's outskirts is Schloss Nymphenburg, the summer palace. Built in 1664 with additions in the 18th Century, it is a beautiful architectural example of baroque and rococo styles. You might also want to detour out to the Olympic Park, site of the 1972 Games.

Munich has a rich selection of places to stay in various price ranges, all within easy walking distance to major points of interest in the old part of town. Look in the back of the book in the *Hotel Description* section to see what appeals to you.

DESTINATION I ISING AM CHIEMSEE

Leave Munich by traveling the autobahn southwest in the direction of Salzburg for an approximate two-hour drive to Chiemsee where the Hotel Zum Goldenen Pflug is a recommended place to stay. The Zum Goldenen Pflug (translated as the golden plow) is a gem of an inn, conveniently located in the little farming village of Ising, just a short distance northeast from the shores of the serene Chiemsee. Another choice of a hotel is the Residenz Heinz Winkler, located southwest of the Chiemsee in the small town of Aschau (the Residenz Heinz Winkler is especially recommended for gourmets—it has been awarded two Michelin stars).

Against a backdrop of magnificent peaks, Chiemsee is the largest lake in the foothills of Bavaria. Although not as beautiful as some of Germany's other lakes that are tucked into mountain pockets, the lake is a draw for sports enthusiasts and has two islands of interest to travelers: Frauenchiemsee and Herren Chiemsee.

As early as the 8th Century, Frauenchiemsee was a home for Benedictine nuns. In 866 Irmengard, a great-granddaughter of Charlemagne, was buried here. Herrenchiemsee is an island chosen by King Ludwig II for the setting of his Bavarian Versailles—Neues Schloss. Although construction ceased at the time of the king's death in 1866 (with only the center of the enormous palace completed), it includes a stunning replica of Versailles' Great Hall of Mirrors with sumptuous and elaborate detailing. The surrounding gardens and forest are most definitely worth a visit. You take a boat to this small island and at the pier are horse-drawn carriages to whisk you to the castle. Of course you can also walk, but should it be a rainy day, the carriages are a welcome sight.

DESTINATION II   BERCHTESGADEN

Leaving the Chiemsee, continue east along the scenic autobahn following the signs for Salzburg. As you near the Austrian border, the Alps are visible in the distance and onion-capped spires crown the rolling hills in the foreground. This is a rich farming area with cattle, sheep, weathered barns and Tyrolean homes dressing the green landscape.

Although in Austria, Salzburg is just on the border and much too close to pass without visiting. This delightful city, located on both banks of the Salzach river, is dramatically set at the base of the Kapuzinerberg and Monchsberg mountains. The ruins of its fortress straddle the city skyline. In the old section of town, narrow streets wind amongst the city's many fine baroque buildings that shelter a number of exquisite shops and boutiques. Salzburg is the birthplace of Wolfgang Amadeus Mozart and when the Mozart Festival is held here in the months of July and August, the town is bursting with song and gaiety (and tourists). Regardless of the season Salzburg is an enchanting city. This itinerary just touches on the glories of Salzburg, one of Austria's many fascinating destinations.

Leave Salzburg and cross the border back into Germany and then travel just a few kilometers south into the Alps to the mountain village of Berchtesgaden. Found at one end of the German Alpine Road, Berchtesgaden, an ancient market town, is now a very popular winter sports resort. Explore the Schlossplatz (the picturesque castle square) and follow the meandering 16th-century arcade to the market place. Berchtesgaden's noblest old inns and interesting houses are located here and many bear the details of weathered woodcarvings that the Augustinian monks introduced to the region in the Middle Ages. Also popular to explore are the Salt Mines of Berchtesgaden, located only a few kilometers away near the Austrian border. Salt was a principal source of the town's prosperity in the early 16th Century. The tour is dramatic and includes a trip down a 500-meter chute, an endless web of tunnels and a journey by raft across an illuminated subterranean lake.

In the center of town, the simple Hotel Watzmann makes a colorful choice for a hotel. If you feel like a splurge, on the north edge of town is a marvelous chalet, the Hotel Geiger. With its weathered exterior, attractively decked with green shutters, wooden balconies and overflowing flower boxes, the Hotel Geiger blends perfectly into this Alpine region. With the Hotel Geiger as your base, you can enjoy the town and its shopping, take advantage of trails that leave practically from the Geiger's doorstep and visit the dazzling lake of Konigsee and the dramatic Eagle's Nest.

Located 5 kilometers south of Berchtesgaden, Konigsee's setting and beauty are comparable to some of the world's most magnificent fjords. Steep Alpine walls enclose this romantic lake that is accessible from the tip of its one small resort village. Traffic on the lake is restricted to electric boats in an admirable effort to minimize pollution. The boats provide the only access and method to fully explore the lake. They glide from the docks across a glass-like, brilliant green lake and wind round the bend to view the picturesque 18th-century chapel and settlement at St Bartholomae where the postcard-pretty little church is built on a pocket of land near the edge of the lake. A backdrop of maple trees and mountains completes the idyllic scene.

The dramatic peak of Kehlstein and the serene pastoral plateau of the Obersalzberg are located just east of Berchtesgaden along a winding Alpine road. The last stretch of just a few kilometers on the approach to the Kehlstein, the highest road in Germany, must be traveled by postal bus. At its crest is a foreboding granite walled structure that was built by Adolf Hitler and understandably labeled the Eagle's Nest. To reach Hitler's retreat, an elevator negotiates the last 400 feet through a shaft in the Kehlstein mountain.

DESTINATION III GARMISCH-PARTENKIRCHEN

Hopefully you will have a sunny day to coincide with your departure from Berchtesgaden. Keep your passport at hand as today you will be criss-crossing back and forth between Germany and Austria. The Alps are incredible against blue skies or dramatic as they break through lingering clouds. Take the Alpine Road (Alpinstrasse) in the direction of Ramsau. Spring weather exposes green foothills and glimpses of jagged peaks struggling with the quickly disappearing fog. The road follows a stream that cuts along and through rocky foothills. Chalets sit perched on knolls as green as a golf course fairway. Ramsau's church has a picture-perfect setting, silhouetted against the Alpine peaks. Take a detour of 6 kilometers at Ramsau to Hintersee, which, on a still morning is a gorgeous lake reflecting the chalet homes and overpowering mountains of Reiter Alps.

An old cobblestoned road winds up from Ramsau in the direction of Traunstein, enhanced by breathtaking views of surrounding peaks. For the photographer, old weathered chalets are tucked on knolls with firewood stacked exactly at their side and milk pails set full and lined up for collection. The German Alpine Road reaches a crest and then descends into a farther valley. The village of Saalachterjeltnberg sits in a shaded valley not far from Saalachsee. Cross the Saalach river and continue in the direction of Traunstein. Soon after a road branches off to Bad Reichenall, look back for a dramatic view of the Gletschhorn framed by the valley walls. Before the village of Rauschberg, turn off towards Ruhpolding, following the Alpine Road signs. There are no major towns along this stretch between Rauschberg and Reit im Winkl—only lakes, hiking trails, breathtaking vistas and an occasional farmer, dressed in Tyrolean green, sitting on a tractor. The road starts to climb again, then levels out following the valley. With every turn of the road, mountains present themselves from a different intriguing perspective. From the small hamlet of Labau, the road twists and winds with the narrow valley and at Seehause you enter the region of lovely small lakes including Lodensee, Mittersee and Weitsee—all especially pretty when the sun shines and the lakes mirror the surrounding scenery.

Ramsau

Bavarian Highlights

Reit im Winkl is a quaint hamlet—a cluster of chalets. The road continues in the direction of Kossen and the Austrian border, with the peaks in the distance ever-beckoning. The road narrows after crossing the border as it follows the path of the Tyrolean Alps.

From Kossen follow signs to Walchsee. Just 7 kilometers away, Walchsee is a small lake with a beautiful setting: the Pyramidenspitze seems to rise right out of the opposite shore. Pass through the town of Durchholzen Niederndorf before crossing back over the Inn River into Germany. Obeandorf is a busy but little village. Continue now in the direction of Niederndorf and then watch for signs to Bayrischzell. Turn onto what seems a small country road and wind through the valley 20 kilometers to Bayrischzell. En route is the hillside village of Wall with spectacular rolling valley vistas and striking snow covered peaks. Reichenau is a hamlet of only two or three chalets. Here the road is dotted with strategically placed benches on which people settle to knit, read the morning paper, or just to soak in the view and let the day pass at will. The road is glorious as it winds through the mountains.

Bayrischzell is an enticing ski village, a perfect spot to picnic. Buy bread at the local bakery, and picnic on the square by the church.

Leave Bayrischzell following the signs to Schliersee and Miesbach. Neuhaus is a town at the tip of Schliersee with a striking 17th-century church set just past the train track. From Neuhaus the road follows the contours of the lake and winds around to its other side where you find the post-card-pretty village of Schliersee, nestled on its shore with two church spires reflecting in the lake.

Hausham is just 1 kilometer away, newer, with industry on its outskirts. From Hausham follow signs to Tegernsee. At Gmund skirt the Tegernsee on its northern shores to Sapplfeld just a few kilometers before the town of Bad Wiessee. This is a resort town of green lawns that roll lazily down to the water's edge—a scene enhanced by mighty mountain peaks towering just a shadow away.

Continuing on, at the town of Weissach turn towards Achensee. The road winds in a valley along the Weissach river and touches the Austrian border at Achenpass. The road soon travels around a dam whose water is a beautiful aquamarine color and the Zwiesler and Demehoch peaks tower above. Scenery now changes to a more wooded landscape; the rolling green pastures simply seem to disappear. At Lenggries Vordereiss pay a nominal toll and take a private road, a beautiful but slow drive, through pine trees and across rugged terrain. Hohergrauwig and Soiernspitze are broad chiseled peaks at the mouth of the valley. This is a lovely approach into the town of Wallgau.

With an absolutely magnificent setting for a village—ringed by the peaks of the Karwendel mountains—Mittenwald is a holiday resort that is known worldwide. In addition to its beauty, this village is famous for the crafting of fine violins, and the Geigenbau (violin) Museum is interesting to visit. Soon after Mittenwald, the rolling green hills return dotted with weathered sheds. It is a gentle half hour's drive on to the Alpine resort village of Garmisch-Partenkirchen.

Framed by some of Germany's most dramatic, jagged peaks, Garmisch-Partenkirchen is backed up against her highest—the towering Zugspitze. At one time two villages, Garmisch and Partenkirchen merged to meet the demands of accommodating the 1936 winter Olympic Games. The distinction between what were once two towns is still apparent. Garmisch is a bustle of activity, with broader, newer streets lined by larger stores and hotels, and closer to the slopes. Partenkirchen, with narrow winding streets and timbered buildings, preserves more old world charm. One of our favorite hotels, the Posthotel Partenkirchen, is located is located on the main street in the "old town" of Partenkirchen. This marvelous hotel reflects the character of its past as a posting station and the tradition of service and standard that four generations of the Stahl family have strived to achieve. The bedrooms are attractively decorated with cherished antiques, lovely prints and nice fabrics. A few rooms enjoy unobstructed views of the Zugspitze. Just down the street from the Posthotel-Partenkirchen is another choice, the Gasthof Fraundorfer, which although a simpler hotel, also offers old world charm. In the "new town" of Garmisch, the Clausing's Posthotel is brimming with antique ambiance.

Note: Although this itinerary suggests overnighting in Garmisch-Partenkirchen, in the *Hotel Description* section, there are other hotel suggestions in Grainau (so close-by it is almost the same town) and Oberammergau (the ever-so-colorful town where the Passion Play is performed every ten years). Any three of these towns (Garmisch-Partenkirchen, Grainau, or Oberammergau) would make an excellent hub for exploring the charming Alpine region of the Oberallgau.

With Garmisch bracketing one end and the Bodensee on the western boundary, this picturesque region of the Bavarian Highlands includes not only such popular destinations as King Ludwig's Neuschwanstein castle, but also some little known mountain villages that are tucked away in a Bavaria of yesteryear. This is a land of flowering meadows and snow capped peaks. The Oberallgau is glorious when blue skies warm endless hiking trails and charming river valleys, and in winter it is a lively sports center. Bavaria's young King Ludwig II's family home, Hohenschwangau, is located here and he chose the region for its splendor and spectacular setting to build his dream castles, Neuschwanstein and Linderhof. This itinerary outlines a circular route to visit the castles and highlights of the region: they are all within an easy drive of Garmisch-Partenkirchen and the trip could easily be scheduled over a few days.

North of Garmisch-Partenkirchen, on the road to Oberammergau, is the small town of Ettal. Ettal is famous for its baroque monastery, pilgrimage church and the herbal liqueur that is produced by the resident monks. It is near Ettal where you will need to watch for a small sign directing you to the isolated castle of Linderhof.

King Ludwig II intended to rule his kingdom from five castles. Ludwig began his reign at the young age of eighteen, but he soon tired of politics and began building castles. Only three were partially completed before his mysterious death at age forty in 1886. Linderhof is the smallest of his accomplishments. Set in the loneliness of the Ammer mountains, this elegant palace is rich in its furnishings and spectacular with its landscaped gardens. It is a lovely shaded walk from where you buy a ticket to the castle. Be sure to buy an English translation of the tour at the entrance, as there aren't always enough English speaking guests to warrant a special guide. Both the interior and gardens are well worth a visit. Ludwig's bedroom looks out onto a dramatic cascading fountain bordered by a wisteria-covered arbor that is beautiful in bloom. A highlight of the grounds includes a man-made grotto on the hillside above the castle that Ludwig commissioned for a dramatic staging of the operas of Richard Wagner.

Continue on from Linderhof in the direction of the Austrian border. This routing affords a tempting glimpse of the peaceful Austrian countryside and avoids backtracking in order to visit Neuschwanstein and Hohenschwangau. The drive through Austria takes you along the shores of a serene lake and onto the village of Reutte, tucked into a valley pocket and shadowed by the towering peaks of the Ammer Range. Musau is another typically charming Austrian village you'll pass before crossing back into Germany and on to the colorful spa town of Füssen. Note: "Konigschlossen" translates as King's Castles. Coming back into Germany directions to the castles are given in German.

Hohenschwangau was built by the Knights of the Swan. It burned in 1600 and was rebuilt from ruins by Maximilian II of Bavaria between 1832 and 1836. He was the father of Ludwig II, and Hohenschwangau became their family residence. There are a few designated parking areas below the castle and it requires a steep climb on foot from any of the parking lots to tour Hohenschwangau. The history of Ludwig's life is outlined on the tour and the rooms that reflect the family's style of living are interesting to visit. It was at Hohenschwangau that Ludwig first met his beloved Wagner.

Neuschwanstein towers above Hohenschwangau. From the bedroom of his family home Ludwig could watch the construction of his fairytale fortress. A visit to both castles requires three to four hours depending on crowds and the season. If time dictates choosing between the two, Neuschwanstein is a must.

To reach Neuschwanstein, you can tackle the half hour walk up a steep path, ride the shuttle bus, or take advantage of the slower but more romantic horse-drawn carriage. Regardless of method of approach, the very last stretch to this fanciful castle must be on foot. Perched on a rocky ledge, high above the valley, Neuschwanstein was Walt Disney's inspiration for Sleeping Beauty's castle. Designed by a theater set designer and an eccentric king, the interior is a romantic flight of fancy whose rooms afford spectacular views. Ludwig lived in a dream world set to music by his adored friend, Richard Wagner, whose work and scenes from his operas are found throughout in the decor.

Leave Hohenschwangau and Neuschwanstein, travel north in the direction of Steingaden and from there continue east following signs to Oberammergau. Soon after crossing the dramatic bridge outside Steingaden, take a short detour to visit Wies and its lovely church. This ornately baroque church is spectacular for the setting it creates—a lovely white facade, capped with an impressive onion dome, set against the rolling Bavarian landscape.

The road winds back in the direction of Garmisch-Partenkirchen through the picturesque village of Oberammergau. Oberammergau is a lovely Alpine resort with stunning murals painted on many of its homes and buildings. Every ten years the "Passion Spiel" (Passion Play), a religious play, is performed here. All the residents in town are involved in the production and performance of this play that celebrates the end of the misery and death associated with the Black Plague. In between plays it seems that everyone in the village carves so the shops are filled with lovely wood carvings, a specialty being nativity scenes.

From Oberammergau it is a short drive to Garmisch-Partenkirchen. Plan to spend several days in this gorgeous region of Germany to enjoy the mountains and explore the many charming villages that are tucked away in the scenic Oberallgau. Venture off on roads that detour through the small hamlets.

From Garmisch-Partenkirchen it is a comfortable drive back to Munich or a convenient drive on to the Bodensee and Constance where you can connect with the Black Forest itinerary.

Bavarian Highlights

Exploring Eastern Germany

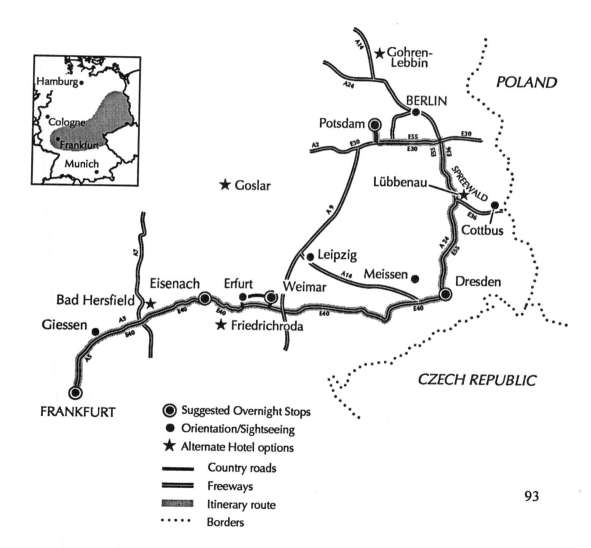

Hamburg
Cologne
Frankfurt
Munich

POLAND

Gohren-Lebbin

BERLIN

Potsdam

★ Goslar

Lübbenau

SPREEWALD

Cottbus

Leipzig

Meissen

Dresden

Eisenach

Erfurt

Weimar

Bad Hersfield

Giessen

★ Friedrichroda

FRANKFURT

◉ Suggested Overnight Stops
● Orientation/Sightseeing
★ Alternate Hotel options
━━━ Country roads
═══ Freeways
▓▓▓ Itinerary route
· · · · · Borders

CZECH REPUBLIC

93

Exploring Eastern Germany

The Brandenburg Gate

For 40 years eastern Germany slept under a mantel of secrecy. Then, in November, 1989, the stunning word spread throughout the world: the infamous "Wall" had been torn down. In October 1990, the reunification became official, and the doors to eastern Germany opened. Two days later, we crossed the now invisible border into what had been for so many years "forbidden territory." The stories we had heard were true: the roads were pot-holed, the buildings dilapidated, the air polluted and the hotels sadly outdated. Three years later we returned to eastern Germany. Miracles had happened: roads smoothly surfaced, gasoline readily available at service stations, buildings freshly painted in bright colors, new restaurants open, and hotels losing their dowdy appearance. Of course, all is not complete: eastern Germany cannot yet compete with the excellence of hotels and perfectly groomed towns in the rest of the country. But don't wait too long to visit—it is fun to be a part of history and see the transition taking place. In this itinerary, we have hand picked for you the destinations we found most intriguing and laced them together along a leisurely loop joining the two major German cities of Frankfurt and Berlin.

ORIGINATING CITY   FRANKFURT

This itinerary begins in Frankfurt, conveniently reached by direct flights from cities throughout the world and by trains racing in from everywhere on the continent. If you arrive into the Frankfurt airport, you can either begin your journey immediately by retrieving a rental car at the airport and starting on your way, or by spending a few days in Frankfurt. Although Frankfurt is a large commercial city rebuilt upon the devastation of World War II, it has at its heart a most appealing old section radiating out from the Town Hall. Here you find a web of pedestrian-only streets lined with enticing shops and dotted with pretty sidewalk cafes. If you have time to linger, a wonderful choice for a place to stay is the Hotel Westend, located just steps from the historic heart of Frankfurt.

DESTINATION I   EISENACH

When you leave Frankfurt, head directly north on autobahn 5. About 60 kilometers from Frankfurt you see signs for the turnoff to Giessen, an old university town whose historical character was almost destroyed in the bombing raids of World War II. Bypassing Giessen, continue on 5 which veers northeast. In less than an hour you see the exit for Bad Hersfeld. Follow the signs into town. Just after going over the overpass, watch for a sign to the left marked "Marktplatz" and follow the signs to the center of town—there are several designated parking areas on the edge of the pedestrian area. Although the surrounding area has grown up with modern buildings, the heart of the Bad Hersfeld still has great old world charm. Wander through the cobbled streets lined with beckoning shops. The aroma of bratwurst grilling might tempt you to stop for a bite to eat from one of the *al fresco* vendors. If you want a more substantial lunch, stop at the quaint Romantik Hotel Zum Stern (easy to spot on one of the main squares, Lingplatz).

After a break for lunch and to stretch your legs in Bad Hersfeld, follow the signs back to the freeway and continue east following the signs for Eisenach. A few kilometers before reaching Eisenach, you might still catch glimpses of the old border control station, high wire fences, and watch towers on the surrounding hills.

As you approach Eisenach, take the first exit you come to, the West Exit. Watch carefully for signs to Wartburg, one of Europe's finest Romanesque castles. The way is well-marked, but stay alert because the route makes several turns. Before long you see the castle perched above you, on the crest of the hill. Leaving the main road, follow the small lane that weaves up through the forest to the castle. You need to drive slowly because the way is frequently blocked by merry-makers happily walking up the hill to see the castle. You soon come to a parking area where concession stands are set up for snacks. There are road signs indicating no through traffic, but if you are a guest of the Hotel auf der Wartburg continue on up the hill and in about 500 meters you come to another parking lot for hotel guests. Again, you think you must certainly stop here, but even though it seems to be a pedestrian path, you can drive on up the hill, through the hoards of tourists on foot, and into the courtyard of the castle. Here you can temporarily park while you unload your luggage before returning your car to the proper parking area. After getting settled in your room, explore the beautiful park-like grounds surrounding the castle.

Many tourists visit the stunning 12th-century Wartburg Castle without realizing that one wing of the castle complex houses the Hotel auf der Wartburg. On our first visit, days after the reunification of Germany, the guest rooms in the hotel were dark and dreary, the furnishings dated and unattractive. But, the hotel has undergone a fabulous transformation and the rooms are now richly decorated in great taste with English fabrics. As the remodeling might not be completed by the time you visit, be sure to ask for one of the newly renovated rooms.

It is a good idea to make an early start today so that you can be at the Wartburg castle gates promptly at 8:30 am to buy your entrance ticket and be among the first group to cross the moat. After purchasing your ticket, go under the portcullis and into the courtyard to stand in line to purchase a second ticket that is necessary for the guided tour of the castle.

Wartburg Castle

You are not allowed to wander around the castle by yourself, but the guided tour is interesting, although in German (buy a booklet in English at the entrance—it will help you understand most of the stories being told). One of the most interesting rooms is the Elisabeth Gallery where six large frescoed murals depict the tale of Elisabeth, a Hungarian princess, who came to live at the castle in 1211. She died when only 24, but became a legend due to her work with the peasants—nursing those who were ill and helping the destitute. Another room in the castle, the Elisabeth room, has a gorgeous mosaic, consisting of more than a million pieces of glass, mother of pearl and gold leaf, which also tells her story.

After leaving the tour, return to the courtyard and take a few minutes to visit the few simple rooms where Martin Luther lived when translating the New Testament into German.

Leaving Wartburg, go into the town of Eisenach. Watch carefully—just a few minutes before entering the town you will see a sign to Bachhaus. Turn left here and follow the road to the small parking area and look for a nearby statue of Bach set in a lovely tiny park. Facing the statue is a cheerful mustard-yellow house where Johann Sebastian Bach lived as a boy. Before you begin the tour, be sure to wander into the enticing rear garden, which in summer is filled with flowers. The tour of Bach's home is not structured. Follow the well-marked signs throughout the house that is furnished in much the same way it was when Bach was a child. The tour ends at the chamber music room where every 20 minutes a program of Bach's music, both live and taped, is cleverly woven together with a presentation about his life and work. This is an experience not to be missed. To sit in this lovely small music chamber dappled with sunlight filtering in from the garden, listening to Bach's music is indeed magical. After the demonstration, you may choose to traverse the garden to another section of the house in which Bach memorabilia and sheet music are displayed. (Open Monday 1:30 pm to 4:30 pm, Tuesday through Friday 9 am to 4 pm; Saturday and Sunday 9 am to 12 noon and 1:30 pm to 4:30 pm.)

Leaving Eisenach, return to the autobahn and continue east. It is only about 45 kilometers to the turnoff heading north to Erfurt. Follow signs into the center of Erfurt. Do not be discouraged by the enormous, ugly apartment complexes, because the heart of Erfurt is full of old world charm. Park in any of the designated parking areas near the old town and set off on foot to explore. Head for the Kramerbruge (Kramer bridge) which is like a stage setting with colorfully painted three story shops lining its sides. A few blocks down the lane from the Kramerbruge you come to the town center, a large square lined with quaint buildings: some ornately painted, others intricately timbered. During the years since World War II, most of the buildings, which were happily spared when many other towns were demolished, fell into great disrepair—roofs caved in, sides of buildings collapsed and nothing was painted. Miraculously after the reunification the original charm of these buildings began to reappear as renovations began on full scale. If you are hungry (and it will probably be about lunch time) stop to eat at the attractive Gildehaus restaurant, facing Fisch Markt Platz, or perhaps you may be tempted to just snack on one of the tantalizing freshly grilled bratwurst sandwiches from one of the street vendors. After lunch, looking up from Fisch Markt Platz you see two very impressive, beautiful churches. Climb the steep steps to visit the dramatic cathedral with its glorious stained glass windows and its neighbor the Church of St Severus—a real beauty. There are several museums in Erfurt, but the town itself is the main attraction.

Leaving Erfurt follow signs for Weimar, 25 kilometers away. It is possible to return to the autobahn, but the most efficient route is a smaller back road that heads directly east from Erfurt to Weimar. When you come to Weimar, continue on to the center of town. (If possible try to purchase a good city map before arriving because the heart of the old town is a maze of one way streets and pedestrian zones.) If you are on a tight budget, we recommend in the *Hotel Description* section, the Hotel Schwartze (6 km south of Weimar near the autobahn). But, our first choice for location is the Hotel Elephant, in center of town on the large Markt Platz. (If you can't secure a room at Hotel Elephant, we also recommend the Weimar Hilton.) As you near the Elephant Hotel cars are not allowed on most of the streets, but you see signs indicating that if you are a guest of the hotel you can drive into the square in order to drop off your luggage. When you check in, the desk clerk gives you a sign to put in behind your windshield and directs you to the hotel's parking area a few blocks away.

There are several excellent places to eat: the Elephantkeller, an informal restaurant on the lower level of your hotel is a convenient choice, but our favorite is just a few minute's walk away at the Zum Weissen Schwan (The White Swan) located opposite

Goethe's house. Goethe frequently dined here and housed his "overflow" of guests for the night. The cozy restaurant has a choice of dining rooms—the least formal, and perhaps the most appealing, is the pub-like small restaurant on the lowest level. The walls are lined with wonderful murals of days gone by. The food is good and the atmosphere delightful.

Plan to spend at least two full days in Weimar—truly a gem: a superb small city laced with wonderful small beckoning streets to explore and graced with a treasure trove of museums. Weimar was home to many of Germany's artistic genius' and as you stroll the streets you slip back in time to the 18th Century and feel touched by the great creativity of the men who lived and worked here. Within a few short blocks you can visit Goethe's house where he lived from 1782 until his death in 1832; Friedrich Schiller's home which is open to the public; Franz Liszt's home, also a museum; and you can also see (but not visit) the home where Johann Bach lived while residing in Weimar. (Note: most of the museums close on Mondays.) While exploring Weimar, be sure to look for the fabulous sculptures of Goethe and Schiller standing side by side in the Theaterplatz.

Along the banks of the Ilm river, which winds through the center of Weimar, is a blissful park with a maze of inviting walking paths meandering through the woodlands and criss-crossing the river. The English-style layout of the park was designed by Goethe who spent much of his time here. Along one of the footpaths is Goethe's garden house (open as a museum) where he lived when he first came to Weimar. Later he married and moved into the larger fancy home, which is now a museum, but he kept his garden cottage as a retreat where he did much of his writing. The country-simple antique furnishings in the garden house are very different from the ornate decor in his later home.

On a sadder note, just a few kilometers northwest of town is Buchenwald. There is an eerie, yet fascinating movie shown at the entrance auditorium showing the history of the camp. Although in German, this jerky, very dated film is somehow more poignant than some slick, commercial production (and it is impossible to miss the story line). The images generated by this concentration camp are horrific, but a part of history not to be forgotten.

DESTINATION III   DRESDEN

Depending upon road conditions, it is about a two to three hour drive from Weimar to Dresden. The distance is 200 kilometers, but you might find delays due to autobahn improvements still in progress. The drive is very pretty: rolling farmland, pasture, forest and low lying hills create a lovely scene. The pastoral beauty is interrupted at times by enormous smoke stacks reaching high into the sky and by a few enormous, awful-looking, concrete housing developments en route—reminders of the Socialist regime.

When you reach Dresden, follow signs for the center of town. You know when you are close because you spot the high spires rising by the river. An excellent choice for a hotel is the Maritim Hotel Bellevue, located at the bend in the river, just across the Georgij-Dimitroff Brucke (bridge) from the Alte-Stadt (Old Town). The Hotel Bellevue is newly built and much larger than the hotels usually recommended in this guide as places to stay, however, it is ideally located along the banks of the Elbe river—just steps across the bridge to the center of all you must see in Dresden. Although the bulk of the hotel is modern, it has cleverly incorporated into its heart one of Dresden's loveliest old buildings, the Royal Chancellery, which was mercifully spared from the bombing raids of World War II. The gardens of the hotel gracefully stretch to the banks of the river along which there is a promenade; perfect for a morning's walk.

Another recommendation, just a 10-minute drive from the center of Dresden in the suburb of Loschwitz, is the Schloss Eckberg. This hotel is much less expensive than the Maritim Hotel Bellevue, and offers not only value, but the fun of living in a castle. Be sure to ask for one of the rooms in the original building. Some of the guest rooms are in a new annex.

Dresden Zwinger Palace

Dresden needs a stay of at least three nights in order to have two full days for sightseeing. When we visited, the city was blackened with grime and many of the monuments were still partial shells—just as they were when the allied bombers left their fires of destruction. Yet it is a fascinating place to visit. The heart of the city is tiny—easily walkable. The most incredible sight is Dresden's greatest treasure, the Zwinger Palace, where you will concentrate much of your sightseeing. Just to walk into the enormous courtyard, which seems the size of multiple football fields, is awesome. Surrounding this lovely garden courtyard is the palace, which contains a mind boggling assortment of museums; twenty-two in all. These will certainly keep you busy (remember that most museums are closed on Mondays). You must also see the gorgeous Semper Opera house, and, if it is the season, try to get seats for a performance.

The Weissen Flotte (White Fleet) is anchored along the river and operates sightseeing excursions from spring to autumn. An especially leisurely excursion is to take one of these boats for a round trip to Meissen and its china factory.

If driving, Meissen, is only 30 kilometers north via the 6 which follows the Elbe river. The heart of Meissen is on a knoll overlooking the Elbe where the beautiful cathedral and the castle decorate the plaza. If you enjoy looking at cathedrals, you might want to come back later for sightseeing, but first go directly to the Meissen factory located at 9 Leninstrasse, a main thoroughfare on the same side of the river as the castle and cathedral. Try to get an early start from Dresden in order to arrive at the factory before the busloads of tourists. Upon entering the building, buy two tickets, one for the museum and one for the work demonstration. Ask for an English booklet that will help you understand the guided tour in German. World famous Meissen china dates back to the very first part of the 18th Century when the art of making the "White Gold" (Meissen china) was discovered. The factory workers were practically kept prisoners in Meissen in order to protect the secret of their craft.

After the tour, follow signs directing you to the museum in the same building. Here you see incredible examples of Meissen china dramatically displayed in the regal setting of these lovely old rooms. Most of the pieces you see date from the 1700's and are extremely ornate: clocks, figurines, dinner ware, candelabrum, statuettes—almost anything you can name has been duplicated in this fine white china. The style might not be your taste. Much is a bit flamboyant to be sure, but you cannot help but appreciate the incredible craftsmanship involved in the making of each piece of art. (At the time of writing, the factory is closed Mondays but is open other days at 8:30 am.) If after visiting the workshop and museum, you are ready for some refreshment, there is a pleasant little cafe operated by the Meissen factory located as you go out the front door.

Leaving Dresden, follow the signs to highway 55 heading north to Berlin. The road is well-maintained and the countryside quite flat so unless there is a lot of traffic, it is an easy drive north. You pass large farms of cultivated fields and drive through some beautiful forests. Watch your map carefully; when highway E55 joins with E36 to Berlin, you turn south toward Cottbus and then almost immediately take the turn off marked to Lübbenau, which is where you will take your boat excursion to explore the water alleys of the Spreewald.

The Spreewald

Follow the road into town and continue to the boat landing (you cannot miss it—there is a large plaza where many boats are tied up along docks lining the Spree River). As you walk along the docks you see a large selection of boats. Each has a sign posted with the price and the length of the trip. When we were there, most of the boats were advertising either 1 1/2 hour or 2 1/2 hour excursions. But, if you are a real enthusiast, some trips are as long as 6 hours. From what I could gather, the boats just leave whenever they fill up with passengers.

The Spreewald is an enormous maze where the Spree River playfully divides into tiny fingers creating a lacy pattern of canal-like waterways which lazily wind in every direction under a canopy of trees. For many centuries the Spreewald has been home to the Sorbs who have their own language and folk customs. (I was told and saw pictures of quaint costumes, but did not see any—perhaps they are only used at festival time.) The Sorbs have built small houses along the banks of the river. These homes vary, but the basic style is a simple wooden house whose high pitched roof is crowned on each corner with a carved snake wearing a crown.

You can only experience the magic of this area by taking one of the boat excursions. First choose your boat (the 2 1/2 hour tour is excellent—giving you a good sample of the area and also time to stop at a Sorb village where you can have a cup of tea and visit the museum made up of a cluster of typical wooden homes furnished with peasant-style antiques). Each canoe is almost identical: a blackened wooden shell—sort of a cross between an Indian dug-out canoe and a Venetian gondola. Benches are set in rows down the length of the canoe and your "gondolier" stands at the back and poles you through the shallow waters. As the boat left the dock, I was reminded of the jungle cruise at Disneyland. The boats pass under many humped bridges from which paths mysteriously disappear into the forest. Your "gondolier" might even make a "pickle stop" for the Spreewald is famous for its pickles and merchants sell these spicy wares along the river banks. As the canoe glides through the water you are surrounded by constant activity: boats pass piled high with hay or filled with laughing children on their way to school, the postman delivering his mail—all attesting to the fact that there are no roads into this world of yesteryear.

Note: If you want to overnight in the Spreewald, the Schloss Lübbenau—a newly renovated castle just steps from the boat dock—is highly recommended.

When it is time to leave the Spreewald, it is an easy drive of about 100 kilometers along the well marked autobahn 55 to Berlin. But, instead of continuing on to the center of the city, we suggest making your home base 25 kilometers southwest of Berlin in Potsdam where you can enjoy a country ambiance at the Hotel Cecilienhof. To reach Potsdam, turn west on highway 30 (about 22 kilometers before Berlin) and watch for signs for the turnoff heading north.

The Hotel Cecilienhof, resembling an English country manor more than a Germany palace, was built by Kaiser Wilhelm in the early 1900's and became the royal residence of the Crown Prince Hohenzollern. The mansion is surrounded by a large park graced with lakes, trees, green lawns and forest. To history buffs, the hotel has an added interest. It was here where Churchill, Truman and Stalin met in 1945 to work out the details for the Potsdam Treaty that proposed the economic and political destiny for the defeated Germany. A section of Cecilienhof is open to the public as a small museum. Although a few years ago there was a fire that destroyed some of the rooms of historical interest, you can still see where the various delegations lived and worked while they planned the Potsdam Treaty. There are many interesting photographs depicting the historical event. The park-like grounds surrounding Cecilienhof are also open to the public, but it is only a lucky few who stay on to spend the night after the other tourists leave.

Besides Cecilienhof, Potsdam offers another regal attraction, the sensational palaces and gardens of Sanssouci. The Prussian King Frederick II chose Potsdam instead of Berlin as his permanent residence and in 1744 began construction on what was to become one of Europe's showplaces, resembling Versailles in its grandeur. Be sure to wear sturdy shoes because it is almost a half an hour's walk between some of the buildings. But it is fun to explore the tantalizing paths (strategically highlighted with sculptures) which weave through forests and glens as they connect some of Germany's most spectacular palaces. You can easily spend a day exploring the gardens and palaces. If you have the stamina, there is Sanssouci Palace (elaborate rooms in the rococo style), the even larger New Palace (don't miss the grotto made from shells and semi-precious stones), the Orangerie (an enormous building used to grow plants plus apartments for royal guests), the Picture Gallery (the first museum built with a sole purpose to display paintings), the Chinese Tea House (with its golden Chinese statues), and the New Chambers (built as a guest house). Plus, of course, you will not want to miss Neptune's Grotto, the Obelisk Portal, the Trellis Pavilion, the Dragon House, the Sicilian Gardens, Charlottenhof Palace, the Temple of Friendship—and on and on. There is a staggering amount to see and do. During the Communist regime, not much money was spent on Sanssouci so the buildings and statues became blackened by pollution, but work is underway scrubbing off the grime.

Although Potsdam is filled with tantalizing sights, Berlin must not be missed. While staying in Potsdam, allow sufficient time for excursions into Berlin. Depending on traffic, it is anywhere from half an hour to an hour's drive away. (It is also possible to go into Berlin by train, bus or boat.)

Berlin is a fascinating city—a dynamic and vigorous survivor, now entering a new chapter of its life. First on your list to visit might be the 200-year-old Brandenburg Gate whose majestic columns support the goddess of peace upon her horse-drawn chariot. During the years when Berlin was divided, the Brandenburg Gate became a symbol of oppression instead of the symbol of peace it was originally conceived to be. Today the fresh breath of freedom again fills the air as tourists and Germans alike stand gazing in awe at this grand monument. Since the reunification, "East Berlin" is bustling with the activity of tourists and the sound of reconstruction as buildings are being brought up to date. The 18th-century Opera House, almost destroyed by Allied bombing raids, has been rebuilt according to the original plans.

Berlin has a wealth of attractions. Stroll down the Kurfürstendamm (the Ku'Damm) which dates back to 1685 when it was a country path amidst asparagus fields. In 1871, Bismarck, decreed that the path be expanded into a fine boulevard—similar to the Champs-Elysees in Paris. Today, the Ku'Damm is a place to see and to be seen: a boulevard lined with chic boutiques, outdoor cafes and grand hotels. Just a short walk from the Ku'Damm are two majestic stone elephants guarding the entrance to Berlin's zoo, which, dating back to 1844, is not only the oldest, but one of Germany's best zoos. Too far to walk to, yet not to be missed is Berlin's Egyptian Museum, worth a visit if for no other reason than to see the incredible bust of Nefertiti, dating back more than 3,000 years yet depicting a woman as beautiful as any modern movie star. Opposite the Egyptian Museum is the Museum of Greek and Roman Antiquities. Across the street from the Egyptian Museum is the Charlottenburg Palace, a most imposing palace whose wings form a courtyard in front while elaborate sculptured gardens, forests and lakes form an idyllic retreat behind. You will certainly want to stroll the inviting paths through the Charlottenburg park, but do not miss a tour of the palace to see the apartments of the Prussian kings. Berlin has many other museums, plus, as mentioned above, fabulous shopping and excellent restaurants.

This itinerary ends in Berlin, but for those who have the luxury of time, drive northwest to Hamburg to follow Schleswig Holstein—The Land Between The Seas or southwest from Berlin to Goslar to join Fairytale Country and The Harz Mountains.

Schleswig Holstein—
the Land Between the Seas

DENMARK

SYLT ISLAND

Westerland

Kietum

Niebull

Glucksburg Castle

Flensburg

Schleswig

A7

Alt Duvenstedt

BALTIC SEA

Kiel

Plon

Eutin

Oldenburg

Timmendorfer

Travemünde

Lübeck

A1

Heide

A 23

NORTH SEA

A7

Quickborn

HAMBURG

⊚ Suggested Overnight S

● Orientation/Sightseein

★ Alternate Hotel option

━━━ Country roads

═══ Freeways

▨▨▨ Itinerary route

• • • • Borders

╫╫╫╫╫ Rail route

Hamburg

Cologne

Frankfurt

Munich

109

Schleswig Holstein–the Land Between the Seas

Thatched Houses, Isle of Sylt

Schleswig Holstein is Germany's most northerly province. With Denmark at its tip, this broad finger of land divides the placid Baltic from the wild North Sea. Along the North Sea shore, dikes protect the sky-wide landscape from being claimed by the sea's crashing waves. Safe behind dikes, sheep and cattle graze while crops grow in serene pastures. Offshore, dune-fringed islands brave the sea. Any visit to Schleswig Holstein would not be complete without a trip to one of the islands, so this itinerary takes you and your car on top of a train for a rocking ride across the Hindenburgdamm to Sylt. This island boasts an impressive landscape of sand dunes and exposed steep cliffs sheltering quaint little thatched villages from bracing sea breezes. In sharp contrast, the Baltic seacoast is hilly with long graceful fjords extending far inland from the gentle lapping ocean. Here kilometer after kilometer of white sand beaches provide a holiday haven for northern Europeans who brave the chilly waters and relax in gaily colored canopied beach chairs while their children decorate sand castles with sea shells. Between these two seas lies Holsteinische Schweiz, "Swiss District," a confusing name as there are no mountain peaks, just a lovely area of wooded rolling hills sprinkled with sparkling lakes.

Northern weather tends to be cool and rainy so pack your warm sweaters and rain gear. But be prepared to be surprised—the weather is unpredictable so hopefully you will have balmy cloudless days as you explore this lovely region far from the beaten tourist paths.

ORIGINATING CITY   HAMBURG

Hamburg is a mighty trading and industrial center on the banks of the Elbe River. Understandably, Hamburg was a target for World War II bombings—by the end of the war the town was little more than a heap of rubble. But with great determination, much of the city has been rebuilt in the old style so that today it has the mellow feel of an older age.

Hamburg's sights are spread around a large area, so the most efficient way to get from place to place is on the U-Bahn, or subway system, whose stations are marked on the city's tourist map. Include the following on your sightseeing agenda: St Michael's church (Hamburg's symbol), the palatial city hall built at the end of the 19th Century, the art museum, an hour-long tour of the harbor to see the boats from the world's great trading nations, a peaceful three-hour tour of the Alster Lake and canals that run through the heart of the city, and shopping along the Spitalerstrasse and Monckebergstrasse.

Just a short walk for sailors from their ships, Hamburg's notorious red-light district has grown up along the Reeperbahn and surrounding streets, where erotic entertainment knows no bounds. This raunchy area, just west of the city center, is just a ripple in what is otherwise a very straight-laced city.

If you are in Hamburg on a Sunday morning, plan on visiting the Altona Fish Market, an open air market at the water's edge, offering everything—fruit, flowers, rabbits, socks, antiques and, of course, fish. The show starts at six, but plan on arriving by nine. No need to eat before you arrive; there are plenty of food stands selling everything from delicious hot grilled sausages to crunchy rolls filled with smoked eel or pickled herring.

Hamburg has many excellent hotels listed in the *Hotel Description* section. Consider also the possibility of staying out in the countryside. The Romantik Hotel Jagdhaus Waldfrieden in Quickborn makes an excellent choice. Another suggestion is the charming Fürst Bismarck Mühle in Aumühle (just a short train commute into the heart of the city).

DESTINATION I   ALT DUVENSTEDT

After a few days of city adventures, you will be ready for a change—something quiet and relaxed, a complete change of pace from the bustling city. Drive into the downtown area and follow signs for the autobahn 1 to Lübeck.

Holstenor Gate, Lübeck

About an hour's drive finds you outside Lübeck's impressive Holstenor Gate, a squat fortress crowned by twin towers shaped like enormous witches' hats. The gate guards the entrance to the medieval old town set on an island surrounded by canals and waterways. This sheltered port was the leading city of the Hanseatic League, a group of towns who banded together for trade advantages during the 13th to 16th centuries. Park your car and head for the marketplace in the old town, where the Rathaus, Lübeck's impressive town hall, covers two sides of the square. Nearby, the tall, slender twin steeples of the Marienkirche, St Mary's church, rise above the town. Step inside to admire the lofty fan ceiling of this majestic building.

Leaving the old town of Lübeck, drive to the north for fifteen minutes to the popular Baltic resort of Travemunde. It is fun to drive along its riverfront road seeing the boats and ferries on one side and the crowded little seaside shops on the other and then to drive along its wide sandy beach fringed by modern hotels.

As you leave Travemunde, follow road 76 that parallels the coastline going north. If the weather is sunny and warm, you may want to get into the German holiday spirit and join the crowds on the beaches at the coastal resorts of Timmendorfer Strand or Scharbeutz-Haffkrug. In pleasant weather sun worshipers soak up the sun from the shelter of their canopied beach chairs while offshore the Baltic waters come alive with the sails of gaily colored sailing boats and wind surfers.

Follow highway 76 as it turns inland at Scharbeutz-Haffkrug. Leaving the flat coastal landscape behind you, enter a region of gently undulating farmland sprinkled with lakes both large and small. Narrow threads of land often separate one lake from another. The region is known as "Holsteinische Schweiz," the "Swiss district," not because of its Alpine peaks, of which there are none, but because it shares a similar rock formation with Switzerland. About a half hour's drive brings you to the lakeside town of Eutin. This is a colorful medieval town with a quaint central pedestrian square. Park by the old moated castle and meander down to the lakefront through a gorgeous forested park, following the promenade that leads you along the shores of the lake (the Eutiner See).

Farther on, lovely lake vistas are provided by the drive around the Keller See to Malente-Gremsmuhlen. Take the road along the northern shore through Sielbeck for the prettiest views. The town of Gremsmuhlen is the departure point for motor-boat tours of the beautiful five lakes to the west of town. The frustration of catching only glimpses of the lakes through the trees is removed when you glide along them on a boat.

Just a short distance to the west is Plon, positioned atop a small hill overlooking the region's largest lake, the Grosser Plonnersee. Drive through the town to the quaint cobbled marketplace near the church. Park your car and walk up the narrow cobblestoned alley to the castle terrace where you have a lovely view of the lake below.

Leaving Plon, you follow the road 76 for the half hour's drive to the outskirts of Kiel. Unless you are interested in busy freight and yacht harbors, do not go into the city but take the road 404 to the B4 and on to the suburban town of Molfsee. Here you will find the Freilichtmuseum, Schleswig-Holstein's Open Air Museum, a collection of rustic farms and country homes dating from the 16th through the 19th Centuries that have been brought here and reassembled. It is great fun to watch the local craftsmen operating the old smithy, potter's shop, mill and bakehouse. You can explore the old houses and barns and retire to the timbered inn for welcome refreshments. Note: The park is closed between November and April and on Mondays except in July and August.

It is only about a half hour's drive from the museum to a hotel we recommend for the night. Take the autobahn 215 south towards Hamburg for just a few kilometers. The autobahn 215 merges with the autobahn 7 and you turn north on the 7 following signs for Flensburg and the Danish border. Take the exit marked Rendsburg and go east on 203 (direction Eckernforde) and after about 3 km you come to the tiny village of Holzbunge. Turn left through the village and follow signs that guide you along a narrow road that leads to the Hotel Töpferhaus. Note: Although the address reads Alt Duvenstedt, do *NOT* go to Alt Duvenstedt—it is on the other side of the autobahn. Hotel Töpferhaus is idyllically located overlooking the Bistensee, and although very isolated, it is loaded with a sophisticated charm.

DESTINATION II   KEITUM-SYLT

When it is time to leave the peaceful waters of the Bistensee, take the autobahn 7 north and exit at the ancient Viking stronghold of Schleswig. Soon after you leave the expressway (before you reach the main town), watch for signs to the road going to the left to Schloss Gottorf, located on a small island at the west end of the town. In a building west of the castle, be sure to see the 4th-century Viking ship, the Nydam Boot. Long and slender, the Nydam Boot conjures up pictures of fast ships and a race of fierce, proud seamen who reached the limits of the known world in their elegant sleek craft.

Schleswig's old town (Altstadt) hugs the northern bank of the Schlei inlet. Its cathedral dates from the 12th Century and is noted for its handsome carved altar. Also in Schleswig, fronting the harbor, is the picturesque fishermen's district called Holm. Don't miss this tiny, but ever-so-special hamlet—it is truly picture perfect. Explore its quaint lanes, follow the circular road that wraps around the park and toy-like church, and stroll down to see the fishing boats at the water's edge.

Return to the autobahn and continue north for about 22 kilometers. Take the exit to Flensburg. Continue through the city and follow signs to Glucksburg Castle, located about 9 kilometers beyond Flensburg near the tip of the Flensburg fjord. When the picturesque castle comes into view, it seems to be floating on the lake that once provided its defenses. The castle and its parklike grounds are open to the public. The furnishings are not outstanding, but the castle is fun to visit and there are many interesting family portraits and old photographs.

Return to Flensburg and follow the signs directing you west across the marshes on road 199 to Niebul. Do not go into the town, but follow the well-posted signs of a car atop a railway car for the train to Sylt. You cannot drive your car to the island, but take it on top of a railway carriage along the causeway that connects the island to the mainland. There is no need to make advance reservations—purchase your round trip ticket as you drive into the railway yard. Do not worry about catching a particular train for there are between eleven and sixteen departures each day. The car-train trip seems excessively expensive for such a short journey, so plan to stay awhile on Sylt.

Leaving the ticket office, you drive your car onto the train and sit in it for the 50-minute bumping ride past fields of sheep and Holstein cows towards the shoals that lead to the Hindenburg Levee that connects the island to the mainland. From your lofty perch atop the train you can appreciate the centuries-long battle to keep the sea from flooding this flat low-lying land. A series of dikes protects the land from the water and the farms are built on earthen banks that become islands if the dikes fail. Crossing the sea dike, the train arrives in the island capital, Westerland, a town of elegant boutiques and sophisticated nightspots.

Schleswig Holstein–The Land Between the Seas

There are many small hotels on Sylt but, if you want to splurge, choose the island's loveliest hotel, the Benen Diken Hof in Keitum. Set in the island's most picturesque village, the hotel is actually several squat thatched Friesian farmhouses joined into a complex by means of glass corridors that appear to bring the outdoors inside. Decorated throughout in white and cream with accents of pale pink and blue, the hotel is "decorator perfect"—warm and welcoming. After a walk along the sand dunes in the bracing sea air, you can return to the hotel to pamper yourself with a sauna and a massage or a relaxing swim.

The hotel's greatest asset is Claas Johannsen, the owner and manager. An avid volunteer fireman, his fondest memory of his one trip to the United States is the morning he spent riding around New York's streets with the fire department. Of an evening he can be found operating the hotel's cozy bar surrounded by his collection of old model fire engines. His warmth and graciousness transcend the language barrier.

The lovely restaurant at the Benen Diken Hof serves only breakfast, but do not worry: the small island abounds with restaurants. A particular recommendation goes to the Restaurant Landhaus Stricker in the adjacent village of Tinnum—gourmet dining in elegant surroundings in an adorable old Friesian farmhouse. Another outstanding, elegant gourmet restaurant is the Restaurant Jörg Müller (also described in the *Hotel Description* section as a place to stay). Note: If you like lots of action, the beautifully decorated, exceptionally well-run Hotel Stadt Hamburg, located in the bustling tourist town of Westerland, is another recommended hotel.

Keitum occupies a sheltered site and remains an old Friesian village of squat thatched cottages, lilac bushes and tree-lined streets. Keitum's low-slung houses are topped by thick roofs of reeds gathered from the tidal marshes, just the kind of house from which you would expect Hansel and Gretel to emerge. High garden walls protect against storm flood tides and winds. The lovely old village has two splendid museums: the Old Friesian House and the Sylter Country Museum. Built in 1739 by a sailing captain, the red brick old Friesian farmhouse passed into the hands of a 19th-century historian who assembled a history of the island. The house and the furnishings are such that a Friesian of two centuries ago would feel immediately at home. Nearby on Cliff Street you find the Country Museum, another old sea captain's home that contains collections of island seafaring memorabilia and coins, porcelain and costumes dating back hundreds of years. Inspired perhaps by their forefathers, modern artisans have set up their shops in nearby houses.

As you explore farther afield, you pass Keitum's St Severin church, a landmark for seafarers since it was built seven centuries ago. The island's days as an important maritime center are long past, yet once a year, on the eve of February 22, the islanders pile straw, reeds and wood into a huge bonfire as a symbolic send-off for the island's sailors.

The island is lovely, a long narrow strip, much of it sand dunes facing the North Sea. Dikes, sand dunes and cliffs protect the island from North Sea storms. Forty kilometers of white sand attract summer sun worshipers—bathing suits are as welcome as none—and canopied beach chairs provide snug shelter from the wind. Hardy Germans enjoy swimming in the chill North Sea waves, but you will probably find the hotel's heated swimming pool more to your liking.

Devote a day to exploring the island and its villages huddled behind the sand dunes, then use the remainder of your stay for relaxation—walking or exploring other islands. Ferries depart from the bustling harbor at Hornum for the nearby island of Amrum or for a sightseeing tour of the "mini islands" known as Halligen. On these little islands, man has battled the sea for centuries. The farmhouses are built on man-made hills because the sea regularly floods the pastures leaving the farmhouses marooned on their own miniature islands.

When your island holiday is over, if your destination is Denmark, you can take a ferry from List or retrace your steps to Niebul for the short drive to the Danish border. For those who are returning to Hamburg, follow the road south across the flat polder lands that have been reclaimed from the sea. The waters offshore are shallow; sea dikes keep them at bay, protecting the lush green pasture and farmlands behind.

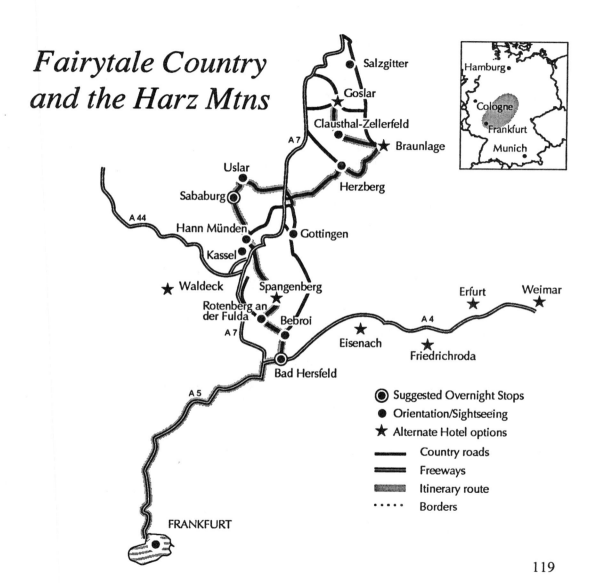

Fairytale Country and the Harz Mtns

Salzgitter

Goslar

Clausthal-Zellerfeld

A 7

Braunlage

Uslar

Herzberg

Sababurg

A 44

Hann Münden

Göttingen

Kassel

Waldeck

Spangenberg

Erfurt

Weimar

Rotenberg an der Fulda

Bebroi

A 7

A 4

Eisenach

Friedrichroda

Bad Hersfeld

A 5

⊙ Suggested Overnight Stops

● Orientation/Sightseeing

★ Alternate Hotel options

――― Country roads

═══ Freeways

▨▨ Itinerary route

····· Borders

FRANKFURT

Hamburg

Cologne

Frankfurt

Munich

Fairytale Country and the Harz Mountains

No less entrancing than Germany's more oft' trod tourist routes is the region between Frankfurt and Hannover—the regions that gave birth to "Sleeping Beauty" and "Little Red Riding Hood," whose tales beginning "Once upon a time" transport us back to childhood memories of wicked stepmothers and handsome princes. But the area has more than fairytales: it is enhanced by its misty mountains, neat small towns of half-timbered buildings and placid shallow rivers flowing quietly through pretty countryside. It was here that Joseph and Wilhelm Grimm pursued their hobby of writing down folk tales told to them by the local villagers. A published collection of these tales is known worldwide as "Grimm's Fairy Tales."

Hann Munden

This itinerary highlights the heart of the German Fairytale Route and then swings east into the Harz mountains. The itinerary does not correspond exactly with the German Tourist Office's fairytale route, yet it is similar, and the German Tourist Office will be glad to provide you with a whimsical pictorial map to lead you down the Fairytale Road that is well marked by signposts with a smiling good fairy.

ORIGINATING CITY   FRANKFURT

Frankfurt is at the crossroads of Germany where transportation routes converge. If you have the inclination to visit the heart of this modern vibrant metropolis, venture downtown. Visit the reconstructed old section, see the house where Johann Wolfgang von Goethe spent his formative years, and browse through Frankfurt's many boutiques and specialty stores—a joy for the ardent shopper.

DESTINATION I   BAD HERSFELD

Leaving Frankfurt, take the autobahn 5 north for about an hour and a half to Alsfeld. The town's lovely historic core is not large and is easily explored on foot. The town hall is raised above the square by tall stone arches, which gave the citizens of old a sheltered place to hold their market day. This half-timbered building, with its peaked turrets looking like witches' hats, is one of the finest in Germany. Explore the streets around the market square for they are full of old leaning houses and cobbles worn smooth by many feet over the centuries. Because of its historic old buildings, the town was chosen to receive a facelift in 1975 to celebrate European Architectural Heritage Year.

The area around Alsfeld is known as Red Riding Hood country. When the Grimm brothers collected their fairytales, they noted that the young girls of the area wore small red cloaks with hoods, and hence the title to the story. At festival times you will see young girls in their traditional costumes topped by small red cloaks.

Following road 62 to the east, about an hour's drive through pretty countryside brings you to the town of Bad Hersfeld. Bad Hersfeld is rather plain in comparison to some of the towns you will see—but handsome nonetheless. At its heart lies a large market square lined with old burghers' houses. Part of the square has been turned into a pedestrian mall and it is in this pedestrian zone, with its tables and chairs spilling over into the square, that you will find the Hotel Zum Stern. Bustling and welcoming, the inn has been offering hospitality to weary travelers for over 500 years. Try to secure one of the darling rooms at the front of the hotel: with their blackened beams, creaking floorboards and antique furniture, they are a real prize.

Your location on the market square is ideal for exploring. Thankfully the town is not a tourist trap, but a busy assortment of everyday shops—butchers and grocers plus wonderful cafes offering coffee and mouth-watering pastries. Admire the architecture of the houses in the old town and do not miss the majestic ruined abbey that makes a splendid backdrop for the famous musical festival held here every July.

It is said that George III of England enlisted many Bad Hersfeld soldiers to help put down the American Revolution—the poor men were so terrified by a dreadful Atlantic crossing that those who survived the war stayed put in America.

DESTINATION II   SABABURG

When it is time to leave Bad Hersfeld, take the road 27 to the north through Bebra where you turn left on the road 83 for the short drive to Rotenberg an der Fulda. As you turn into this old town you will see ancient houses sheltered beneath the cliff that rises dramatically from the River Fulda.

Next, follow country roads north for the short drive to Spangenberg. Stroll amidst the old houses on the town's main street, the Klosterstrasse, and then drive up the winding road to the Schloss Spangenberg that looms above the town. From the castle ramparts the tiny brown and black timbered houses of the town below look as if they belong in a child's toy box. If the weather is fine, the restaurant on the ramparts makes a perfect refreshment stop: the town is spread before you and the castle rises steeply to your back.

Continue to the north through the town of Hessisch Lichtenau for the short drive to Kassel. The town has centuries of history but is now modern in style largely because the Allies flattened most of it during World War II. This modern sprawling metropolis is the heart of German fairytale country for it was here that the great folklorists Jakob and Wilhelm Grimm worked as court librarians between 1805 and 1830. In their spare time the congenial brothers walked the countryside collecting myths, legends and folk tales. Pausing for a glass of beer at the Knallhutte (brewery) in the nearby town of Baunatal, they met Dorothea Viehmann, an old lady with a passion for yarns. She was born at the brewery and over the years had picked up stories from travelers. The brothers were attentive listeners—and even better writers. In 1815 they published a collection of their tales that is known the world over as "Grimm's Fairy Tales." If you are interested in their writing, you will want to visit the "Bruder-Grimm Museum" with its memorabilia of their lives and works: it is well marked from the center of town. Otherwise it is best to avoid Kassel's urban sprawl and let the autobahn whisk you northwards to Hann Münden.

Where the Weser and the Werra rivers converge, the town of Hann Münden has grown—a town of graceful old houses embellished with figures, animal heads and curlicues. Walking along some of the old side streets, you will notice the fronts of the houses look like the prows of a fleet of old galleons leaning against the wind. The old town has survived turbulent centuries intact—all that has been needed is a touchup coat of paint here and there. The eccentric "quack" Dr Eisenbart is buried in the town. In the 17th Century he was a successful surgeon and doctor—although his doctoring was somewhat unorthodox: "I give back the blind the use of their legs, the paralyzed their sight, I give shots in the middle of the stitch, for anesthesia I use ten pounds of opium." Apparently proud of its rather unorthodox surgeon, the town honors him with summer performances of the play "Dr Eisenbart."

Follow the River Weser to the north as it leaves Hann Münden. A left turn in the nearby village of Reinhardshagen takes you through the "enchanted" forest of the Rheinhard to your hotel for tonight, the Burghotel Sababurg, more often referred to as Sleeping Beauty's Castle. The Brothers Grimm visited Sababurg Castle and used it as the setting for their famous story. Plan on arriving late in the day to avoid the coach loads of daytime tourists that flock to this attraction.

Burghotel Sababurg, Sababurg

What was once a proud fortress is now largely a romantic ruin—a shell of towers and walls. Fortunately one wing has been restored as a hotel. The dining room serves superb venison and provides lovely views of the countryside and distant forest. There is no lounge or bar to gather in before or after dinner, so splurge and request a larger room. The romance of staying in Sleeping Beauty's castle cannot be denied, but be aware that the castle is very isolated.

Bid farewell to Sleeping Beauty's domain and retrace your steps into the forest taking the road north to the Weser River. Cross the river and follow signs that lead you east to Uslar, an enchanting town of many half-timbered houses.

From Uslar it is about a 45-minute drive to Gottingen, an old university town where the Brothers Grimm taught. Apart from admiring its old and very lovely architecture, you must visit Liesel, the Goose Girl, whose statue stands atop the fountain in front of the town hall on the market square. She is reputed to be the most kissed girl in the world. This is no small surprise for the story says that anyone who kisses Liesel will enjoy good luck the rest of his life.

Leaving Gottingen, main roads take you east for the half-hour drive to Herzberg located at the foot of the Harz Mountains. From Herzberg, continue east upwards into the mountains to St Andreasburg. High on top of a hill, the town's streets drop steeply to the old Samson Silver Mine in the valley. Since the mine closed in 1910, the little town has become an attractive tourist center.

A few kilometers beyond St Andreasburg

Liesel, the Goose Girl of Gottingen

is Braunlage. On the town's main street you will find the small Romantik Hotel zur Tanne. The owners, Helmut and Barbel Herbst, are perfect hosts whose warm welcome, excellent English, and concern for their guests' comfort add to an enjoyable stay. The dining room is the center of activity for the hotel and has gained a well-deserved reputation for fine cuisine and excellent service. The choice bedrooms are found at the front; cozy little rooms in the tiny old section of the hotel.

DESTINATION IV   GOSLAR

The Harz Mountains offers abundant wild mountain scenery to explore: deep gullies, tumbling mountain streams, green forests, and cool blue lakes—ideal country for hiking in the summer and cross country skiing in the winter.

The Brothers Grimm did not come this far north and thus missed a myth that was saved for Goethe who used it as a basis for the witches' Sabbath in "Faust." It is said that on Walpurgisnacht, April 30, cackling witches astride their broomsticks gather on the summit of Mount Brocken to cavort and cast their wicked spells.

As the itinerary's final destination lies only 40 kilometers north, take the opportunity for some leisurely sightseeing of this lovely region. Buy a walking map of the area and combine today's sightseeing with a walk to one of the lakes whose warm summer surfaces welcome swimmers but whose depths remain icy cold.

Leave Braunlage driving north along road 4, skirting the Harz's highest mountain, the Brocken. In Torfhaus, the busy small tourist center for the mountains, turn left along the Altenau road: the views of the valleys are quite breathtaking along this narrow road. In the ski resort of Altenau, bear left along the road 498 and shortly right along road 242. As the road descends into Clausthal-Zellerfeld you have beautiful views across forested high mountain valleys.

The twin towns of Clausthal and Zellerfeld were the capital of the Harz mining region, and the Oberharzer Museum in Zellerfeld is dedicated to mining in the Harz. Apart from displays of rock specimens and old-fashioned mining paraphernalia, rooms have been set up to give you a glimpse of eras long past showing how the miners lived and worked. Leaving the first museum, you cross a rustic courtyard and enter a mock-up of an old-fashioned underground mine. Here, as you wind up and down through the tunnels, a venerable old miner gives a discourse in German. It is all very self-explanatory so do not worry if you understand not a word.

Just on the southern outskirts of Zellerfeld, take the road to the right to Schulenberg and the Oker Dam. The road traces the dam and, as the valley narrows, follows the Oker river as it cascades and tumbles down from the mountains to the plain below. Linger in this wild and romantic river valley, an understandable favorite of visitors to the Harz.

Saving the best for last, you come to the capital of the region, the old imperial town of Goslar. Ambling through the town past half-timbered houses on crooked streets is like taking a walk back into the Middle Ages. The River Gose tumbles through the town past quaint red-tiled houses to the majestic 11th-century imperial palace, once the largest non-church building in the empire.

Occupying a corner of the market square, the old town merchants' guildhall is now the Hotel Kaiserworth where statues of German emperors guard the portals. Here you are only steps away from the town's main sights: the town hall, the market church and the Goslarer Museum with its fascinating displays of life in old Goslar. Step outside your hotel at six in the evening and watch the concert of the city clock whose four different scenes represent the 1,000-year-old mining history of the region. In such a colorful town, it is no wonder the bedrooms overlooking the market square are so popular with guests (ask for our special favorite—room 110).

Hotel Kaiserworth, Marketplatz in Goslar

Leaving Goslar, it is only a few kilometers to the autobahn where you have the choice of going south to Frankfurt, north to Hamburg or east to Berlin.

Hotel Descriptions

If you are looking for an isolated hideaway far from the oft' trod tourist paths, the Hotel Töpferhaus fits the bill. Hugging the shores of the tranquil Bistensee and surrounded by manicured gardens, the Hotel Töpferhaus commands a serene setting. On our first visit, the Töpferhaus was a small hotel with guest rooms in a simple white-washed farmhouse. This original part of the inn remains, but a new section has been built, adding 21 deluxe guest rooms and a restaurant with a view of the Bistensee gently lapping at the lawn in front of the hotel. As a result of the expansion, the hotel has gained a sophisticated elegance, but happily there is no jarring commercial feeling to spoil the mood. The setting remains superbly pastoral, the warmth of welcome sincere, and the furnishings throughout extremely tasteful. All the guest rooms are appealing, but I especially love number 30—on the ground floor with French doors opening out to the garden. The Töpferhaus is not the kind of hotel for an overnight stop, but rather an enchanting place to stay for at least several days to enjoy the unspoiled solitude of the countryside. The Töpferhaus is quite difficult to find: Take the autobahn 7 north from Hamburg and get off at the Rendsburg exit. Turn east on 203 (direction Eckernforde) and after about 3 km you come to the tiny village of Holzbunge. Turn left through the village and follow signs that guide you along a narrow road that leads to the Hotel Töpferhaus. Note: Do *NOT* go to Alt Duvenstedt—it is on the other side of the autobahn.

HOTEL TÖPFERHAUS
Owner: Ulrich Harms
34701 Alt Duvenstedt am Bistensee, Germany
tel:(04338) 402, fax:(04338) 551
35 rooms, Double: DM 230-DM 250
Open all year
Credit cards: all major
Restaurant-closed Mondays
120 km N of Hamburg, 22 km W of Kiel

On a hillside dotted with grazing sheep, near the village of Amorbach, is Der Schafhof, one of Germany's loveliest hotels. Built in 1721, it originally belonged to the estate of the Amorbach Benedictine Abbey. Now the flag bearing the crest of the Winkler family, who were once the titled millers of the region, is proudly raised out front. Der Schafhof is still an operating farm with sheep, hens and ducks, but the Winkler family also provide excellent accommodations and cuisine. There are fourteen guest rooms in the hotel. Their decor is consistently beautiful: a harmony of natural dyes in tones of brown, cream and white. The restaurant, decorated in warm colors with soft lighting, lovely flower arrangements and intimately placed tables, is captivating. The cuisine is exceptional and the wine cellar boasts an excellent selection of regional wines. Space is provided in the stables for guests' horses. Der Schafhof also has horse-drawn sleighs for country rides through snow or across lush green farmland and there are kilometers of undeveloped land to explore. Guests may also enjoy tennis in the garden, or simply relaxing on the terrace. A very handsome couple, the Winklers offer travelers a splendid retreat.

DER SCHAFHOF
Owner: Dr. Winkler
Otterbachtal
63916 Amorbach, Germany
tel: (09373) 80.88, fax: (09373) 41.20
14 rooms, Double: 220-350 DM
Closed January to mid-February
Credit cards: all major
Restaurant-open daily
tennis, boccia, garden chess
3 km W of Amorbach
80 km SE of Frankfurt, 67 km NE of Heidelberg

The Residenz Heinz Winkler, conveniently located just south of the expressway that links Munich and Salzburg, is a real charmer. The hotel is easy to find: as you drive into Aschau you will see a small hill rising from the town. Perched on this hill is a picturesque church with twin onion domes, and right next to the church is the Residenz Heinz Winkler. This stately home was at one time an annex of Hohenaschau Castle whose history dates back to the early 15th Century. From the moment you enter, the mood of sophisticated elegance is set. Light streams through large plate-glass windows into a spacious lobby with a marble floor enhanced by a handsome Persian carpet. The hotel is showcase for several dining rooms. Each has its own personality—from elaborately formal to cozy-Bavarian. On warm summer days, you have the option to dine outside on a protected terrace that affords a sweeping view of the mountains. And, if you appreciate truly fine cuisine, you will be pleased to note the hotel has the remarkable accomplishment of being awarded two coveted Michelin stars! The mood of subdued grandeur continues in the bedrooms. Each is appointed with fine furniture and lovely fabrics—every detail of this Relais & Chateaux hotel exudes quality.

RESIDENZ HEINZ WINKLER
Owner: Heinz Winkler
Kirchplatz 1
83229 Aschau, Germany
tel: (08052) 17.990, fax: (08052) 17.99.66
32 rooms, Double: 280-450 DM
Suites to 640 DM
Open all year
Credit cards: all major
Restaurant-open daily
Located 82 km SE of Munich
Gast im Schloss; Relais & Chateaux

The tiny wine village of Assmannshausen has grown up at a slight widening of the narrow Rhine river gorge. Limited by its geographic location, the village has not been spoiled by modern development and remains as a cramped cluster of old houses overlooking the river. Fronting the Rhine river, the Hotel Krone has been providing bed, food and drink to weary travelers since 1541. The hotel's vine-covered terrace and raised restaurant provide lovely places for dining while watching the busy river life glide by. Much of the building dates from the turn of the century. The interior is perfectly in keeping with the exterior, with large, rather heavy, pieces of lovingly polished furniture against dark paneled walls. Some of the bedrooms are in the main building while others are located in the adjacent annex—all have been beautifully refurbished and are "decorator perfect." All of the rooms are attractive, but the 14 luxury suites, furnished with antiques, are especially appealing. The rooms in the front are choice since these offer the added advantage of a view of the Rhine. Rhine river steamers arrive and depart from the dock just a five-minute walk away: if you arrive by boat the hotel will gladly send someone to meet you and tend to your luggage. (Note when the Rhine is low, the steamers cannot dock at Assmannshausen so stop in the nearby town of Rüdesheim.) Assmannshausen is not on most maps. It is on the Rhine, 5 km NW of Rüdesheim.

HOTEL KRONE
Owner: Family Hufnagel-Ullrich
65385 Rüdesheim-Assmannshausen, Germany
tel: (06722) 40.30, fax: (06722) 30.49
55 rooms, Double: 294-424 DM
14 Suites 440-820 DM
Closed January & February
Credit cards: all major
Restaurant-open daily, pool
70 km W of Frankfurt, 31 km W of Mainz
5 km NW of Rüdesheim

Come dream a romantic dream or two in this imposing hillside fortress. Surrounded by dense forest, the Burg Schnellenberg has been in existence since 1255. Over the years it has been altered, added to and finally restored into an elegant castle hotel. The halls display enormous old oil paintings. The bedrooms vary in their size and aspect: you may find yourself in a cozy paneled room with a window seat overlooking the trout ponds or high atop a winding turret staircase in a room with twenty-foot-high ceilings and a lofty view over the surrounding countryside. The furniture is large and old, not as old as the castle but very old nonetheless. The main dining room is splendid: several rooms with lofty ceilings, an enormous old tapestry decorating the main wall, and groupings of elegant tables and chairs. A further dining room is decorated in a hunting lodge motif and beneath it lies a cozy wine cellar bar. Other cellars comprise a museum where rows of cases are filled with weapons and suits of armor. Tucked away in the upper castle is a 17th-century family chapel whose vaulted ceiling is covered with decorative Biblical frescoes.

BURGHOTEL SCHNELLENBERG
Owner: Family Bilsing
57439 Attendorn, Germany
tel: (02722) 69.40, fax: (02722) 69.469
42 rooms, 5 suites; Double: 210-300 DM
Open mid-January to December 20
Credit cards: all major
Restaurant-open daily, tennis
3.5 km E of Attendorn
131 km E of Düsseldorf, past the Biggesee
Gast im Schloss

If your heart always longs to be in the countryside, on your next visit to Hamburg stay at the Fürst Bismarck Mühle. It is just a five-minute walk to the station where you can hop on a train for the half-hour ride to the heart of the Hamburg. The Fürst Bismarck Mühle, a charming cottage-like white mill with a gabled roof, is set in a forest overlooking a peaceful pond. On the side of the inn, a stream rushes by—a reminder that in days-gone-by, this was a mill for grinding corn. The entrance is accented by cheerful bright-red double doors. Excellent meals are served in the beamed-ceilinged dining room that has an heirloom armoire, carved chests, portraits, and oil paintings (all authentic antiques from the Bismarck family). Tall windows on three sides capture the sunlight and views of the pond and forests. A flight of stairs leads up to the seven, comfortable, home-like guest rooms. All are furnished with antiques, and have traditional, color-coordinated fabrics used for the draperies, upholstery and bed coverings. I loved room 5, overlooking the pond, but it really doesn't matter what room you choose—they are all appealing. In 1871 King Wilhelm I gave the Sachsenwald Forest (which included the old corn mill) to Chancellor Otto von Bismarck and the property still belongs to the family. Although the inn is filled with memorabilia from the Bismarck family, the old mill has been leased and superbly managed by Jochen Dölger and Monika Diehl for nearly 20 years.

FÜRST BISMARCK MÜHLE
Monika Diehl & Jochen Dölger
Mühlenweg 3
21521 Aumühle, Germany
tel: (04104) 20.28, fax: (04104) 12.00
7 rooms, Double: 190 DM
Open all year
Credit cards: EC, MC, VS
Restaurant-closed on Wednesdays
25 km W of Hamburg

The Brauerei-Gasthof-Hotel Aying is a famous brewery, restaurant and hotel, all rolled into one typically Bavarian package. The hotel's wisteria-covered facade is easily spotted thanks to a giant, blue-striped flagpole marking the entrance. The front doors and entry area are painted a bright blue, complemented by many decorative flower designs and German proverbs inscribed on the ceiling beams. Fresh bouquets and large dried flower arrangements abound in all the public areas, and traditional "hearts and flowers" painting adorns most every nook and cranny—on armoires, beams, staircases and old chests. The restaurant offers candlelit dinners in front of a large, open fireplace. The romantic scene is completed with Dutch-blue tablecloths set with pretty china and glassware. Traditional Bavarian specialties of ham and pork (and of course all varieties of the famous Ayinger beer) are offered with pride. The guest rooms are all extremely inviting. Some are decorated with Bavarian-style painted furniture. Others have a more traditional elegant look. One of my favorites is room 1, with pretty fabrics in tones of peaches and greens. As a special little touch, beer is left as a gift in each room. Aying is a pretty, Bavarian brewery town, with the advantage of being in the country, yet very convenient to Munich.

BRAUEREI-GASTHOF-HOTEL AYING
Owner: Family Franz Inselkammer
Zornedinger Strasse 2
85653 Aying bei Munchen, Germany
tel: (08095) 705, fax: (08095) 20.53
28 rooms, 2 suites; Double: 220-300 DM
Closed last 2 weeks in January
Credit cards: all major
Restaurant & beer garden-open daily
25 km SE of Munich

The Romantik Kurhotel was built by Herzog Friedrich Franz von Mecklenburg in 1793 as a holiday retreat where he would come to the Baltic Sea for his health. Thus started the concept in Germany of a spa holiday, a trend that continues to be extremely popular today. During the Communist regime, the Kurhotel was confiscated, but with the re-unification, the Metz family returned to Bad Doberan to reclaim their family home. They found it a disaster: dark, dingy and very depressing. Happily, Dr Metz's wife (who oversaw the renovation) has impeccable taste. After studying both Scandinavian and English decorating journals, she came up with her own style, combining the fresh clean, uncluttered look of Scandinavian design with lovely traditional English fabrics. The mood of understated elegance is set as you enter the reception hall where classical music is playing. Soft-white predominates throughout with bouquets of freshly cut flowers and pretty slip-covered chairs in handsome English stripes adding just the right dash of color. There are main two dining rooms. Each is traditional in feel, with Biedermeyer-style chairs, handsome draperies, pastel colors and fresh flowers. The guest bedrooms continue the country-manor-look with English fabrics in color schemes of soft yellows or pretty greens. Note: The hotel is located in the center of town facing the small park.

ROMANTIK KURHOTEL
Owner: Family Metz
Am Kamp
18209 Bad Doberan, Germany
tel: (038203) 30.36, fax: (038203) 21.26
60 rooms, Double: 198-248 DM
Open all year
Credit cards: all major
Restaurant-open daily
17 km W of Rostock, 210 km NW of Berlin
USA Rep: Euro-Connection 800-645-3876

Bad Hersfeld is a handsome North German town. At its heart lies a large market square lined with old burghers' houses, part of which has been turned into a pedestrian mall. It is in this pedestrian zone, with its tables and chairs spilling over onto the square, that you find the Romantik Hotel Zum Stern. Bustling and welcoming, the inn has been offering hospitality to weary travelers for over 500 years. In recent years, as the volume of trade has grown, the hotel has expanded back from the square so that accommodations are provided both in the old section and a modern extension. An indoor swimming pool is found at the rear of the building overlooking the garden. Try to secure one of the darling rooms in the original hostelry. With their blackened beams, creaking floorboards and antique furniture, they are a real prize. Regional specialties highlight the extensive menu. What is special here is the kindness and hospitality of the Kniese family who have owned this inn for four generations.

ROMANTIK HOTEL ZUM STERN
Owner: Family Kniese
Linggplatz 11
36251 Bad Hersfeld, Germany
tel: (06621) 18.90, fax: (06621) 18.92.60
45 rooms, Double: 190-230 DM
Open all year
Credit cards: all major
Restaurant-open daily, indoor pool
170 km NE of Frankfurt
126 km W of Erfurt, 69 km SE of Kassel
USA Rep: Euro-Connection 800-645-3876

Romantik Hotel "Der Kleine Prinz" (The Little Prince) is an appealing small hotel, conveniently located close to shopping, parks and spa facilities in the popular resort town of Baden Baden. The inn's ambiance is more French than German, its mood set by the pretty facade topped by a mansard roof. The Gaelic mood continues as you walk up the front steps and into the hotel and are welcomed by a salon-like room decorated in soft pink tones offering chairs set around small tables and a fireplace. The reception desk is located beyond this inviting lounge, and the owners, Edeltraud and Norbert Rademacher, are often present to personally greet each new arrival. The guest rooms are comfortable, and each has its own special feature such as an open fire-place, tower, balcony or whirlpool-bath. Some are decorated with antiques, others with reproduction light pine furniture. All have cable TV, and minibars. Norbert Rademacher worked in hotels in the United States for many years so he knows and caters to American tastes and preferences. "Der Kleine Prinz" is named after the irresistible red-haired hero of St. Exupéry's heartwarming fable, and as whimsical touch, a memento of this delightful little fellow appears in every guest room. It is refreshing to find such a warm and friendly hotel in the somewhat formal spa town of Baden Baden.

ROMANTIK HOTEL "DER KLEINE PRINZ"
Owners: Edeltraud & Norbert Rademacher
Lichtentaler Strasse 36
76530 Baden-Baden, Germany
tel: (07221) 34.64, fax: (07221) 38.264
39 rooms, Double: 325-375 DM
Open all year
Credit cards: all major
Restaurant-open daily
112 N of Freiburg, 39 km S of Karlsruhe
USA Rep: Euro-Connection 800-645-3876

I postponed writing the description of the Hotel Sonne, not because of the task, but out of a desire to make the description the best it could be—to do justice to the excellence of the hotel and the hospitality of its owner. Herr Fischer continues a tradition begun by his grandfather some hundred years ago. This is an inn where guests are welcomed year after year, where a sense of home is created. The Sonne is the oldest gasthaus in Badenweiler and Herr Fischer has a greeting and a loving smile for all. He and his wife are ever present among their guests, selecting wines, suggesting outings and even sometimes escorting excursions themselves. A walk into the Black Forest is always more special with their company. Very caring hosts, the Fischers offer accommodations of comfort that vary from simple guest rooms to beautiful, traditionally decorated rooms. There are even a few commodious apartments. Of the restaurants, one is cozy and intimate, and the other (a larger, more formal, dining room) is for pension guests. The Fischer family once also had vineyards, but now Herr Fischer is dedicated solely to the hotel business—and it shows. Note: The hotel is located in the old part of Badenweiler, up a small lane above the church.

ROMANTIK HOTEL SONNE
Owners: Family Fischer
Moltkestrasse 4
79405 Badenweiler, Germany
tel: (07632) 75.080, fax: (07632) 75.08.65
40 rooms, 10 suites; Double: 145-225 DM
Closed mid-November to mid-February
Credit cards: all major
Restaurant-closed on Wednesdays
35 km S of Freiburg, 40 km N of Basel
USA. Rep: Euro-Connection 800-645-3876

Bamberg is an absolute delight, a medieval city exuding the appeal of yesteryear. It is almost too picturesque to be real with the Rathaus (city hall) perched on a tiny island in the middle of the river that flows through the center of town. In fact, to cross the river one follows a tunnel through the arcaded Rathaus, which also forms one of the walled entrances to the city. Just a few minute's walk from the Rathaus, marvelously positioned fronting the Regnitz River, is the Hotel Brudermühle. It is an attractive three-story light yellow building, with green shutters and dormer windows peeking out from under the steeply pitched red roof. Originally a mill dating from the early 14th Century, the structure now houses a small, modern hotel. The owners, Erna and Georg Vogler have increased the hotel's charm with a few well-chosen antiques. Just off the lobby is an attractive restaurant where good "home-cooking" of regional specialties is served. The guest rooms are small and the decor is simple, but you'll be quite happy if you're lucky enough to snare one the choice rooms: number 5 (overlooking the river) or number 1 (a sunny corner room with a view of both the river and the famous Rathaus).

HOTEL BRUDERMÜHLE
Owners: Erna & Georg Vogler
Schranne 1
96049 Bamberg, Germany
tel: (0951) 54.091, fax: (0951) 51.211
16 rooms, Double: 160 DM
Open all year
Credit cards: VS, DC, MC
Restaurant-closed Mondays
61 km NW of Nürnberg, 230 N of Munich

Bamberg is a beautiful town and a destination that deserves more attention than given in travel literature. From a distance, the six spires of its church pierce the skyline. At its center, Bamberg is a complex of quaint cobbled pedestrian streets, outdoor cafes, bridges and enchanting houses that grace and line the waterfront. Not more than a few blocks from the old section of town is a simple hotel with wonderful restaurant—the Romantik Hotel Weinhaus Messerschmitt. The charming, well-known, Franconian-style restaurant (in the Pschorn family since 1832) always includes local specialties on the menu. The hotel has only fifteen rooms for overnight guests. The bedrooms are found up a marvelous wooden handcarved stairway and are identified from other offices and private rooms by numbered wine bottles that hang over each door. The bedrooms are simple but sweet in decor. Down comforters deck the beds and the bathroom facilities are modern but enhanced by lovely old fixtures. At night it is difficult to shut out the street noise but a welcome cognac left by the considerate management might be all you need to sleep.

ROMANTIK WEINHAUS MESSERSCHMITT
Owners: Lydia & Otto Pschorn
Langestrasse 41
96047 Bamberg, Germany
tel: (0951) 27.866, fax: (0951) 26.141
14 rooms, 1 suite; Double: 190-218 DM
Open all year
Credit cards: all major
Restaurant-open daily
61 km NW of Nürnberg
USA. Rep: Euro-Connection 800-645-3876

The Jagdschloss Thiergarten is a small, ever-so-pretty hunting lodge (well-known for its excellent cuisine) that has converted eight rooms to accommodate overnight guests. The spacious bedrooms are individually furnished, not with a sleek elegance, but more like guest rooms in a country home. There are several intimate, pastel-toned dining rooms, just brimming with charm. The "Kamin" (translates as fireplace) has just a few elegantly set tables warmed by a dramatic fireplace. The "Venezianischer Salon" highlights a dramatic, very intricate, two-tiered hand-made Venetian glass chandelier that dates back approximately 300 years. The "Barocksaal," used for brunch on Sundays and also banquets or weddings, is found in the imposing rotunda, open to a meticulously restored, detailed ceiling. In days-gone-by, when the hotel was primarily a hunting lodge, guests actually shot from the vantage point of a balcony that wrapped around the rotunda. In warm weather tables are set out on a stretch of grass behind the castle, under the blossoms of cherry and apple trees. Open as a hotel for more than 40 years, the Schloss Hotel Thiergarten provides a delightful retreat from the neighboring city of Bayreuth. Note: The hotel is very easy to find. Driving south from Bayreuth on expressway 9, take the Bayreuth-Sud exit and follow signs to Thiergarten.

SCHLOSS HOTEL THIERGARTEN
Owners: Renate & Harald Kaiser
Obertheirgärtner Strasse 36
95406 Thiergarten-Bayreuth, Germany
tel: (09209) 13.14, fax: (09209) 18.29
8 rooms, Double: 220-260 DM
Open all year
Credit cards: all major
Restaurant-closed Mondays
75 km NE of Nürnberg, 6 km S of Bayreuth
Gast im Schloss

The Hotel Haus Lipmann, dating back to 1795, has been in the same family for many years: Frau Lipmann, her son Joachim and her gracious daughter Marion are the sixth and seventh generations of the family to run this inn and tend the family vineyards that rise steeply above the banks of the Moselle river. This small hotel is especially appealing because it is located at the heart of one of the prettiest village along the Moselle. With its picturesque medieval buildings, church and ruined castle, Beilstein is a gem. The dining rooms are just as quaint as the exterior: you may find yourself in a small farmhouse-style room before an old fireplace, in the warm paneled main dining room or feasting in the knights' hall surrounded by collections of old weapons. When weather permits, you can move out of doors to the terrace and watch the life on the gentle Moselle river glide by as sip a glass of Moselle wine produced from the Lipmann's own grapes. Upstairs are five nicely decorated guest rooms. Ask for one of the bedrooms in the front of the house with an antique bed and a splendid river view. The Haus Lipmann makes an excellent base for exploring the Moselle. Note: There are additional rooms available in a nearby annex, but our preference is for one of the five bedrooms in the main building. Beilstein's wine festival takes place during the first weekend in September.

HOTEL HAUS LIPMANN
Owner: Family Lipmann
Marktplatz 3
56814 Beilstein, Germany
tel: (02673) 15.73
5 rooms, Double: 120–150 DM
Open mid-March to mid-November
Credit cards: none accepted
Restaurant, garden terrace
111 km NW of Mainz, 11 km SE of Cochem

The Hotel Geiger, located at the Austrian-Bavarian border, is a large mountain cabin with the elegance of a fine city hotel. Set on the hillside on the outskirts of Berchtesgaden in the direction of Bad Reichenall, the hotel is a weathered chalet attractively decked with green shutters, wooden balconies and overflowing flower boxes. With its traditional Bavarian decor, the Hotel Geiger blends perfectly into this Alpine region on the Austrian-German border. The entrance into the main building exposes the richness of a wood-paneled dining room with handsome painted ceilings, planked floors, heart-carved chairs, red print cushions, Oriental carpets, hand carved figurine chandeliers, pewter, candles, antlers and the peaceful background of ticking old clocks—an atmosphere reminiscent of one of Scotland's finest hunting lodges. A sitting area adjoins the restaurant and its decor is consistent in rich tones and quality. Like a private library, the salon is warmed by an open fire, with heavy fabrics, wood paneling and large windows opening onto Alpine views. There are forty rooms in the old house and ten in a neighboring new annex. All the rooms enjoy views of the mountains.

BERCHTESGADEN HOTEL GEIGER
Owner: Hugo Geiger
Stanggass
83462 Berchtesgaden, Germany
tel: (08652) 96.53, fax: (08652) 96.54.00
50 rooms, 2 suites; Double: 160-400 DM
Closed mid-November to mid-December
Credit cards: VS
Restaurant-open daily, pool
150 km SE of Munich, 25 km S of Salzburg
USA Rep: Euro-Connection 800-645-3876

The atmospheric Hotel Watzmann is centrally located in Berchtesgaden across from the Franziskaner Kirche on the main road through town. It was originally built as a beer brewery in the 1600s and is now a family-run hotel filled with antiques, memorabilia and charm. The yellow facade with its green shutters and bright red geraniums is set back from the road behind a large terrace filled with tables, umbrellas, and, on a warm day, many patrons. The public areas and two dining rooms contain plenty of old prints, painted antique furniture and hunting trophies, as well as beamed ceilings and old ceramic stoves. Menu selections are traditionally Bavarian, featuring delicious pork and game dishes. The hotel has 38 bedrooms, only 17 of which have private baths, and none of which are equipped with phones or televisions. Bedrooms are comfortable, clean, and well appointed with reproduction Bavarian-style furniture, and large family suites are also available. The upstairs hallways are decorated by door panels painted with Bavarian floral designs and a collection of colorful old archery targets. Antique chests, armoires, and paintings are also displayed in abundance. This is a very warm Bavarian inn, owned and managed with personal care by the English speaking Piscantor family.

HOTEL WATZMANN
Owner: Family Hinrich Piscantor
Franziskanerplatz 2
83471 Berchtesgaden, Germany
tel: (08652) 20.55, fax: (08652) 51.74
38 rooms, 1 suite; Double: 108-158 DM
Closed October 31 to December 23
Credit cards: all major
Restaurant, open daily
150 km SE of Munich, 25 km S of Salzburg

Many hotels with super-expensive rates claim to be deluxe, few deliver. Not so with the Maritim Grand Hotel. This truly outstanding hotel gives you everything you could possibly expect in an elegant hotel—and more. Although large, the Maritim Grand Hotel has the warmth and friendliness usually only encountered in small, family-run establishments. From the front desk receptionist to the maid who brings fresh towels, every one exudes a caring, yet professional manner. You enter into one of the grandest lobbies imaginable with a broad staircase sweeping majestically up to the second level that forms a galleried balcony. As you gaze far above to the domed skylight, the floors rise ever higher like a tiered wedding cake, each level with a balcony overlooking the lobby below. The architectural effect is reminiscent of the "Hyatt" style, but the mood is sophisticated and traditional instead of contemporary. Although large, the lobby is cleverly designed with intimate nooks and crannies that encourage friends to gather and talk quietly. The beautifully decorated guest rooms offer more amenities than I have ever seen in a deluxe hotel: large bath towels, towel warmers, tooth brushes, combs, hair dryers, fancy soaps and shampoos, and even such a thoughtful extra as an umbrella to use on a rainy day.

MARITIM GRAND HOTEL
Manager: Thomas Wachs
Friedrichstrasse 158-164
10117 Berlin, Germany
tel: (030) 23.270, fax: (030) 23.27.33.62
350 rooms, 20 suites; Double: from 536 DM
Suites from 756 DM
Open all year
Credit cards: all major
Restaurant-open daily
3 blocks E of the Brandenburg Gate

Because so many buildings in Berlin were demolished in World War II, most of the hotels are of necessity, comparatively new construction. Such is the case with the Hotel Mondial. But happily, it is very inviting and instead of being starkly modern, has an appealing warmth. The location is ideal, on the nicest stretches of Berlin's fascinating shopping street, the Kurfürstendamm. The hotel sits far enough back from the street to allow space for a sidewalk cafe where tables are set under shady trees, a favorite place for guests to sip a glass of wine or glass of beer while watching the world of Berlin pass by. The exterior is mostly glass, but it is not gaudy. Bronzed green trim, marble, and dark glass create a sedate, somewhat traditional feel. The attractive reception area and intimate bar are modern, but not starkly so, and have a predominantly rose color-scheme. To the left of the lobby, excellent meals are served in the "Krautergarten" restaurant, which is decorated in shades of green. There is a parking garage, not free, but still a blessing as it is a convenient, safe place to park your car. All the double rooms have private baths and are offered at a range of prices. None of the rates are a bargain (everything in the heart of Berlin is expensive), but the lowest priced rooms continue to offer one of the best values for a quality hotel in Berlin. .

HOTEL MONDIAL
Manager: Herr U. Hayer
Kurfürstendamm 47
10707 Berlin, Germany
tel: (030) 88.41.10, fax: (030) 88.41.11.150
75 rooms, Double: 280-480 DM
Open all year
Credit cards: all major
Restaurant-open daily, indoor pool
In the heart of Berlin

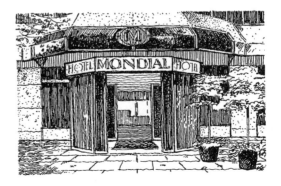

Berlin is a large, bustling city, yet incredibly close-by, is an oasis of forests and lakes called the Grunewald. If you don't mind a short drive into the city, you can stay in the Grunewald (Green Forest) at the Forsthaus Paulsborn, and not only spend much less than you would for a comparable hotel in Berlin, but also have the fun of staying in a 19th-century hunting lodge, surrounded by woodlands and just steps from the Grunewaldsee (Grunewald Lake). In addition to being a hotel, the Forsthaus Paulsborn is well-known as a restaurant where the talented Bernd-Peter Heide (manager of Forsthaus Paulson) has been chef for many years. On weekends the dining room is bustling with guests who come to enjoy a meal in the countryside. When the weather is warm, meals are also served outside. The Forsthaus Paulsborn is an appealing small lodge-like building, painted white with two small turrets and a steeply pitched red tile roof. The approach to the restaurant (which also serves as the reception desk for the hotel) is through a beautifully tended garden. On the ground floor of the hotel is the main restaurant, plus a series of small dining rooms for private parties. A staircase leads to the bedrooms. Although the bedrooms are simple and the decor rather dated, they all have private bathrooms, television, and direct dial phone. One of my favorites, room 14, has a view of the lake from the pretty sitting area in the round bay window.

FORSTHAUS PAULSBORN
Innkeeper: Bernd-Peter Heide
Am Grunewaldsee
14193 Berlin, Germany
tel: (030)81.38.010, fax: (030) 81.41.156
10 rooms, Double: 185-230 DM
Open all year
Credit cards: all major
Restaurant-closed Mondays
10-minute car ride from downtown Berlin

No sightseeing excursion to Berlin would be complete without a visit to the nearby suburb of Potsdam to see the sensational palaces and gardens of Sansouci and Schloss Cecilienhof. Most tourists linger along the paths of the Schloss Cecilienhof, never realizing that if they had planned ahead, they could have spent the night. This historic castle, the very place where Truman, Churchill and Stalin signed the Potsdam agreement in 1945, now takes overnight guests. The setting of this lovely timbered manor-house hotel is magnificent—not one, but two lakes are on the property plus beautiful forests laced with walking paths. Only a part of the castle is operated as a hotel, the remainder and the surrounding park are open to the public. Most of the guest rooms are alike, pleasantly decorated with modern wooden furniture, writing desk, mini bar, television, table and two chairs. What makes these rooms so appealing are the views out over the park. There is also a lovely "bridal suite" available that has a canopied king-size bed and is quite special. The paneled dining room is very appealing, especially in the evening when the cozy room glows from the candles on each table. On warm days, lunch is served on a pretty garden terrace. This is a serene, pleasant hotel that offers a wonderful alternative to staying in nearby Berlin.

HOTEL SCHLOSS CECILIENHOF
Manager: Adolf Bismark
Neuer Garten
14469 Potsdam, Germany
tel: (0331) 37.050, fax: (0331) 22.498
40 rooms, 3 suites; Double: 250-380 DM
Open all year
Credit cards: all major
Restaurant-open daily
24 km SW of Berlin
USA Rep: Euro-Connection 800-645-3876

Bernkastel is one of the most charming of the larger towns along the Moselle River. Fronting the river are large turn-of-the-century hotels, venture behind them and you find winding, cobblestoned streets lined by 400-year-old half-timbered houses. In amongst these side streets is found the Doctor Weinstuben. Named after the local tax collector, Doctor Wein, who lived here in the 17th Century, the house went on to become a wine room and in 1974 became a hotel when a modern block of rooms was built across the courtyard. While an effort was made to put an old world exterior on the annex, the accommodations are modern, functional hotel rooms. Their decor is clean and bright but far from memorable. Each room has a private bathroom. By sharp contrast, the hotel has put a great deal of effort into making the restaurant in the old wine room reflect the atmosphere of this pretty little wine town. A large hay wagon stands as a decorative centerpiece and around it the lofty room has been divided into intimate dining nooks with beams and dark wood.

HOTEL DOCTOR WEINSTUBEN
Owner: Manfred Schantz
Hebegasse 5
54470 Bernkastel-Kues, Germany
tel: (06531) 60.81 (06531) 62.96
19 rooms, Double: 140-160 DM
Open March to December
Credit cards: all major
Restaurant-closed Thursdays
75 km SW of Koblenz
On the Moselle river

The Hotel Zur Post is lovingly and professionally looked after by owners Frau and Herr Rossling. True hoteliers, the Rosslings do a superb job and are always striving to improve their charming hotel. Located slightly away from the center of town and right on the banks of the Moselle, the Zur Post has a mustard colored facade that is complemented by dark green shutters and window boxes of red geraniums. In the oldest part of the Zur Post, dating from 1827, guests climb a narrow old stairway to spotless rooms that have been recently renovated so that all now have private baths. An adjoining annex is located just beside and behind the hotel, and is skillfully done so that from the exterior the entire ensemble looks original. The annex rooms combine modern appointments with tasteful decorating, adding up to a level of comfort that is truly a treat. The Zur Post's excellent kitchen serves a generous breakfast buffet as well as savory lunch and dinner specialties. Guests may choose to dine in any one of the three warm dining rooms. The informal restaurant has walls and ceilings entirely of carved pine complemented by dried flower arrangements and bright tablecloths. Usually full of fun-loving guests, the restaurant is also a cozy spot for an afternoon sampling of the crisp, white regional wines. The other two dining rooms offer a slightly more refined atmosphere with table side service and attentive waiters.

HOTEL ZUR POST
Owner: Family Rossling
54470 Bernkastel-Kues, Germany
tel: (06531) 20.22, fax: (06531) 29.27
42 rooms, 1 suite; Double: 150-180 DM
Closed month of January
Credit cards: all major
Restaurant-open daily, sauna
75 km SW of Koblenz
on Moselle River

The Störzer family have lovingly converted a building that dates from 1500 and added an annex to offer guests 43 delightful rooms in a village whose inhabitants probably number even fewer than the guests in the hotel. In this rural setting, mornings might be disturbed by the sound of milkcarts or a tractor. The Romantik Hotel "Die Bierhütte" incorporates the Bavarian theme throughout in its decor. Stenciling, found bordering doorways, is used to identify rooms, and furnishings are in light wood enhanced by lovely handpainted designs—so typical of the region. All the rooms in the new annex have either a balcony or terrace depending on whether they are found on the ground or first floor and the entire basement of the annex is devoted to a playroom equipped with toys, sauna, solarium, ping pong table and fitness room. In the main building, the restaurant, "Wappenstupen," is named for the coats of armor displayed on the walls, the "Gaststube" is a cozy room available for either a meal or refreshment, and the cheery breakfast room benefits from the morning sun. A lovely terrace, over looking the lake, is used on warmer days for dining.

ROMANTIK HOTEL "DIE BIERHÜTTE"
Owner: Family Störzer
94545 Bierhütte
Hohenhau, Germany
tel: (08558) 315, fax: (08558) 23.87
43 rooms, Double: 150-296 DM
Open all year
Credit cards: all major
Restaurant-open daily
205 km N of Munich
135 km E of Regensburg
USA Rep: Euro-Connection 800-645-3876

A wonderfully rustic, country home atmosphere prevails at the Landhotel Schindlerhof. A recently renovated and enlarged farm complex, it is built around a large open courtyard where tables are set in summer for cocktails and evening barbecues. Inside, the two dining rooms are "country cozy," yet also retain a certain elegance. The walls and ceilings are warm knotty pine, matched by light pine furniture throughout. Hanging baskets, shafts of harvest wheat, dried and fresh flowers brighten all corners of the rooms, while charming rose and white checked tablecloths are complemented by lace curtains and pink candles. Waitresses are introduced by name, and are all attired in pretty, traditional dirndls. The menu is imaginative and varied, offering cosmopolitan gourmet selections as well as fresh, health-food entrees. In all areas of the Schindlerhof, host Klaus Kobjoll's attention to the smallest detail is infallible. From thoughtful touches such as welcoming fruit baskets in each guest bedroom, packets of German gummy bears underneath the pillows, to a complimentary glass of sherry or champagne upon arrival, every comfort is attended to. Guest bedrooms are all fresh and new, but never sterile. Light pine antique reproductions furnish the spacious rooms, all of which have a writing table, good lighting, discreet color television, minibar, and telephone.

LANDHOTEL SCHINDLERHOF
Owner: Klaus Kobjoll
Steinacher Strasse 8
90427 Nürnberg-Boxdorf, Germany
tel: (0911) 30.20.77, fax: (0911) 93.02.620
71 rooms, Double: 225-260 DM
Open all year
Credit cards: all major
Restaurant, bicycles
10 km NW of Nürnberg, near airport

The little town of Braubach lies on the Rhine almost opposite Koblenz. In amongst a mixture of modern and old houses you find the Zum Weissen Schwanen leaning against the old city wall where the large tower extends into the street. Step behind the half-timbered facade and you enter a gem of a country rustic tavern: warm pine paneling, bottle-glass dimpled windows hung with hand-crocheted curtains, and simple pine tables and carved chairs. Your genial hosts, Erich and Gerhilde Kunz, will probably be there to welcome you. Although they speak but a few words of English, their warm smiles and exuberant gestures overcome any language barrier. A few bedrooms are found in the converted stables behind the tavern. While these are charming, the inn's choice rooms lie in a nearby watermill where a huge wooden waterwheel slowly turns at the building's center. Around the waterwheel passages and staircases lead to the bedchambers. The bedrooms are delightful—rustic handicrafts surround old pine beds topped with plump gingham pillows and comforters. The Kunz family has a restaurant at the heart of the mill. The hotel gives you a wonderful feel of days gone by. There is nothing pretentious about the Zum Weissen Schwanen: it is just an old-fashioned inn in a picturesque, but non-touristy, town run with great pride by very nice people.

HOTEL ZUM WEISSEN SCHWANEN
Owners: Gerhilde & Erich Kunz
Brunnenstrasse 4
5423 Braubach, Germany
tel: (02627) 559, fax: (02627) 88.02
14 rooms, 1 suite; Double: 120-140 DM
Open all year
Credit cards: AX, DC
Restaurant-closed Wednesdays
130 km NW of Frankfurt, 13 km SE of Koblenz

You will have no problem finding the Romantik Hotel Zur Tanne; its pretty little facade graces the town's main street. Probably one of your genial hosts, Helmut and Barbel Herbst, will be there to greet you. Their warm welcome, excellent English and concern for their guests' comfort add to an enjoyable stay. From a tiny entrance the hotel opens up to reveal a large dignified dining room. This is the center of activity, for the hotel has gained a well-deserved reputation for excellent meals and impeccable service. Up the winding front staircase you find a few country-cozy bedrooms. I suggest you request one of these when making a reservation. A wing of modern rooms, decorated in shades of green, stretches out from the rear of the old inn. The hotel's most rustic room is its cheery bar where guests gather for after-dinner drinks and discussions of the day's events. Budget travelers can find more simple accommodations at the Guesthouse Zur Tanne on the edge of town. Braunlage is in the heart of the Harz Mountains. In summer, besides sightseeing, delightful trails in the forests beckon, while winter offers the opportunity for cross-country skiing. Since the opening of the German border, the Harz region presents an appealing ring of quaint towns dating from the Middle Ages to explore such as Goslar, Duderstadt, Wernigerode and Quedlinburg. Last, but not least, don't miss the nostalgic steam engine train ride through the lovely Harz mountains.

ROMANTIK HOTEL ZUR TANNE
Owners: Barbel & Helmut Herbst
Herzog-Wilhelm-Strasse 8
38693 Braunlage, Germany
tel: (05520) 10.34, fax: (05520) 39.92
21 rooms, Double: 165-215 DM
Open all year
Credit cards: all major
Restaurant-open daily
69 km S of Braunschweig, in the Harz mountains
USA Rep: Euro-Connection 800-645-3876

The name of this delightful 17th-century inn, "Die Grüne Bettlad" ("Green Bed"), refers back to the early history of the inn, when, so the story goes, the beautiful wife of the dipsomaniac innkeeper blatantly entertained her suitors in a green bed conveniently set next to a large ceramic oven in the tavern. For the past two generations the hotel has been owned by the gracious Günthner family and is now ably run by Peter, the talented chef, along with his lovely wife and hostess. The small front lobby sets the mood of the inn with a gaily painted reception desk and a large antique cradle. Through adjoining doors, guests find the intimate and charming restaurant where, in the evening, candlelight casts a romantic glow over tables set with crisp, pretty linens and fresh flowers. Whitewashed walls set off the cheerful red and green color scheme and a clutter of artistically placed prints, religious statues, copper molds, and wall sconces. Peter is a fine chef and his cuisine does credit to the inviting surroundings. From the lobby, an old wooden spiral staircase leads to an upper lounge and bedrooms. Each of the guest rooms is spotlessly clean and features hand painted furniture. Although the food is superb and the accommodations delightful, the nicest aspect of this tiny inn is the warmth and caring of the owners who truly want their guests to be happy.

HOTEL "DIE GRÜNE BETTLAD"
Owner: Family Günthner
Blumenstrasse 4
77815 Bühl-Baden, Germany
tel: (07223) 24.238, fax (07223) 24.247
6 rooms, Double: 190-260 DM
Closed Dec 23 to mid-Jan & mid-Jul to end-Jul
Credit cards: AX
Restaurant-closed Sundays & Mondays
14 km south of Baden-Baden

The Alte Rheinmuhle is in a little niche of Germany, practically surrounded by Switzerland, only 3 kilometers east of Schaffhausen. The distance between the countries is so short and the town so Swiss that customs are friendly and casual although you do need your passport to cross the border. The Alte Rheinmuhle is a transformation of an old mill to an inn whose emphasis in on its restaurant. The building dates from 1674 and sits right on the edge of the Rhine. On the first floor is a beautiful dining room whose large windows overlook the river. The hotel has earned an outstanding reputation for its cuisine and extensive wine cellar. Some of the restaurant's specialties include superb venison and wild rabbit, and the highlight for dessert is the most scrumptious cassis sherbet to be found anywhere. I discussed the rooms with the management and was told that all rooms are decorated in a country style and furnished with antiques—some even have four-poster beds. Our room, number fourteen, with twin beds, is set under old heavy beams. However, other rooms seen in passing were more modern in decor and style. Do request a room facing the river—it would be a shame not to take advantage of the mill's serene setting. While the rooms are relatively inexpensive in price the restaurant is very expensive.

ALTE RHEINMUHLE
Manager: Fredy Wagner
Junkerstrasse 93
94545 Busingen, Germany
tel: (07734) 60.76, fax: (07734) 60.79
15 rooms, Double: 180-250 DM
Closed December 15-January 15
Credit cards: all major
Restaurant-open daily
5 km E of Schaffhausen, Switzerland

Hotel Descriptions

The Alte Weinschänke, a pretty, appealing cream-colored building accented by rich green trim and cheerful flower boxes, is located in the heart of the charming medieval town of Celle. The Alte Weinschänke, dating from 1566, is primarily a cozy wine house where wine, beer, coffee, tea and light snacks are served. The pub-like interior (including the low ceiling) is covered in wood paneling that has the marvelous patina that only age can achieve. A long bar stretches across the length of the room and small antique tables and chairs complete the scene. Outside, more tables are set where you can sip your cappuccino and watch the parade of people pass by. Although this is a tiny, well-priced inn, the guest rooms are exceptionally pleasant and decorated in excellent taste. There are only two double rooms and two single rooms. All are bright and pretty and have an old world ambiance that is accomplished by the use of antiques such as lovely old desks, prints on the walls, chests, etc. My favorite double room opens out onto a small terrace that is tucked in amongst the roof tops. The owner, Annette Heilmann, looks after both the guests in her bar and those spending the night with the same gracious warmth. Note: You cannot drive to the Alte Weinschänke, which is located in a pedestrian-only area. Park your car and ask for directions to the narrow side-street where the hotel is located, then retrieve your luggage.

HOTEL ALTE WEINSCHÄNKE
Owner: Annette Heilmann
Piltzergasse 9
29221 Celle, Germany
tel: (05084) 28.381, fax: (05084) 42.28
4 rooms (2 singles, 2 doubles), Double: 154 DM
Open all year
Credit cards: EC, MC, VS
No restaurant-breakfast only
45 km NE of Hannover, 118 km S of Hamburg

If your taste is for fancy, sophisticated decor, the hotel for you in the lovely town of Celle should be the Fürstenhof Celle. Whereas most of the buildings in Celle are quaint timbered houses, the Fürstenhof is a stately 17th-century, peach-colored palace that reflects the influence of its famous Italian architect, Stechinelli. For many years the estate belonged to one of Europe's well-known aristocratic families, the Hardenbergs, but it was only recently that Count Christian-Ludwig von Hardenberg took over the property and converted it into a luxury hotel. Two timbered buildings (in days-gone-by the stables and carriage house) stretch out in front of the pink two-story palace forming a courtyard where tables are set in the shade of a 300-year-old chestnut tree. Inside, the hotel is ornately glamorous—especially the grand salon where Grecian columns support a mirror-paneled ceiling and comfortable leather chairs form intimate groups for afternoon tea. From the salon, a dramatic staircase leads up to the only four bedrooms located in the original building. Be sure to ask for one of these spacious, antique-filled bedrooms (all of the others are located in a modern, hotel-like wing without much personality). There are two places to dine: an elegant gourmet restaurant (with a well-deserved Michelin star) in addition a charming, rustic restaurant (in the what were once the stables) serving regional specialties.

FÜRSTENHOF CELLE
Owner: Count von Hardenberg
Hannnoversche Strasse 55-56
29221 Celle, Germany
tel: (05141) 20.10, fax: (05141) 20.11.20
71 rooms, 5 apartments; Double: 260-430 DM
Open all year
Credit cards: all major
Restaurant-open daily
45 km NE of Hannover, 118 km S of Hamburg
Relais & Chateaux

The two-tone-green facade of the Hotel Utspann (a narrow, colorfully-painted, timbered house dating from 1644) reflects the marvelous character of old Celle. At first glance, the hotel looks small, but as you walk through the entrance and into the back courtyard, it is evident that the hotel actually incorporates six 17th-century houses, cleverly renovated into one building by the owner-architect, Andreas Mehls. The cluster of houses form a central patio with tables and chairs set for a relaxing moment under the trees. The bedrooms are all different in decor, yet each has a similar folksy-cute look. Ursula Mehls is an avid collector, and all of the rooms are brimming with antique toys, old plates, copper pots, baskets of silk flowers, country-style fabrics, painted tables, hanging plants, and oriental throw rugs. My favorite is the prettily decorated "Rostock" room, tucked under the eves with windows overlooking the street. An added bonus is the Hotel Utspann's intimate little restaurant where there are only five small antique tables set for dining. An upright piano along one wall, framed musical manuscripts, fresh green plants set in the deep window niches, fresh flowers, pretty linens, and soft candlelight set a romantic ambiance for excellent, home-cooked meals. Note: You can drive to Hotel Utspann, which is located on the edge of the pedestrian-only section of town.

HOTEL UTSPANN
Owner: Family Mehls
Im Kreise 13
29221 Celle, Germany
tel: (05141) 92.77.20 fax: (05141) 92.72.52
17 rooms, Double: 203-295 DM
2 suites: 300-450 DM
Open all year except Christmas & New Year
Credit cards: all major
Restaurant-open daily except holidays
45 km NE of Hannover, 118 km S of Hamburg

Cochem hugs the banks of the winding River Moselle. It is a delightful village that thrives on the production of wine and the influx of tourists who come to wander through its streets lined by old houses and to climb to the castle that guards the heights. Leaning against the remnants of the old town wall, the Alte Thorschenke is a lovely old-fashioned German inn. From the tiny lobby, a beautifully carved, creaking wooden staircase spirals up to the old-fashioned bedchambers. Several have romantic antique four-poster beds and French armoires. Request one of these older rooms as the majority of the hotel's accommodations are "dated-modern" rooms built at the rear of the hotel. A special treat is the hunting-lodge-style dining room with its handsome oil paintings, great old portraits, hunting trophies and oriental carpets accenting beautiful planked wooden floors. Surrounding the village, steep vineyards produce excellent white wines, for Cochem is at the heart of the Moselle wine region. Consequently wine sampling from the hotel's long wine list or in one of the taverns along the river is a popular pastime. The Alte Thorschenke has its own 500 year-old winery where the best Moselle-wines can be tasted and bought at low prices.

ALTE THORSCHENKE
Managers: Annegret & Walther Kretz
Bruckenstrasse 3
56812 Cochem, Germany
tel: (02671) 70.59, fax: (02671) 42.02
45 rooms, Double: 165-225 DM
Closed January 5 to March 15
Credit cards: all major
Restaurant-open daily
51 km SW of Koblenz, on Moselle River
USA Rep: Euro-Connection 800-645-3876
Gast im Schloss

Miraculously, Cologne's cathedral was not flattened by the Allied bombers that devastated the rest of the city during the Second World War. Its tall, delicate spires still rise above the skyline and the pedestrian square surrounding the cathedral is still the meeting point for visitors from all over the world. Jutting out into the square is the Dom Hotel, one of the grand old stylish hotels of Europe. The public rooms are gracious and formal. Relaxed and informal dining can be enjoyed in the wintergarden restaurant with its natural plants and palm trees, comfortable rattan chairs and a breathtaking view of the cathedral. In summer the terrace cafe provides a less formal dining spot: from here you can almost touch the cathedral—a perfect spot for watching busy Cologne whirl by. Heavy marble stairways lead to wide, recently renovated hallways and grand, high-ceilinged bedchambers. Large windows hung with beautiful full length drapes, and elegant antique furniture add to the luxurious ambiance. One warning: the rooms are not soundproofed and while the noise of the square recedes late at night, the cathedral bells continue to ring.

DOM HOTEL
Manager: Herr Horst Berl
50667 Cologne, Germany
tel: (0221) 20.240, fax: (0221) 20.24.444
125 rooms, 2 suites; Double: 410-600 DM
Open all year
Credit cards: all major
Restaurant-open daily
Near the cathedral in heart of Cologne
USA Rep: Forte Hotels 800-225-5843

The Haus Lyskirchen is an excellent choice for a moderately priced hotel in Cologne. The hotel occupies a quiet side street just off the River Rhine. From the pier, only a short distance from the hotel, steamers depart for the popular Rhine river day trip from Cologne to Mainz. A ten-minute stroll through the old town brings you to the cathedral, just far enough away that you can hear the distant echo of its bells. The Haus Lyskirchen is a blend of styles: ten guest rooms have a mountain-chalet style, others, furnished in white-ashwood, are brighter. To the left of the modern lobby is a small country-style dining room where, if you are too tired to venture out after a busy day's sightseeing, you can enjoy an intimate dinner. Next door an appealing little paneled bar provides a cozy spot for after-dinner drinks. In sharp contrast, a display of modern art leads you to the stark modern breakfast room where you enjoy a sumptuous buffet style breakfast. Some bedrooms are just like a mountain chalet (all in pine and cozy); the others, which are brighter, have been completely renovated and are furnished in white ash-wood. A large indoor swimming pool and underground parking are added bonuses. Cologne hosts conventions during January, February, March, April, September and October: if you plan to visit during these times, book well in advance.

HAUS LYSKIRCHEN
Owner: Family Marzorati
Filzengraben 26-32
50676 Cologne, Germany
tel: (0221) 20.970, fax: (0221) 20.97.718
94 rooms, Double: 199-340 DM
Closed December 23 to January 1
Credit cards: all major
Restaurant-closed Sunday, indoor pool
10-minute walk to the city center

One of the most charming places in Cologne is Fish Market Square, a tiny cobbled plaza lined with tall, narrow buildings, all colorfully painted. On sunny days the plaza blossoms with small tables covered with cheerful checked tablecloths. Three sides of this miniature old square are lined with houses and the fourth side fronts the Rhine Garden—the park that borders the Rhine River. The Stapelhäuschen das Kleine is formed by two separate houses, one pale blue the other pale yellow, standing side by side with matching window boxes brimming with red geraniums at each white curtained window. The entry leads into a cozy restaurant and bar with a wooden spiral staircase winding up to an open balcony where extra seating is available. This lovely old staircase also leads to an inner, rather dimly lit and drab, staircase that continues up to the guest rooms on the five floors above. "Das Historische Turmzimmer" (historical tower room) is a small but romantic guest room tucked up under the roof of massive dark beams and old crane wheel. For a more spacious bedroom with bath, room 24 is especially nice, a sunny corner room in shades of blue with a view out over the square to the Rhine. This is not a deluxe hotel, but if you would like to sample a slice of simple life in a picturesque location, the Stapelhauschen das Rheine is special.

STAPELHÄUSCHEN DAS KLEINE
Owner: Family Frömmter
Fischmarkt 1-3 am Rheinufer
50667 Cologne, Germany
tel: (0221) 25.77.862, fax: (0221) 25.74.232
30 rooms, Double: 110-195 DM
Closed December 21 to January 17
Credit cards: all major
Restaurant, open daily
Near waterfront; short walk from the Cathedral

"Die Deutsche Weinstrasse" means "German Wine Road" and is written on the signposts leading through a string of unpretentious wine-producing villages set amidst the vineyards of the Palatinate. Ambling from village to village, with stops for wine tasting at taverns and open-to-visit vineyards, is great fun. A most appropriate base for such pursuits is a charming country inn, the Deidesheimer Hof owned by the Hahn Wine family. Occupying a corner of the village square, the hotel has a formal appearance, for this was once a Bishop's residence. The inside is all country warmth and good cheer. The informal dining room—my favorite room—is hung with gay garlands of bread sculptures and wine jugs; the furniture is rustic pine and the food simple and delicious. As you might expect, there are many cozy spots where you can sit and consume wine—the cavernous cellar, the dark beamed bar or, better still, the flower decked terrace that spills into the cobblestoned square in front of the hotel. The bedrooms come in all shapes and sizes; most are furnished in a very pleasing country modern decor. Deidesheim's wine festival takes place during the second week of August.

HOTEL DEIDESHEIMER HOF
Owner: Anita Hahn
Am Marktplatz
67146 Deidesheim, Germany
tel: (06326) 18.11, fax: (06326) 76.85
26 rooms, Double: 160-290 DM
2 suites 330-400 DM
Closed first week of January
Credit cards: all major
Two restaurants-one open daily
88 km S of Mainz, 23 km SW of Mannheim
Relais & Chateaux

Rarely do we include hotels of this size (the Bellevue has 340 rooms), but until some romantic small hotel opens its doors, this is definitely the best choice for sightseeing while in Dresden. And, in spite of only being "born" as a hotel in 1985, its history goes back much further. Instead of building a contemporary concrete monstrosity, architects cleverly blended the modern hotel with one of Dresden's beautiful old buildings, the Royal Chancellery, mercifully spared from World War II bombs. This lovely yellow palace-like building is joined to the new hotel with garden courtyards which lead into the attractive airy lobby. Guests are welcomed by comfortable seating nooks adorned with a few antiques to relieve the completely modern mood. The bedrooms have attractive, built-in furnishings and all the modern amenities that one expects in a deluxe hotel. A few suites, which are much more expensive, are elaborately decorated with antique furnishings. Located across the bridge from Dresden's wealth of palaces and museums, the Hotel Bellevue enjoys an enviable location for a city hotel. It is convenient to tourist sights yet retains a tranquil ambiance with lawns and gardens stretching down to the river.

MARITIM HOTEL BELLEVUE
Manager: Herr Hans-Joachim Herrmann
Grosse Meissner Strasse 15
01097 Dresden, Germany
tel: (0351) 56620, fax: (0351) 55997
340 rooms, Double: 448-538 DM
Open all year
Credit cards: all major
Restaurant-open daily
Across the river from city center

For only a fraction of the cost of staying in a deluxe hotel in Dresden, you can drive ten minutes across the Carolabrucke and stay in Schloss Eckberg, a handsome castle perched on the slope of the Elbe River. This 19th-century castle was originally a private residence until in the 1960's it became a youth hostel. Happily, now that private enterprise is again a motivating factor in what was "East Germany," the Schloss Eckberg has been converted to a hotel. The castle, an exceptionally picturesque honey-toned stone structure with crenolated roof, is set in a 37 acre park laced with paths for walking through the forest. There is a new annex on the property where 60 of the 80 guest rooms are located. Although the bathrooms are more up-to-date in the new wing, I prefer the characterful castle. Here you will find the furniture a bit old-fashioned and the decor not "decorator perfect," but the ambiance more interesting—ask for one of the rooms (such as 415) that overlooks the Elbe River. You enter Schloss Eckberg through a massive carved doorway into an octagonal foyer. Located on the ground floor, overlooking a formal garden, is an intimate dining room where the food is delicious and beautifully served. From the foyer, a magnificent staircase, accented by a rich blue carpet and enclosed by a handsome carved-stoned banister, leads to the guest rooms.

SCHLOSS ECKBERG
Manager: Frau Janija Jegovnik
Bautzener Strasse 134
01099 Dresden-Loschwitz, Germany
tel: (0351) 52.571, fax: (0351) 55.379
80 rooms, Double: 233-295 DM
Open all year
Credit cards: EC, MC, VS
Restaurant-open daily
10-minute drive E of downtown Dresden
Gast im Schloss

It was in 1990 (only a few days after the reunification of Germany) when we first stayed at the Hotel auf der Wartburg, located in what was formerly East Germany. On our second visit a few years later, we were astounded at the miraculous changes. Bathless guest rooms with out-dated, dreary decor had emerged like butterflies from their cocoons into some of the best-looking rooms in all of Germany. Each of the bedrooms is individual in decor, yet they all have the same refined English country manor look with beautiful fabrics used in the color coordinating draperies and upholstered chairs. One of my favorites, number 104 (a deluxe corner room decorated in rich blues and yellows) looks out to the forest. Less expensive room 102 (overlooking the front courtyard) is also a charmer in tones of reds and golds. Some of the most romantic rooms are tucked up under the eaves with tiny garret windows capturing miniature views of the wooded hills. Just steps from the hotel is the museum section of Wartburg Castle, one of Germany's real gems. The hotel is easy to find. As you leave the motorway at Eisenach, follow signs to "Wartburg." As you near the castle, follow the small signposted lane that winds uphill through the forest to the castle. There is a parking area at the top with a barricade. Continue about 500 meters past the barricade to the hotel guest parking area.

HOTEL AUF DER WARTBURG
Manager: Hans Joachim Hook
Wirtschaftsbetriebe
99817 Eisenach, Germany
tel: (03691) 51.11, fax: (03691) 51.11
32 rooms, 5 suites; Double: 260-280 DM
Open all year
Credit cards: all major
Restaurant-open daily
On a hilltop, 3 km S of Eisenach
Gast im Schloss

We searched in vain for a small hotel with charm in the large city of Nürnberg, and finally settled on a delightful alternative only 22 kilometers to the north. The Schwarzer Adler exudes country charm even though it is located near the large city of Nürnberg and Erlangen (home of the enormous Siemens company). The facade of the Schwarzer Adler is prettily laced with intricate timbering and has green shuttered windows above window boxes full of bright red geraniums in summer. A small stream flows behind the inn and a pretty church sits nearby. Once inside, you will not be disappointed for the inn is beautifully decorated in a cozy style perfectly suited to its picturesque facade. An antique wooden spiral staircase winds up from the lobby to the Mulle family's quarters on the second floor, and continues to the third floor where the guest accommodations are tucked into cozy dormers. Although these guest rooms are not large, they are spotlessly clean and very appealing; decorated with tasteful light pine furniture, fluffy down comforters with crisp white duvet coverings, and white crocheted curtains at the windows. The owner of the Schwarzer Adler, Christiane Müller-Kinzel, has renovated this historical Frankonian framework house (dating back to at least 1702) with such loving care and attention to detail that this it has won several well-deserved awards.

SCHWARZER ADLER
Owner: Christiane Müller-Kinzel
Herdegenplatz 1
91056 Erlangen-Frauenaurach, Germany
tel: (09131) 99.20.51 fax (09131) 99.31.95
8 rooms, Double: 170-190 DM
Closed Christmas & Aug 13-Sep 9
Credit cards: DC, VS
Restaurant serving snacks
22 km N of Nürnberg

The Romantik Hotel Voss Haus is located on the main road through Eutin, an ever-so-quaint medieval town with pedestrian-only lanes and a picturesque square lined by 17th-century houses. The hotel fronts onto the street, but backs onto a garden with a path leading down to an exceptionally picturesque lake. The 300-year-old building is chock-full of character. The lower part of the building is brick while the upper floors are vertical panels of wood painted a deep blue, enhanced by white-framed windows and a steeply pitched red tile roof. You enter into a large reception room (with dark red walls) that also serves as a lounge for guests of the hotel's restaurant. There are five dining rooms. Each is individual in decor, but all are brimming with a stunning romantic charm: dark woods, soft lighting, beamed ceilings, many oil paintings, antiques galore, pretty white dotted-Swiss curtains, fresh flowers throughout. It is no wonder that the Voss Haus restaurant is so popular: the food, the service and the ambiance are all faultless. In the summer, meals are also served in the back garden overlooking the lake. A curving staircase (that could use a coat of paint and new carpeting) winds up to the guest rooms that, although a bit dated in decor, are spacious and quite pleasant. The choice rooms are those in the rear overlooking the garden.

ROMANTIK HOTEL VOSS HAUS
Manager: Herr E B Mommsen
Vossplatz 6
23701 Eutin, Germany
tel: (04521) 17.97, fax: (04521) 13.57
15 rooms, Double: 170-190 DM
Open all year
Credit cards: AX, VS
Restaurant-open daily
40 km N of Lubeck, 106 km NE of Hamburg
USA Rep: Euro-Connection 800-645-3876

Four generations of the Lorentz family have perfected a tradition of a welcome and quality that is ever present in their hotel. Referenced in local records as early as 1369, the Post now offers extremely modern comforts and facilities. The inn has a number of intimate rooms that serve as restaurants. The main restaurant is very elegant with heavy beams and hand-painted scenes that stage an attractive atmosphere. Downstairs is a spectacular bar grill: overlooking the pool through stone arched windows, tapestry covered high back chairs are set around a large open fireplace used to grill steaks and cutlets. Also indoors, the adjoining swimming pool resembles a Roman bath house. The Greifen Post has 35 rooms, which can be grouped by decor: the "Biedermeier Zimmers," (with Biedermeier antiques) the "Himmelbett Zimmers" (with charming four-poster beds) and "Laura Ashley" (with English-style fabrics). I could not decide what style of room I liked best—every one is beautiful. The entire hotel shows the touch of owners who strive to have every detail of their inn perfect. Each morning, a large table is artfully spread with one of the most generous breakfast buffets I saw in Germany. As a special touch, bikes are available for exploring the "Romantic Road."

ROMANTIK HOTEL GREIFEN POST
Owner: Edward Lorentz
Marktplatz 8
91555 Feuchtwangen, Germany
tel: (09852) 20.02, fax: (09852) 48.41
35 rooms, 3 suites, Double: 175-395 DM
Open all year
Credit cards: all major
Restaurant-closed Sundays & Mondays, indoor pool*
**Smaller restaurant open daily for guests*
170 km NW of Munich, 70 km SW of Nürnberg
USA Rep: Euro-Connection 800-645-3876

On the outskirts of Frankfurt, conveniently located about fifteen minutes from Frankfurt's popular international airport, is the very polished, sophisticated, well-run Hotel Gravenbruch-Kempinski Frankfurt. Although much larger than most hotels included in this guide, the hotel has so much to offer that we decided to include it. Most of the hotel is new, but the nucleus is old. The architects have constructed the additions to this inn very cleverly, mindful of its origins, combining the best of modern conveniences while still achieving old world ambiance. The hotel has a resort atmosphere with various dining rooms, enormous lobbies and a swimming pool. Another plus, the Gravenbruch-Kempinski is set in a forest with excellent paths for strolling or jogging. After a long airline journey, it is quite refreshing to take a walk in the woods before a bite to eat and going to bed. You will find yourself refreshed the next day and ready to "hit the road." If you are on your way home, then you will find the Hotel Gravenbruch-Kempinski very handy: there is even a Lufthansa counter where you can check in for your flight home and limousine service to the airport.

HOTEL GRAVENBRUCH-KEMPINSKI FRANKFURT
Manager: Gunther Haug
Neu-Isenburg 2
63263 Frankfurt, Germany
tel: (06102) 50.50, fax: (06102) 50.54.45
288 rooms, Double: 526-576 DM
Open all year
Credit cards: all major
Restaurant-open daily
tennis, 2 pools (indoor & outdoor), health club/spa
Near Frankfurt Airport,
On Rte 459, 11 km SE of Frankfurt
USA Rep: Kempinski 800-426-3135

We thought the ideal little inn could not exist in the heart of Frankfurt where most of the buildings are new and without charm. But, happily, we were proved wrong. Not only does a gem of a small hotel exist, but it is splendidly located in a very nice neighborhood, only three blocks from the train station, and within easy walking distance to shopping and sightseeing. Your heart will be won at first glance at the Hotel Westend—a pretty pastel-pink house, reminiscent of a small villa. There is a small front lawn and steps leading up the side of the house to a long, marble-floored entry accented by Persian carpets. Three intimate little parlors are at guests' disposal, each prettily decorated with antique furniture, bouquets of fresh flowers, oriental carpets, crystal chandeliers, handsome mirrors and oil paintings. The overall effect is one of quiet elegance, somewhat formal yet welcoming and homelike. Guest rooms are located upstairs and all have an old world ambiance created by pretty pastel color schemes, white curtains at the windows and liberal use of authentic antiques. The mood is one of refinement, quiet comfort, and the loving touch of an owner who really cares about guests. An added bonus is a secluded back garden where breakfast is served during the warm summer months. Hotel Westend is truly an oasis in the busy city of Frankfurt, but with so few rooms available, you need to book far in advance for this very special hotel.

HOTEL WESTEND
Owner: Frau Elinor Mayer
Westendstrasse 15
60325 Frankfurt 1, Germany
20 rooms, Double: 250-330 DM
tel: (069) 74.67.02, fax: (069) 74.53.96
Closed for Christmas
Credit cards: all major
No Restaurant, breakfast only, free guest parking
3 blocks from train station, central location

How fortunate that driving rain drove us into Oberkirchs Weinstuben for a fortifying drink, for we discovered that it is also a darling inn. Oberkirchs Weinstuben is actually located in two buildings. The principal building sits on Munsterplatz in the shadow of Freiburg's impressive cathedral, the other just a short cobblestone block away. The Weinstuben serves a very satisfying lunch or dinner in a congenial, cozy atmosphere. Beamed ceilings, wooden tables, white linen and contented chatter set the mood for the charming restaurant. It is a popular place to dine in the marvelous medieval town of Freiburg and understandably so. In addition to the restaurant, there 26 guest rooms, found either directly above the weinstube or in the neighboring building. All have been recently refurbished and are very attractive. The nine rooms above the weinstube have been redecorated more recently and are slightly more expensive. My special favorite is number 55, a gem of a room with a romantic view out over the square to the cathedral. Freiburg is one of the most attractive walled cities in the Black Forest region of Germany, and the Oberkirchs Weinstuben makes an excellent choice for overnight accommodation. It is somewhat difficult to maneuver by auto through the pedestrian district, but the hotel provides a map and directions for parking.

OBERKIRCHS WEINSTUBEN
Owner: Helmut Johner-Oberkirch
Munsterplatz 22
79098 Freiburg im Breisgau, Germany
tel: (0761) 31.011, fax: (0761) 31.031
26 rooms, Double: 220-290 DM
Closed January
Credit cards: all major
Restaurant-closed Sundays
208 km SW of Stuttgart, 71 km N of Basel

One of the most recent castles to open its doors to guests in what used to be "East Germany" is the Schloss Reinhardsbrunn. Although parts of the foundation date back almost 1,000 years, the elaborate castle as you see it today was built in 1828 for the Dukes of Gotha. The light beige-colored stone structure overlooking a small lake is not foreboding at all as some fortified castles tend to be, but rather an inviting friendly castle set in a large park laced with trails that wind through the forest. Just up the path from the castle, in what was previously the "Kavaliershaus" (the Duke's guest house), are the first of the 19 rooms to undergo beautification. These deluxe rooms are completely renovated with double insulated windows, televisions, mini-bars, built-in safes, direct-dial phones, and modern tiled baths. These rooms are all similar in ambiance with a modern, sophisticated look created by fine fabrics in pastel color schemes and light-toned wooden furniture. If you are on a tight budget, there are some guest rooms (without private bathroom) in the main castle, which although a bit old fashioned and rather drab, are spacious, impeccably clean, and a good value (I especially liked room 39 with large windows overlooking the forest). But, no matter what category of accommodation you choose, you will certainly find the castle dramatic and the staff especially friendly.

SCHLOSS REINHARDSBRUNN
Manager: Klaus Kraft
99894 Friedrichroda, Germany
tel: (03623) 42.53, fax: (03623) 42.51
19 rooms with private bath; Double: 250-320 DM
35 rooms without private bath; Double: 98 DM
Open all year
Credit cards: all major
Restaurant-open daily
57 km SW of Erfurt, 290 W of Dresden
Gast im Schloss

The Wald & Schlosshotel Friedrichsruhe, a complex of buildings set on spacious grounds in a very idyllic and rural setting, is run along the lines of a deluxe hotel as opposed to an inn. The reception is efficient, but somewhat formal and impersonal. Managed for many years by Herr Eiermann, the Waldhotel Friedrichsruhe provides deluxe room accommodations, excellent dining, facilities for sportsmen, a beauty farm and a peaceful environment. The main dining room is very elegant: walls covered in rust colored material to match the floor-to-ceiling drapes, gilded chandeliers, and tables set with white linen and dramatic fresh flower arrangements. The breakfast room, by contrast, is very simple and opens onto the lush green gardens. The Hunters Restaurant is a charming gathering spot, more country in decor, with wood backed chairs and green print fabrics. The bedrooms, ranging in decor from traditional to modern, are found in various buildings on the property. Set in a rotunda and exposed to the garden through floor to ceiling windows are a lovely indoor—outdoor swimming pool and a sauna.

WALD & SCHLOSSHOTEL FRIEDRICHSRUHE
Manager: Lothar Eiermann
74639 Friedrichsruhe, Germany
tel: (07941) 60.870, fax: (07941) 61.468
50 rooms, 12 suites; Double: 295-580 DM
Closed last two weeks of January
Credit cards: all major
Restaurant-closed Mondays & Tuesdays
Pool, golf, tennis, beauty farm
70 km NE of Stuttgart, between
Heilbronn & Schwäbisch Hall

There is something very endearing about the simplicity of the Schloss Fürsteneck. One would never just happen upon this hotel. It is set in the Bavarian Hills in a village that is mostly comprised of a castle and a church. By no means luxurious, this hotel, has appeal for those on a budget. The exterior is accented by colorful window boxes while inside there are twelve spotless guest rooms. Under arched ceilings, the restaurant is very cozy. Tables are appealingly decked with either blue or red checked cloths. There are actually three adjoining dining rooms to choose from: the "Gaststube," the "Jagerzimmer" (a round room with a hunting motif that overlooks a steep drop to the River Ohr), and the "Kaminzimmer" (named for the fireplace that warms it). The menu highlights the regional specialties and garden fresh vegetables. This hotel has only two rooms with full bath and private toilet, the rest share facilities. Again, I stress the rooms are simple but sweet, with matching prints used for the comforter covers and the curtains. In this region one can hike between hotels. Set out with only a luncheon pack and have your bags delivered to your next hotel. Contact the hotel for specific details and arrangements.

SCHLOSS FÜRSTENECK
Owner: Adrian Forster
94142 Fürsteneck, Germany
tel: (08505) 1473
12 rooms, Double: from 80 DM
Open all year except January
Credit cards: all major
Restaurant
195 km NE of Munich, 125 km E of
Regensburg
Near Czech Republic border

Set under the shadow of Germany's highest peak, the Zugspitze, Clausing's Posthotel affords a convenient, but somewhat busy location on one of the main streets in the town of Garmisch. Just steps away from elegant boutiques and ski slopes, this colorfully painted, small hotel, once a postal station, has been managed by the Clausing family for five generations. Members of the family can be seen welcoming guests in the reception area, or assisting with a selection from the menu in one of their fine restaurants. The hotel offers a wide variety of places to dine or enjoy a beer: Oom-pah music tempts one into the ever popular "Post Horndl," unobstructed views of the Zugspitze and town's street activity are the reasons that many settle at the glassed-in "Terrace," "Stüberls" prides itself on atmosphere and fine cuisine. Clausing's Posthotel is loaded with charm. Throughout the hotel the decor reflects the cozy, romantic ambiance that makes Bavaria so special. The bedrooms are large, spacious and well appointed. Although rooms at the front of the hotel enjoy breathtaking views of the Zugspitze, the rooms in the back avoid the constant sound of traffic.

ROMANTIK HOTEL CLAUSING'S POSTHOTEL
Owner: Marianne & Anton Weinfurtner
Marienplatz 12
82467 Garmisch-Partenkirchen, Germany
tel: (08821) 70.90, fax: (08821) 70.92.05
42 rooms, Double: 186-256 DM
Open all year
Credit cards: all major
Restaurant-open daily
89 km S of Munich, near Austrian border
USA Rep: Euro-Connection 800-645-3876

Located in the historic section of Partenkirchen, the Gasthof Fraundorfer has been in the Fraundorfer family since 1820 and is still very much a homey, family-run inn. Its facade is decorated with murals and window boxes of red geraniums, while inside a marvelously atmospheric restaurant awaits. Walls and ceilings entirely in mellow knotty pine foster a warm, rustic feeling here, where tradition is taken seriously. Frau Fraundorfer explained that one of the wooden tables in the room is what is called in German a "Stammtisch." This table is the exclusive territory of a specific group of regulars, and each person in the group has his own place at which he always sits. In fact, some of the chairs have brass plaques engraved with the occupant's name. Photos of "Stammtisch" regulars adorn the wall above the table, some dating back 50 years. Home-cooked meals accompanied by German beers and wines are served in this charming dining room. Some of the guest rooms are located in Gästehaus Barbara, a new annex located just behind the hotel; others are in the original Gasthof. The guest rooms vary in size and furnishings, although most are in a reproduction Bavarian style. Do not expect elegance, but homey comfort. All rooms have private bath, phone, and television, and some have balconies. This inn is truly a friendly place and a very good value, especially for being in the center of such a popular tourist site.

GASTHOF FRAUNDORFER
Owners: Barbara & Josef Fraundorfer
Ludwigstrasse 24
82467 Garmisch-Partenkirchen, Germany
tel: (08821) 21.76, fax: (08821) 71.073
32 rooms, Double: 120-140 DM, apt 180 DM
Open all year
Credit cards: AX, MC, VS
Restaurant-closed Tuesdays, sauna, steam
89 km S of Munich

In the charming village of Partenkirchen, just across from the picturesque church whose bells toll the hour, the Posthotel Partenkirchen reflects its colorful heritage history as a postal station. Four generations of the gracious Stahl family have maintained the old world tradition and excellent standard of service. Cherished antiques are beautifully displayed in all the public rooms and maids are forever busy polishing and scrubbing each and every corner. A cozy bar sits just off the grand entry and is warmed by a lovely oven. Trunks and painted armoires line the hallways that lead to delightful accommodations. Rather than a particular one or two, it seemed that the majority of the hotel's 60 rooms were decorated with cherished antiques and lovely prints and fabrics. The bathrooms have all been recently remodeled in a luxurious style. On the first floor, the largest room is number 2. Wood-paneled, it looks out over the back streets through thick walls. Although smaller, my favorite is number 53, a corner room on the top floor. It is cozily paneled both on the walls and ceiling with antique wood that is set off by handsome tapestry-like spread and draperies. Sliding doors lead our to a wrap-around balcony that enjoys an unobstructed view of the Zugspitze. However, no matter what room you have, you will certainly be enchanted by this very special hotel.

POSTHOTEL PARTENKIRCHEN
Owners: Lisa & Otto Stahl
Ludwigstrasse 49
82467 Garmisch-Partenkirchen, Germany
tel: (08821) 51.067, fax: (08821) 78.568
60 rooms, Double: 180-350 DM
Open all year
Credit cards: all major
Restaurant-open daily
89 km S of Munich

Like so many of the hotels in what used to be "East Germany," the handsome Schloss Blücher has undergone a tremendous face lift since the return of free enterprise. During the days of communism, Schloss Blücher, which is serenely located amidst forests and lakes, was used by the government as a holiday retreat. The castle was not well-tended and looked quite dreadful when first taken over by the present owner. Today, with a complete face-lift, the castle has returned to its former glory. You enter a very large, quite formal, reception hall with an intricately paneled ceiling that soars two stories high. The reception area has ornate, upholstered furniture in a deep red fabric that sets off the rich blue carpet. A majestic wide staircase with beautiful wooden banisters leads to the second level where a balcony wraps around the room, open to the floor below. Beyond the reception area is a lounge with large windows looking out to a peaceful wooded landscape. The hotel is well-known for its kitchen, and to the right of the foyer, there is a series of dining rooms, formal but extremely attractive. My favorite is one fashioned from the original chapel with an intricately sculpted ceiling and stained glass windows. The guest rooms were designed by an Italian decorator: the custom-made, ultra modern furniture is obviously very expensive, and although not to my taste, is undoubtedly popular with many guests.

HOTEL SCHLOSS BLÜCHER
Manager: Wolfgang A. Werner
Schlossplatz
17213 Göhren-Lebbin, Germany
tel: (039932) 81.941, fax: (039932) 90.28
40 rooms, Double: 220-265 DM
Open all year
Credit cards: AX, VS
Restaurant-open daily
150 km N of Berlin, 86 km S of Rostock
Gast im Schloss

Often I have included a town because of a wonderful hotel but in this case I am including a hotel because of a wonderful town. Made rich by mining in the nearby Harz Mountains, Goslar was a flourishing regional capital before Columbus set sail for America. Time has been kind, and wandering the narrow cobbled streets is like taking a walk into a history book. Occupying a corner of the large pedestrian market square, the Kaiserworth was built in 1494 as the guild house of the cloth-workers. The impressive facade, with carvings of emperors beneath the eaves, was completed in the 17th Century. The Oberhuber family purchased the hotel a few years ago and are in the process of renovating this potential jewel. Sparing no expensive, the exterior has been meticulously restored and repainted to perfection. Inside, the public rooms do not yet live up to the promise of the splendid exterior, but plans are on the books for remodeling. At our last visit, the somewhat bedraggled guest rooms were well underway to regaining their former grandeur. Renovation has been completed in several rooms, including my favorite, number 110 (a lovely corner room overlooking the square). Step outside your hotel at six in the evening and watch the concert of the city clock whose four different scenes represent the thousand year-old mining history of the region.

HOTEL KAISERWORTH
Owner: Karin Oberhuber
Markt 3
38640 Goslar, Germany
tel: (05321) 21.111, fax: (05321) 21.114
51 rooms, Double: 240 DM
Open all year
Credit cards: all major
Restaurant, historic bar
250 km S of Hamburg
70 km S of Braunschweig

It is always a real delight to discover a newly built hotel that blends all the latest up-to-date comforts without sacrificing an old world ambiance. A fine example is the Hotel Alpenhof, which does not pretend to be old, yet maintains a romantic mood of Bavarian country charm. Soaring mountain peaks form the backdrop for this modern chalet-style hotel that has balconies both in front and back, accented by window boxes filled with red geraniums. You enter into a cheerful reception area that opens onto a cozy yet sophisticated bar where a fireplace warms the room in winter. From the bar, steps lead down to a series of dining rooms, each a masterpiece of design. My favorite is an intimate, wood-paneled (both walls and ceiling) dining room adorned with pewter trays, antique mugs, brass lamps, a cozy antique tile oven and tables colorfully set with blue table clothes and napkins. When the weather is warm, meals are also served outside in a pretty rear garden. This is a deluxe hotel with many amenities including a solarium, a sauna and magnificent indoor pool with arched windows looking out to the trees. The bedrooms continue the standard of excellence: the furnishings are new, but are traditional in style and of excellent quality. Although more expensive, splurge and request a bedroom in the back with a balcony that captures the majestic soaring granite peaks of the Zugspitz.

HOTEL ALPENHOF
Owners: Margret and Albert Falkenstein
Alpspitzstrasse 34
82491 Grainau, Germany
tel: (08821) 80.71, fax: (08821) 81.680
36 rooms, Double: 250-330 DM
Closed mid-Nov to mid-Dec
Credit cards: EC, MC, VS
Restaurant-open daily
94 km S of Munich, 6 km SW of Garmisch

It is rare to discover a hotel with guest rooms that offer an unobstructed view of the mountains, but the Hotel Post, located in the small village of Grainau, just a few kilometers from the famous resort of Garmisch-Partenkirchen, is a happy exception. If you love collecting memories of dramatic mountain peaks, ask for room 20. From your balcony there are no commercial buildings to sully the perfection of green meadows stretching up the hillside, ending only at the enormous soaring, granite peaks of the Zugspitz. The Hotel Post is a very simple hotel—not for those expecting luxury or quaint accommodation. The guest rooms are fresh and clean, but basic and with very dated decor. However, the breakfast room is much more appealing with beamed ceiling, provincial print tie-back curtains, attractive wooden chairs, tables set with linen cloths, and oil paintings and copper pots adorning fresh white-washed walls. The thick walls of the Hotel Post attest to the fact that is it around 300 years old. The first two centuries it was a sturdy farmhouse. Then, in 1890 it was bought by the Seufferth family who decided to take in "paying guests." The family still owns the hotel. You will usually find Frau Seufferth at the front desk. She speaks perfect English and is an exceptionally gracious hostess who has the knack of making guests feel very welcome.

HOTEL POST
Owner: Family Seufferth
near Garmisch-Partenkirchen
82491 Grainau/Zugspitzdorf, Germany
tel: (08821) 88.53, fax: (08821) 88.73
20 rooms, Double: 115-150 DM
Open May-Nov, Dec 15-Jan 15, Feb 10-Mar 30
Credit cards: AX, VS
No restaurant-breakfast only
94 km S of Munich, 6 km SW of Garmisch

The Stadtschänke is truly a gem, a superb tiny hotel that brims with charm inside and outside. Your heart will be won from the moment you wind your way to the colorful little market place in the center of Grossbottwar and discover the picture-perfect Stadtschänke. The facade is a whimsical delight—a narrow timbered building that rises five stories high, ending in a steeply pitched roof. A huge bucket of flowers, hanging from a wrought iron brace, completes the story-book look of this house that dates back to 1434. The first two floors are dedicated to the restaurant, and you must plan to dine here. Hans Könneke is the master chef, and not only is the food outstanding, but the dining rooms exude an oh-so-appealing rustic elegance. The candle-lit tables, dressed with fine linens and fresh flowers, set off to perfection the rough-hewn, exposed timber walls. The inn's own local red wine from the cask completes a delicious dinner. The guest rooms are located on the third level. They are small and simple, but each is decorated in perfect harmony with the mood of the house. Beamed ceilings, simple white walls, embroidered tie-back curtains, comfortable beds and soft pink linens create a most inviting look. My favorite room is number 3, a darling corner room that overlooks the square. As a final bonus, the Stadtschänke is run by the very gracious Könneke family who add their warmth of hospitality to make your visit even more special.

STADTSCHÄNKE GASTHOF
Owners: Sybille & Hans Könneke
Hauptstrasse 36, am Marktplatz
71723 Grossbottwar, Germany
tel: (07148) 80.24, fax: (07148) 49.77
4 rooms, Double: 120 DM
Open all year
Credit cards: all major
Restaurant-closed Wednesdays
30 km S of Heilbronn, 35 km N of Stuttgart

A curved, dark wooden staircase leads to the first floor of the Schloss Hotel Grünwald, where the atmosphere is more like a museum that takes in guests than a hotel. Each room has very high ceilings and is uniquely furnished in priceless antiques. The hallways are also filled with old paintings, carved wooden statues, and large antique pieces. The second floor is the former maids' quarters, thus the ceilings are lower and rooms smaller in their dimensions. Rooms are not as lavishly furnished, although all have antique touches and are very tasteful and refined. The hotel's beautiful setting high on a hillside overlooking the Isar river affords gorgeous views from the pleasant outdoor terrace, where guests can sit under the chestnut trees and enjoy an open air lunch or perhaps a before dinner cocktail. Inside, the ambiance of the dark wood paneled restaurant is more that of a Bavarian hunting lodge than of an elegant museum as in the upstairs rooms. Warm rose tablecloths complement pretty flower arrangements, gleaming silver, china, and glassware. Traditional regional cuisine is served here as well as a fresh, "nouvelle cuisine" style of cooking. Great arched windows frame the breathtaking view over the terrace to the forested hills and down to the Isar River. Relax in this inviting restaurant and enjoy a delicious meal without fear of the bill, as the menu is very reasonably priced.

SCHLOSS HOTEL GRÜNWALD
Owner: Frau Sigrid Bayer
Zeillerstrasse 1
82031 Grünwald, Germany
tel: (089) 64.17.935, fax: (089) 64.14.771
16 rooms, suites; Double: 190-320 DM
Closed January 1-15
Credit cards: all major
Restaurant-closed Wednesdays
10 km S of Munich

The Hotel Abtei is one of the finest small city hotels in Germany. Situated on a quiet, tree-lined street north of the center of Hamburg, the hotel seems far removed from the confusion of the city, yet is quickly accessible either by car, subway, or boat. Every detail of the Abtei, originally a gracious private home, is of the highest quality and taste: gorgeous fabrics, exquisite antiques, fine linens, comfortable mattresses (replaced every two years), fresh flower arrangements throughout, and exceptional service. Herr Lay's goal is to provide the old-fashioned quality of excellence rarely found today—his goal is to have the "Smallest GRAND Hotel" in Europe. The Abtei is not inexpensive, yet when compared with all the other hotels in the costly city of Hamburg, it offers real value for the price. It was voted the best hotel with under 50 rooms in Germany—and was among the top 25 of all German hotels. The guest rooms are beautifully decorated suites with well-equipped, attractive bathrooms ensuite. Guests may enjoy breakfast in their room, in one of the guest dining rooms, or if the weather is warm, in the pretty garden behind the hotel. Homemade baked goods are offered in silver bread baskets, and delicious coffee or tea is served in antique pots. In the evening, dinner is served in the intimate dining room. If you like refinement, and exceptional service, you will love this tiny hotel.

HOTEL ABTEI
Owner: Fritz Lay
Abteistrasse 14
20149 Hamburg, Germany
tel: (040) 44.29.05, fax: (040) 44.98.20
12 rooms, Double: 420 DM
Open all year
Credit cards: DC, MC, VS
Restaurant-closed Sundays & Mondays
In the Harvestehude section of Hamburg
NW of the Alster Lake

Hamburg is the hub of northern Germany. Far more than an important seaport and business center, it is a city of great beauty offering a rich and varied social and cultural menu. Just north of the city center you find Alster Lake: with this expanse of water at its front and a tranquil garden at its rear, the Hotel Prem occupies a handsome downtown Hamburg location. What were originally two large townhouses were converted into a small hotel by Herr and Frau Prem more than 75 years ago. The downstairs is small: a lounge area leads to a bar and beyond an airy restaurant overlooks the garden. The restaurant, decorated in shades of beige and white and with arrangements of fresh flowers, brightens even the gloomiest Hamburg day. In summer the pretty garden is set with tables and chairs for outside dining. Accented with fine antiques, the bedrooms retain their high ceilings, which give a spacious feeling. A few lovely rooms have retained their original ornate plaster work ceilings. The staff speak excellent English and really care that you enjoy your holiday. You can easily walk to the heart of Hamburg, or, if you prefer, one of the ferry stops is very close. Also, only steps from your front door are the walking paths that encircle the lake. As an added bonus, the hotel provides discounted rates for guests staying on weekends.

HOTEL PREM
Manager: Ulrich Void
An der Alster 9
20099 Hamburg, Germany
tel:(040) 24.17.26, fax: (040) 28.03.851
59 rooms, 3 suites; Double: 275-535 DM
Open all year
Credit cards: all major
Restaurant, garden
N of city center
On SE shore of Alster Lake

This guide usually features small, intimate inns rather than grand hotels, but sometimes a hotel is so lovely that we feel compelled to make an exception. Such is definitely the case with the Vier Jahreszeiten. Although a large hotel, it maintains the quality and ambiance of a small inn. If you don't mind spending the money for a very deluxe hotel and want to be in the heart of Hamburg, the Vier Jahreszeiten is a wonderful choice: it is proudly positioned on the banks of the Alster Lake near the picturesque boats that ply the rivers and canals, and minutes from Hamburg's elegant shops. From the moment you enter into the exquisite lobby you are surrounded by the warmth and charm of a lovely country home. A dramatic hallway stretches beyond the reception counter with an exquisite Persian carpet in shades of gold and cream reflecting the color scheme of a gorgeous tapestry dominating the end of the room. To the left of the reception area is a cozy club-like lounge with mellow paneling, a grandfather clock, lovely fresh flowers and comfortable chairs and couches. Several restaurants offer a delicious variety of dining options, from casual to more elaborate meals. As you might expect, the Vier Jahreszeiten's guest rooms are beautiful and the service refined.

VIER JAHRESZEITEN
Manager: Moreno Occhiolini
Neuer Jungfernstieg 9-14
20354 Hamburg, Germany
tel: (040) 34940, fax: (040) 34.94.602
172 rooms, 11 suites; Double 534-664 DM
Open all year
Restaurant-open daily
Credit cards: all major
On the shore of SW shore of Alster Lake
USA Rep: LHW 800-223-6800

One of our favorite places to stay along the Rhine has always been the beautiful Krone in Assmannshausen. Now the Hufnagel-Ullrich family (who own the Krone) have opened a second hotel nearby, the deluxe Kronen Schlösschen. This attractive mansion, painted white with brown trim, is set in its own intimate park, across the highway from the Rhine. The Kronen Schlösschen has a whimsical look with jaunty towers topped by peaked onion domes and a stepped roof line. From the courtyard, you enter into a pretty foyer with ornate stucco design and marble floors. A staircase leads up to the guest rooms, each one absolutely stunning in decor. Your choice of rooms depends upon what style appeals to you—some are smartly tailored in dark colors, others are spring-like with a pastel color scheme, some are modern, some antique. One of my favorites, mini-suite 29, has pale-yellow wallpaper, rich natural-silk lemon-toned draperies, soft green carpet and comfortable, off-white matching sofas. No matter what room you choose, you will find glamorous marble bathrooms, truly fit for a king. The Kronen Schlösschen has two excellent restaurants: one an elegant gourmet dining room, the other "The Bistro," a less formal, pub-like room that is enclosed on two sides with windows. Note: Hattenheim is so small it is not on most maps. It is located on the Rhine just west of Eltville.

KRONEN SCHLÖSSCHEN
Owner: Family Hufnagel-Ullrich
Rheinallee
65347 Hattenheim-Eltville, Germany
tel: (06723) 640, fax: (06723) 76.63
18 rooms, Double: 298-368 DM
7 suites 408-728 DM
Open all year
Credit cards: all major
Restaurant-open daily
39 km to Frankfurt airport
12 km W of Wiesbaden

The Weinhaus "Zum Krug" is located in Hattenheim, a the tiny wine town along the Rhine, just west of Eltville. The village has many very old buildings with character, but only a few of them have been restored to reflect their historic past. Happily, the Weinhaus "Zum Krug," that dates back to 1720, is an absolute jewel, an intriguing little inn that sits right on a bend of the main road through town. The first floor is painted white and has dark green shutters framing leaded windows. The timbered second floor has a fairy-tale quality. It is painted a dark green that is merrily set off by an intricate design of gold grape vines. To add the finishing touch to this quaint house, bright red geraniums overflow from green boxes below each of the windows. There is no doubt about what awaits the guest within—suspended over the entrance is a jug of wine, enclosed in a wreath of grapes (as might be guessed, the restaurant has its own winery). Inside, the decor is appropriately rustic with a beamed ceiling, small tables with wooden chairs, oriental throw rugs, and a dark green tile stove along the wall. This is not a deluxe hotel, nor is it meant to be. However, upstairs there are 8 guest rooms. Although simple, each has its own private bathroom. For a reasonable-priced place to stay along the Rhine, Weinhaus "Zum Krug," makes an attractive choice.

WEINHAUS "ZUM KRUG"
Owner: Josef Laufer
Hauptstrasse 34
65347 Hattenheim-Eltville, Germany
tel: (06723) 28.12, fax: (06723) 76.77
8 rooms, Double: 180-200 DM
Closed January & last 2 weeks July
Credit cards: all major
Restaurant-closed Sunday evenings & Mondays
39 km to Frankfurt airport, 12 km W of Wiesbaden

The 300-year-old Zur Backmulde enjoys a quiet location off the main pedestrian street of Heidelberg's picturesque "old town." This lovely small and atmospheric establishment offers an intimate restaurant and thirteen bedrooms. From the street, guests pass under the old stone arched doorway to enter the softly lit restaurant filled with fresh flowers, antique pieces, old mirrors, photos and paintings from Heidelberg. The restaurant, decorated in tones of red and green, offers excellent food in a cozy atmosphere. The hotel section faces its own quiet, enclosed courtyard (a convenient, free parking area for guests). A staircase, whose dark blue walls are brightened by an overhead sky light, leads up one floor to the reception area and the breakfast room. With new ownership, the entire hotel has been totally renovated. A blue color scheme prevails throughout, including an excellent quality, patterned carpet. Each of the bedrooms is attractively decorated in pretty blue floral draperies (with white sheer curtains beneath) and color-coordinating fabrics on the bed covers (room 1 is a special favorite). The bathrooms are not large, but each is brand new and spotlessly clean. With its recent face-lift, the Zur Backmulde has emerged as one of the best small hotels in Heidelberg, and the price is excellent for the value received.

ZUR BACKMULDE
Owners: Bernhard Zepf & Alex Schneider
Schiffgasse 11
69117 Heidelberg, Germany
tel: (06221) 53.660, fax: (06221) 53.66.60
13 rooms, Double: 145-155 DM
Open all year
Credit cards: all major
Restaurant-closed Sunday evenings
In the old town of Heidelberg
80 km S of Frankfurt

Heidelberg is a romantic, beguiling old university town with one main street, the Hauptstrasse, that captures most of the atmosphere. It is here that you will find the Romantik Hotel Zum Ritter St Georg afforded one of the best locations in town. From its roof-top garden you will have an incomparable view of the old city. Owned by the Kuchelmeisters, the Zum Ritter is managed as a very professional and first class city hotel. The majority of the accommodations are comfortable, but sterile and modern in decor (room number 100, a spacious double overlooking the street, offers a bit more old world ambiance). The hotel serves a nice standard breakfast that is included in the price of the room. In the evening the restaurant is lit with candles and takes on a very intimate and romantic atmosphere. The public areas are decorated with antiques and the hotel's stately facade dates from 1592 when the master builder, Carolus Belier, imprinted the gold sign still hanging above the door. Official records show the building served as a town hall for a decade before it became the Hotel Zum Ritter. If driving, follow signs to Parkhaus 12. From there it is only a few blocks to the hotel.

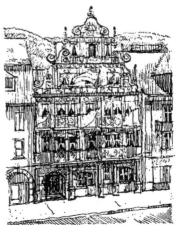

ROMANTIK HOTEL ZUM RITTER ST GEORG
Owner: Georg Kuchelmeister
Manager: H.J. Gerber
Hauptstrasse 178
69117 Heidelberg, Germany
tel: (06221) 24.272, fax: (6221) 12.683
38 rooms, Double: 250-325 DM
Open all year
Credit cards: all major
Restaurant-open daily
80 km S of Frankfurt
USA Rep: Euro-Connection 800-645-3876

Staying in a castle almost always guarantees an adventure, but not always a comfortable night's accommodation. All too often the knights in armor are ever present, but not the firm mattress and the welcome hot and cold running water. Near the Neckar River there are numerous castle hotels. One of these, Schloss Heinsheim (in the von Racknitz family for over 350 years), is especially appealing because of its excellent accommodations and outstanding cuisine. The hotel is surrounded by a forest and has all the ambiance of a large country estate. Horses frequently frolic in the fields visible from your bedroom window, enhancing the "country mood." There is a small circular pool that is favored by children and a lovely terraced area set with tables for enjoying meals outside in warm weather. There are two attractive restaurants: one is in a rustic decor and one is a bit more modern. The bedrooms are beautifully furnished with fine fabrics and many antiques—one of my favorites, room 15, is especially attractive. There is a small, baroque chapel on the grounds and on weekends you might well have the fun of witnessing a wedding celebration. Note: The town of Heinsheim is quite small and not on many maps. From Bad Rappenau (which you can find on most maps) go east for 5 kilometers to Heinsheim (signposted to Gundelsheim, a town beyond Heinsheim).

SCHLOSS HEINSHEIM
Manager: Peter Messner
Gundelsheimer Strasse 36
74906 Heinsheim, Bad-Rappenau, Germany
tel: (07264) 10.45, fax: (07264) 42.08
40 rooms, 1 suite; Double: 190-290 DM
Closed month of January
Credit cards: DC, MC, VS
Restaurant-open daily, pool
74 km N of Stuttgart, 55 km E of Heidelberg
Gast im Schloss

If your arrival at the Sassenhof is midday you will most likely find Frau Pfeiffer dressed in a starched lace apron, supervising the cleaning and presentation of each of her guest rooms. An extremely handsome woman, she strives to achieve an atmosphere of a private home with the advantages of very personalized service. Richly polished woods and antique furnishings adorn the public rooms and artistic fresh flower arrangements prepared by Frau Pfeiffer add splashes of color everywhere. The Sassenhof has a pretty dining area where breakfast is unfortunately the only formal meal served. Tea, however, can be enjoyed in the afternoons and each room is thoughtfully provided with freshly pressed linen and dishes. Drinks and bread are conveniently available upon request, encouraging guests to buy their own meats and cheeses and to prepare their own light suppers or lunches. The halls that lead to the bedrooms are warmed by soft lighting, handsome prints, red carpet covered in Oriental throw rugs, and heavy wooden doors and doorways. Each room is individual in its decor but all are tastefully and attractively decorated and arranged by Frau Pfeiffer. In this small guest house it is surprising to find a very large, attractive swimming pool.

SASSENHOF
Owner: Irmgard Pfeiffer
Alderweg 17
79856 Hinterzarten, Germany
tel: (07652) 15.15, fax: (07652) 484
24 rooms, 6 suites; Double: 130-185 DM
Closed November to mid-December
Credit cards: none accepted
No restaurant-breakfast only, pool, sauna
161 km SW of Stuttgart, 26 km SE of Freiburg

High above the beautiful Moselle Valley is one of those rare, perfect hideaways—the Historische Schlossmühle. It is a little complicated getting to the hotel; a detailed map will certainly aid you in finding the Rhaunen turnoff from the road 327 that runs to the south of the Moselle. You will find the Historische Schlossmühle a short drive from the junction, about half a mile beyond the tiny village of Horbruch. The Historische Schlossmühle was once an old mill. Bedrooms in the old mill (named after country animals) are stocked with thoughtful little extras that make a stay memorable—proper sewing kits and hair spray. The four new rooms in the granary are equally as lovely. There is no need to splurge on a suite—standard doubles (especially those overlooking the back pond) are most appealing. Rüdiger and Anneliese Liller are your charming hosts—Anneliese is responsible for the creative decor. A little corner room honors Napoleon, for the mill has associations with this famous soldier. The story goes that in 1804 Napoleon sold the mill to raise money and the enterprising new owner had the foresight to realize that once Napoleon had left, the original owner would reclaim his property. To guard against this happening, he had the mill taken apart and erected 25 kilometers away in this quiet green valley outside the village of Horbruch.

HOTEL HISTORISCHE SCHLOSSMÜHLE
Owners: Anneliese & Rüdiger Liller
55483 Horbruch-Hunsruck, Germany
tel: (06543) 40.41, fax: (06543) 31.78
10 rooms, 1 suite; Double: 195-286 DM
Open all year
Credit cards: AC, MC, VS
Restaurant-closed Mondays,
63 km NE of Trier, 20 km SE of Bernkastel-Kues
Gast im Schloss

Just 30 kilometers from the fascinating city of Würzburg, the Zehntkeller, Romantik Hotel and wine house, is also convenient to the wine region at the foot of the Schwan mountains. Once a tax collection point for the church, and hence a most unpopular building, the Zehntkeller (made into a hotel in 1910) is now a chosen destination of many. Iphofen is a small quiet village and it is amazing to find the traffic coming and going from the inn: the specialties of the menu attract diners from the outlying regions. The restaurant is actually a number of rooms on the first floor and serviced by gracious girls dressed in attractive dirndls. The hotel rooms found in the main building above the restaurant are all lovely and are well appointed with modern bathrooms. Single rooms are found on the top floor. In an annex that backs onto a walled garden, a new wing of rooms has been added to accommodate guests who want to linger for a stay of more than a few days.

ROMANTIK HOTEL ZEHNTKELLER
Owner: Heinrich Seufert
Bahnhofstrasse 12
97346 Iphofen, Germany
tel: (09323) 30.62, fax: (09323) 15.19
43 rooms, Double: 140-220 DM
Closed last 2 weeks of January
Credit cards: AX, DC, EC, VS
Restaurant-open daily
248 km NW of Munich, 72 km NW of Nürnberg
30 km E of Würzburg
USA Rep: Euro-Connection 800-645-3876

Under the management of Wilhelm Ritter, pride and care are evident in every aspect of the Hotel Zum Goldenen Pflug (translated as the "golden plow"). This gem of a hotel is located in the little farming village of Ising not far from "Mad Ludwig's" dramatic castle on a tiny island in the Chiemsee. The reception area and spacious inviting bar are found in what were once the cow byres. The charming dining rooms: Fischer Stube, Gaststube and Jagerstube are in the barn. Although all three restaurants have a different theme of decor, the food is good and attractively presented in each. The bedrooms are scattered around the complex and, depending on their location, vary in theme but are all exceptional in comfort and decor. Accommodations are found in the stables, in the old blacksmith's abode—cozy under beams and country in decor—and some dear rooms are located in a house set all on its own. Off the reception area is a wing of rooms more recently built but traditional in decor. Surrounding the hotel is a large estate. The hotel also offers its own riding stables and trainer for guests on a longer stay who wish to ride.

ZUM GOLDENEN PFLUG
Manager: Wilhelm Ritter
Kirchberg 3, Ising am Chiemsee
83339 Chieming, Germany
tel: (08667) 790, fax: (08667) 79.432
88 rooms, 7 suites; Double: 227-327 DM
Open all year
Credit cards: AX, DC, VS
Restaurant, golf, beach
104 km SE of Munich, on the Chiemsee

If you admire dramatic settings, the Parkhotel Wasserburg will certainly impress you. At first glance, this huge red brick castle appears to be floating in its own lake. The hotel entrance is, of course, over a proper drawbridge and through an arched tower. Inside, the castle has a sophisticated aura, somewhat commercial, but pleasing. There is a pretty lounge where light pine furniture, floral print chairs and a fireplace provide an inviting refuge. Another cozy spot is found in the rustic "Pferdestall" bar. The formal dining room is decorated in pastel tones and offers refined dining illuminated by candlelight and glowing chandeliers. There is a less elegant, but still very inviting restaurant on a lower level that has a sunny terrace where tables and umbrellas are set right out over the water. Guest bedrooms are contemporary in style, but tastefully decorated in muted colors. The tower suite has a canopy bed, pretty floral wallpaper and a crystal chandelier. Part of the castle is open to the public as a museum and offers beautiful examples of German and Italian master painters from the 17th and 18th Centuries, Chinese porcelains from the 18th and 19th Centuries, and Flemish tapestries from the 18th and 19th Centuries, all displayed in historic rooms among period furniture. Outdoors, a large park including an 18-hole golf course surrounds the lake and castle.

PARKHOTEL WASSERBURG ANHOLT
Manager: Heinz Brune
46419 Isselburg, Germany
tel: (02874) 45.90, fax: (02874) 40.35
28 rooms, Double: 200-370 DM
Open all year
Credit cards: EC, MC, VS
Restaurant-closed Mondays, golf
87 km NW of Düsseldorf, 13 km SW of Bocholt
On IsselRiver near Dutch border
Gast im Schloss

The introduction to this marvelous castle hotel is first an expanse of lawn, intricate turrets and then an old timbered courtyard. Up a flight of stairs, the hotel entrance is a majestic banquet hall. The dining room is very regal. Take notice of a handsome, intricately inlaid door, lovely flower arrangements and the crest of the family above both entrances. The present family has lived in the castle as far back as 927. Herr Bircks, both manager and chef, is a charming man, exuding pride in the castle and offering a warm welcome for each guest. The breakfast room looks out through large windows onto the lush surrounding countryside. Climb a steep staircase in the direction of the bedchambers onto a terrace that also enjoys an expansive view and is used in warmer months for dining. Down a timbered hallway, the bedrooms are all named for renowned actors and many overlook either the valley or the weathered tiles of another castle wing. The least expensive rooms are those without a private bathroom. The highlight of the adjoining armament's museum is an iron hand, unique because of its moveable parts. In summer months the courtyard becomes a stage for afternoon and evening plays. Also, to the delight of children and adults, a steam train provides scenic rides through the valley.

BURGHOTEL GÖTZENBURG
Owner: Family von Berlichingen
Manager: Herr Bircks
74249 Jagsthausen, Germany
tel: (07943) 22.22, fax: (07943) 82.00
17 rooms, Double: 135-260 DM
Closed November to mid-March
Credit cards: all major
Restaurant-open daily
82 km N of Stuttgart

The lush Ruhr region is beautiful. Especially appealing is the landscape around Kettwig. Here, far from the smokestacks of the industrial area, you find the Schloss Hugenpoet, an imposing fortress surrounded by a water-filled moat where large carp swim lazily. There has been a fortification on this site for over one thousand years, and during violent periods of history several castles on the site were destroyed. The present structure has existed since 1650. The interior, rich in tradition, presents a castle in tiptop condition. The lobby is dominated by an impressive black marble staircase; a grouping of fine furniture stands in front of the huge carved fireplace, while the surrounding walls host a picture gallery of fine oil paintings. This is a grand castle where the bedchambers were given spacious proportions. Many are furnished with authentic 16th-century furniture. Down stairs, the dining rooms are baronial in their size, each dominated by a grand carved fireplace. Boasting famous chefs and gourmet cuisine, the dining rooms command a large, loyal, local following while still giving impeccable service to the hotel residents. The Schloss Hugenpoet is a member of the prestigious Relais & Chateaux group of outstanding hotels.

SCHLOSS HUGENPOET
Owner: Jürgen Neumann
August-Thyssen Strasse 51
45219 Essen (Kettwig), Germany
tel: (02054) 12.040, fax: (02054) 12.0450
19 rooms, Double: 335-470 DM, Suite 730 DM
Closed first week in January
Credit cards: AX, DC, MC
Restaurant-open daily, tennis
60 km NE of Cologne, 11 km SW of Essen
Between Wuppertal & Mülheim
Gast im Schloss

Our visit to the Schloss Hotel Kronberg coincided with that of visiting delegates and bedrooms were closed off for security reasons. However, based on the few rooms I saw and the sumptuous sophistication of the public rooms, I feel comfortable in recommending the Schloss Hotel Kronberg as an excellent choice for a hotel. Northwest of Frankfurt, a convenient half an hour drive by the autobahn from the Frankfurt airport, this was once a gathering place for European royalty and most of the ruling monarchs were at one time guests here. Today, it is a member of the prestigious Relais & Chateaux group, an indication of its outstanding attributes. The Schloss Hotel Kronberg has a number of grand halls, impressive with their high ceilings and adorning tapestries. A typical "English-Afternoon-Tea" is served on weekends in the stately library in front of its large stone fireplace (it is advisable to book a table in advance). The adjoining Blue Parlor room is frequently reserved for private functions and luncheons. At the end of the hall a beautiful wood paneled dining room achieves intimacy and grandeur in its decor. The Schloss Hotel Kronberg was built originally in 1888 as a private home, and has been offering rooms to guests for over fifty years.

SCHLOSS HOTEL KRONBERG
Manager: Hartmut Althoff
Hainstrasse 25
61476 Kronberg in Taunus, Germany
tel: (06173) 70101, fax: (06173) 70.12.67
58 rooms, Double: 519-679 DM
7 suites from 949 DM
Open all year
Credit cards: all major
Restaurant-open daily, golf
17 km NW of Frankfurt
USA Rep: Utell International 800 448-8355

If you are a castle connoisseur, the Schlosshotel Lembeck is worth a detour to see. It is a real winner. This 12th-century, moated castle is awesome in size yet not in the least foreboding as some German castles tend to be. Somehow, as you approach over the moat and through the gate, this massive building of mellow cut stone and dark gray slate roof with perky pointed cap-like domed towers is irresistible. The castle is also a sightseeing attraction—the museum and grounds are open to the public, but at the gate just say you are a guest of the hotel and there is no charge to enter. A door in the gate leads down to the small restaurant which is also where you register. The restaurant is informal and very inviting with a vaulted brick ceiling, wooden chairs and tables, soft lighting from rustic chandeliers, and a cozy fireplace. In the summertime, snacks are also served outside on the lawn overlooking the moat. The guest rooms are located in the rear wing of the castle. Splurge on one of the best rooms and you will be treated to antique furniture and an ambiance of days gone by. The bridal suite (Hochzeitszimmer mit Himmelbett) has a large canopied bed, tapestry chairs and windows looking out over the countryside. The Schlosshotel Lembeck is surrounded with lovely grounds and woods where kilometers of footpaths meander beneath the trees.

SCHLOSSHOTEL LEMBECK
Owner: Josef Selting
46286 Dorsten, Lembeck, Germany
tel: (02369) 72.13, fax: (02369) 77.370
10 rooms, bridal suite
Double: 118-178 DM
Open all year
Credit cards: DC, MC, VS
Restaurant-open daily
61 km N of Düsseldorf
10 km N of Dorsten, 29 km N of Essen

An old commercial hotel near the railway station does not seem a likely candidate for inclusion in a book of country inns, but the interior of the hotel is so charming and the nearby old town so picturesque that I could not exclude it. Limburg is quite a large town but you will have no difficulty finding the Hotel Zimmermann as it is sign-posted from the time you leave the autobahn. The hotel is decorated in the prim and proper style of an English Victorian house: dark wood bow-back chairs with deep cushions and velour coverings, prim striped wallpaper and ornate lamps. Downstairs is a parlor and a dining room, and upstairs are nicely decorated bedrooms, each with its own sitting area. Some of the rooms are designated non smoking. Triple glazing on the windows eliminates all noise, ensuring a quiet night's sleep. Frau Zimmermann cooks dinner only during the week, so on the occasion of my weekend visit, she directed me to the Golden Lion, a historic restaurant in the old town amongst half-timbered houses and narrow cobbled streets leading to the River Lahn. The nearby cathedral is seven stories high and ornately painted in coral and white; a splendid example of 13th-century architecture.

ROMANTIK HOTEL ZIMMERMANN
Owner: Dieter Zimmermann
Blumenröder Strasse 1
65549 Limburg, Germany
tel: (06431) 46.11, fax: (06431) 41.314
25 rooms, Double: 158-295 DM
Closed Christmas through New Years
Credit cards: AX, DC, VS
Restaurant-for guests only
74 km N of Frankfurt
52 km N of Wiesbaden, 50 km E of Koblenz
USA Rep: Euro-Connection 800-645-3876

An unknown, yet absolutely fascinating niche in Germany is the Spreewald, an area south of Berlin. Here the Spree River fans out into a spider web of waterways bordered by quaint houses, many only accessible by boat. Until recently we could not find a place to suggest to overnight in the vicinity, but now we heartily recommend a small castle has been converted into a deluxe hotel. When we stayed at Schloss Lübbenau in 1990, it was a drab, dismal hotel with rooms so bedraggled we felt we could not include it in our guide. But with the reunification, the Counts Lynar reclaimed their property that has belonged to their family since 1621. In World War II, Wilhelm-Friedrich, their father, was one of the few men who had the astounding courage to resist the Nazi movement, and subsequently lost his life. What a remarkable man! During the absence of the Lynar family, the castle became dilapidated—being used as a school then later a cheap hotel, but now it is rapidly resuming its former glory. One of the wings is completely renovated and guest rooms that were quite dismal are now bright and cheerful. Italian, antique-style furniture gives a pleasing traditional look, enhanced by fine-quality carpets and drapes that are in restful tones of green. Countess Lynar's hobby is dried-flower arranging, and she is personally responsible for the pretty floral arrangements in the hotel.

SCHLOSS LÜBBENAU
Owner: Graf zu Lynar
Schlossbezirk 6
03222 Lübbenau, Germany
tel: (03542) 81.26, fax: (03542) 33.27
52 rooms, Double: 194-271 DM
Open all year
Credit cards: all major
Restaurant-open daily
Midway between Berlin & Dresden
Gast im Schloss

The Hotel Jensen enjoys a choice location just across the river from the dramatic walled entrance to the town of Lübeck. The hotel is one of many tall narrow buildings lining the canal, and, like its neighbors, this slim and appealing building has the characteristic steep roof that forms a "stair step" gabled effect in the front. The main thrust of the Jensen seems to be the dining rooms: there is "The Cabin," the "Yacht Room," the "Fireside Room" and the "Patrician's Room," each with its own personality. The bedrooms are located up a stairway leading from the reception area. They are small and do not exhibit much character in their decor, yet they are clean and adequately furnished. The rooms in the front of the building overlook the canal and the twin-towered Hostentor (Holsten Gate), affording good views of the boats and quayside activity. Although these front rooms face the busy street, they are very quiet due to well insulated windows. Handily, the pier for the ferry excursion boats (a must for enjoying the colorful town of Lübeck) is located just across the street from the hotel. Recommended mainly for travelers seeking a convenient location from which to enjoy Lübeck, the Jensen is a very modest hotel offering friendly management and a fun place to stay.

HOTEL JENSEN
Owner: Wilfried Rahlff-Petersson
Manager: Dietrich Bergmann
Am der Obertrave 4-5
23552 Lübeck, Germany
tel: (0451) 71.646, fax: (0451) 73.386
42 rooms, Double: 170-190 DM
Open all year
Credit cards: all major
Restaurant-open daily
66 km NE of Hamburg, 92 km SE of Kiel

The Hotel Kaiserhof is located just across the canal and a short walk from the historic old city of Lübeck. The hotel is a clever combination of two stately 19th-century homes that have been joined with a central core serving as lobby and reception area. The hotel has grown over the years and now has amenities such as a large indoor swimming pool and sauna, yet it still retains the home-spun ambiance and warmth of a small hotel. This homey feeling is undoubtedly due to the owner, Ruth Klemm, who cares deeply about the comfort of each guest. Her staff is carefully chosen and taught to give "service with a heart," thus making this a hotel with a special level of service. The reception area is light and airy with oriental carpets setting off the polished marble floor. The intimate lounge has a magnificent sculpted ceiling, fully restored including the 24 caret gilt paint, yet this room's pièce de résistance is a superb, intricately formed Meissen porcelain fireplace. Each of the bedrooms is individually decorated and the ones I saw were spacious and filled with light from large windows. The Hotel Kaiserhof is not a showplace of antique furniture or a decorator's dream, yet these two lovely old buildings are beautiful and Frau Klemm has gone to great effort to restore all of the architectural details to their original elegance.

HOTEL KAISERHOF
Owner: Ruth Klemm
Kronsforder Allee 11-13
23560 Lübeck, Germany
tel: (0451) 79.10.11, fax: (0451) 79.50.83
70 rooms, suites, Double: 180-225 DM
Open all year
Credit cards: all major
Restaurant-closed Saturdays & Sundays
Indoor pool
66 km NE of Hamburg, 92 km SE of Kiel

The tiny village of Marienthal is little more than the Haus Elmer, an antique shop and a craft shop clustered around what was once a thriving Augustinian monastery. The hotel is a clever blend of an old and new building. Bedrooms in the old house are smaller and exude country charm; those in the new section are larger and decorated with new country-style furniture. There are two especially romantic rooms with old four-poster beds making them favorites with honeymooners. There are several dining rooms. One is on the upper story of the new wing and has delightful views of the surrounding countryside through its large picture windows, another is paneled and cozy. The surrounding sky-wide landscapes are perfect for cycling: cyclists pedal easily along, enjoying the country sounds and smells that are lost to speeding motorists. The hotel has plenty of bicycles for you to use during your stay. If you prefer to venture farther afield, the hotel offers a four-night cycling holiday in conjunction with two other hotels in the area. The package includes bicycles, maps, accommodations and the transportation of your luggage from hotel to hotel.

ROMANTIK HOTEL HAUS ELMER
Owners: Marlies & Karl-Heinz Elmer
An der Klosterkirche 12
46499 Hamminkeln-Marienthal, Germany
tel: (02856) 2041, fax: (02856) 20.61
31 rooms, Double: 180-250 DM
Open all year
Credit cards: DC, MC, VS
Restaurant-open daily, golf, bikes
100 km NW of Cologne, near Wesel
USA Rep: Euro-Connection 800-645-3876

The Gasthof Zum Bären is a postcard-perfect, 15th-century inn. The hotel would be a real gem even if it didn't have the added bonus of being in the heart of Meersburg, an absolutely stunning small medieval village hugging the shore of Lake Constance. In the Gilowsky family for five generations, the Zum Bären is now smoothly run by Michael Gilowsky (who is also the chef) and his attractive wife, Heike. Upstairs, a treasure chest of bedrooms awaits. Our room had a beautifully carved wooden ceiling, country pine furniture, dainty print wallpaper and lace curtains. Some rooms have old painted furniture and all have antique touches and pretty wallpapers. The Zum Bären is a "gasthof" not a hotel, thus bedrooms are not equipped with telephones, although all have color televisions and a private bath or shower. Downstairs, the two cozy dining rooms are decorated with pewter plates and typical blue stoneware filling shelves above carved wooden furniture, fresh flowers, and comfy window benches with pretty print pillows. A wood parquet floor, low, beamed ceiling and white tile stove add to the pervading feeling of "gemütlichkeit." Both dining rooms contain only large tables for six to eight persons. This is purposely done to encourage guests to share a table, perhaps some wine, and certainly good conversation. A very warm and charming inn, the Gasthof Zum Bären is one of Germany's very special small inns.

GASTHOF ZUM BÄREN
Owners: Heike & Michael Gilowsky
Marktplatz 11
88709 Meersburg, Germany
tel: (07532) 60.44 fax: (07532) 22.16
17 rooms, Double: 125-135 DM
Closed December, January & February
Credit cards: none accepted
Restaurant-closed Mondays
170 km SE of Stuttgart, 31 km SW of Ravensburg

The Hotel Weinstube Löwen, located in the heart of the pedestrian section of the fairy-tale-like walled town of Meersburg, sits across the street from one of our favorite small inns, the Hotel Bären. Both adorable hotels are similar in ambiance: dining rooms filled with charm and guest rooms that are simple, but very comfortable (the guest rooms in the Bären offer a more traditional ambiance). The Hotel Löwen's appeal is immediate: you cannot help being captivated by the wisteria-laden, deep salmon-colored facade, green shutters, and steep gabled roof. You step inside to an attractive reception area where chances are you will be warmly greeted by one of the Löwen's greatest assets, the pretty and ever-so-gracious, Frau Bauer, the front desk manager. The owner, Sigfrid Fischer, is also exceptionally friendly, and although he speaks little English, his warmth of welcome crosses all language barriers. The romantic dining room with its low beamed ceiling and cozy tables set with fresh flowers, serves marvelous food, including of course, many fish specialties from adjacent Lake Constance. The guest rooms are modern in decor, lacking old world ambiance. One that has the most personality is number 36, tucked up under the eaves with the gears of an antique hoist (used in days-gone-by to bring up goods from the street) incorporated into the design.

HOTEL WEINSTUBE LÖWEN
Owner: Sigfrid Fischer
Manager: Frau Bauer
Am Marktplatz 2
88709 Meersburg, Germany
tel: (07532) 43.040, fax: (07532) 43.04.10
21 rooms, Double: 145-185 DM
Open all year
Credit cards: EC, MC, VS
Restaurant-open daily
191 km SE of Stuttgart, on Lake Constance

On the left bend of the Main river, Miltenberg is a charming mix of cobblestoned streets and sloping slate and tile roofs. It is a quick and rewarding hike up from the market place to the castle ruins for a splendid view overlooking this picturesque village. On Haupstrasse, a street reserved for pedestrians, you will enjoy a number of quaint shops and discover a dear little inn. With its timbered facade and charming decor, the Hotel Zum Riesen has served as a welcome travelers' retreat for close to 400 years, but it has only been the last 15 years that it has profited immensely from the efforts and care of Cilly and Werner Jost. Preserving the weathered beams of the ceilings and walls, the Josts have added plumbing and heating throughout. In each of the 15 rooms the beds are decked with plump down comforters. The decor is further enhanced by some handsome antiques and Oriental rugs cover the hardwood floors. Breakfast is served on the third floor. Easter morning we were greeted with a stunning breakfast setting: tables were laid with fresh linens, candles and flowers, and thoughtfully wrapped Easter gifts were set out for all. Fresh jams, rolls, meats, cheese, juice and an egg were served and Frau Jost was there to welcome and seat her guests—with a warm smile.

HOTEL ZUM RIESEN
Owners: Cilly & Werner Jost
Hauptstrasse 97
63897 Miltenberg, Germany
tel: (09371) 3644
15 Rooms, Double: 115-185 DM
Closed December to mid-March
Credit cards: DC
No restaurant-breakfast only
160 km SE of Frankfurt,
41 km S of Aschaffenburg

The Acanthus Hotel was a non-descript, commercial hotel (formerly called the Sendlinger Tor) until Carola Günther (a retired Lufthansa stewardess) and her husband Jörg took over. Under their loving care, the hotel has developed real heart and is now a wonderful option for those looking for a not-too-expensive place to stay in Munich's inner ring. You enter into an intimate reception area where the front desk is managed by a warm, gracious staff. There is no restaurant, but just off the lobby, a cozy bar opens into a breakfast room. Each morning a bountiful buffet is set up in the bar and guests can help themselves to a delicious array of tempting foods. A tiny elevator takes guests to the upper floors where the bedrooms are located. The least expensive rooms are decorated in "Rustikana" style using attractive, pastel-colored fabrics and modern furniture. Costing just a little bit more are the guest rooms displaying the "Alba-Rose" theme. These are ever-so-prettily decorated and have an English-country look. In the "Alba-Rose" rooms there are accents of antiques (such as desks or tables), pretty wall papers, and Laura-Ashley-like fabrics. All the rooms have modern bathrooms, good lighting, comfortable mattresses and down pillows. The Acanthus is not a luxury hotel, but for an especially friendly, well-located place to stay with charm, it can't be beat.

ACANTHUS HOTEL
Owners: Carola & Jörg Günther
Manager: Carola Günther
Blumenstrasse 40
80331 Munich, Germany
tel: (089) 23.18.80, fax: (089) 26.07.364
36 rooms, Double: 190-350 DM
Open all year
Credit cards: all major
No restaurant-breakfast only
Heart of Munich, just off Sendlinger-Tor Platz

If money is no object and you are looking for an intimate, small, deluxe hotel in the heart of historic old Munich, the Hotel Rafael makes a superb choice. Tucked away on a quiet side street, catty-corner from a tiny park where children play, the hotel offers every luxury—definitely designed with the discriminating traveler in mind. One enters into a two-story lobby. The registration desk is of cherry wood with inlaid ebony. From the reception area a sweeping staircase of pewter-toned marble imported from France leads up to the mezzanine to "Mark's," the hotel's gourmet restaurant. Throughout the hotel there are authentic antiques plus a treasured art collection of original prints and etchings that even includes some by Raphael. The ambiance throughout is one of subdued elegance. This refined mood extends to the guest rooms that are decorated in tones of parchment and blue. Over half of the rooms are either junior or executive suites. To complement the luxury, every extra has been provided: each room has four telephones, a fax/computer outlet, color television with VCR, mini bar, and electronic safe. In summer, guests enjoy a swimming pool tucked on the roof terrace. Although definitely a posh, deluxe establishment, the Rafael prides itself on a warm, home-like atmosphere.

HOTEL RAFAEL
Manager: Karl-Heinz Zimmermann
Neuturmstrasse 1
80331 Munich, Germany
tel: (089) 29.09.80, fax: (089) 22.25.39
74 rooms, Double: 520-750 DM
20 suites 750-2,000 DM
Open all year
Credit cards: all major
Restaurant-open daily, pool
Located in the heart of Munich
USA Rep: LHW 800-223-6800

Frau Furholzner solicitously takes guests under her wing at the Pension Schubert, and she spoils them with generous breakfasts and comfortable, spotless rooms. Located on a quiet side street, the atmosphere at the Pension Schubert is not at all hotel-like. There is no lobby or public area to speak of, but if you are looking for homey comfort and a place to rest your head at night, this is a reasonably priced alternative. The pension is found on the second floor of a former villa, thus the rooms are all high-ceilinged and vary in size. Furnishings are a mixture of antiques and contemporary pieces, complemented by pretty drapes and Oriental rugs. Only three of the six rooms have private bath. The foyer displays many family knickknacks and mementos and creates a cheerful, informal atmosphere. The tiny breakfast room has lace covered tables and antique furnishings and is an agreeable place to meet other guests and plan sightseeing excursions for the day. The Pension Schubert is a good choice for travelers who prefer to spend their time and money outside of their hotel, appreciate a home-like ambiance, and do not require all the services offered in a hotel. However, Frau Fürholzner seems to be constantly booked, so early reservations are advised.

PENSION SCHUBERT
Owner: Frau Fürholzner
1 Schubertstrasse
80336 Munich, Germany
tel: (089) 53.50.87
6 rooms, Double: 95 DM
Open all year
Credit cards: none accepted
No restaurant-breakfast only
About 5 blocks S of the main train station

A somewhat sterile city facade hides this traditional and cozy hotel. With the river just to its left and the Marienplatz a few blocks to its rear, the Splendid is an ideally located treasure. The entrance and downstairs salon are inviting, giving only a glimpse of the mood of furnishings to be found in the individualized bedrooms. Oriental carpets enhance hardwood floors, lovely antiques grace the walls and clusters of tables and chairs upholstered in tones of pink make the salon an inviting place to rest after the inevitable city wandering. An outside terrace is a treat on warm days and an ideal spot for tea or an afternoon refreshment. The Splendid does not have a restaurant though a buffet breakfast is offered. This is a small hotel with only 40 bedrooms and one suite, but each a jewel with beautifully painted armoires, traditional to the region of Bavaria, lovely wooden beds, and sitting areas. Everything is spotless, and bathrooms have modern facilities. This hotel is an extremely convenient and comfortable place to reside in Munich and very pleasing to the eye as well. Traditional decor permeates every room—a surprise and unexpected discovery in a large city. A delight.

SPLENDID HOTELL
Owner: Klaus Lieboldt
Maximilianstrasse 54
80538 Munich, Germany
tel: (089) 29.66.06, fax: (089) 29.13.176
40 rooms, 1 suite
Double with bath: 335 DM
Double without bath: 230 DM
Open all year
Credit cards: all major
No restaurant-breakfast only
10-minute walk to city center

For years our friend Judi has been extolling the merits of her favorite hotel in Munich, the Torbräu, where she has returned again and again. Now that we have finally had the opportunity to inspect it, we agree. The Torbräu (whose history dates back to 1490) has much to offer. For location, it can't be surpassed. The attractive five-story, ocher-colored building with red tiled roof sits on sits on a corner in the heart of Munich at the historic Isator (originally one of Munich's main tower gates) and just two blocks from the colorful Marienplatz. The lobby has a tiled floor, Oriental scatter rugs, mirrored panels on the walls, recessed lighting, and formal groupings of fancy French-style chairs in light wood. From first impression, one might think this is a staid, rather impersonal hotel. But in fact, the opposite is true. One of the nicest aspects of the Hotel Torbräu is the warmth and friendliness of its staff. The guest rooms vary from a somewhat dated ambiance with built in beds and old-fashioned wall paper to rooms with a more modern, traditional hotel look. No matter what the decor, all the rooms have modern bathrooms. Breakfast is served each morning in an especially attractive dining room that has a balcony over-looking the street. At 11am (when breakfast is over) this room converts to a tea room where a stunning selection of scrumptious pastries (fresh from the hotel's own bakery) are served. There is also an outstanding Italian restaurant located below the hotel.

HOTEL TORBRÄU
Owner: Family Kirchlechner
Tal 41
80331 Munich, Germany
tel: (089) 22.50.16, fax: (089) 22.50.19
100 rooms, Double: 220-300 DM
Open all year
Credit cards: all major
Restaurant-open daily
In heart of Munich, 2 blocks to the Marienplatz
USA Rep: Euro-Connection 800-645-3876

The Hotel Schloss Wilkinghege is located just 6 kilometers from Münster (with regular bus service available to the city). Although considered a castle, the handsome red brick building with red tile roof is really more reminiscent of a country estate. A pretty moat and lots of trees and gardens surround the castle, and an 18 hole golf course is situated behind the hotel. The castle has changed hands many times and undergone several architectural alterations in the years since built in 1719. Lubert Winneken bought the property in 1955 and turned it into a hotel and restaurant, preserving the style and feeling of this romantic home's former grandeur. The restaurant at Schloss Wilkinghege is well-known for the quality of its nouvelle cuisine. Reservations are needed to dine in the atmospheric restaurant that has been completely renovated, reflecting the authentic mood of the late renaissance period. There are some guest rooms in the main house with lofty ceilings and fancy decor. Especially dramatic is one new suite, resembling the style of 1759 with original furniture of the epoch of the commander General d'Armentier. In addition to the main house, there are some modernly-furnished apartments in the annex. Note: the Hotel Schloss Wilkinghege is not located in the heart of town, but just on the outskirts, signposted off road 54.

HOTEL SCHLOSS WILKINGHEGE
Owner: Lubert Winneken
Steinfurter Strasse 374
48159 Münster, Germany
tel: (0251) 21.30.45, fax: (0251) 21.28.98
33 rooms, suites, Double: 290-320 DM
Open all year
Credit cards: all major
Restaurant-open daily, golf
70 km N of Dortmund, 164 km N of Cologne
Relais & Chateaux

The Hof Zur Linde is as lovely inside and out as the brochure depicts. It is a complex of old farm buildings connected by courtyards and surrounded by grassy lawns and woodlands leading down to a river. At dinnertime you can choose from a selection of dining rooms. These are all actually adjacent, but each has been done in a totally different style so that you move from a light pine-paneled room with gay red gingham curtains where you dine in cozy booths to one with stucco walls and beams, a huge walk-in fireplace, flagstone floors and hams hung from the ceiling. The main dining room is more formal with its tapestry-covered chairs and starched white linens. The menu is extensive, the food delicious, and the service friendly and efficient. Bedrooms are upstairs in the main building or in a lovely old farmhouse just a few steps away. You may find yourself sleeping in a bed that was made for British royalty or in a rustic pine bed beneath a curtained canopy. Summer mornings find Herr Löfken, the hotel owner, busy adjusting bicycles and providing maps for guests setting off to explore the area.

ROMANTIK HOTEL HOF ZUR LINDE
Owner: Otto Löfken
Handorfer Werseufer 1
48157 Münster-Handorf, Germany
tel: (0251) 32.750, fax: (0251) 32.82.09
30 rooms, 14 suites; Double: 190-320 DM
Closed Christmas
Credit cards: all major
Restaurant-open daily, bikes
164 km NE of Cologne, 70 km N of Dortmund
7 km NE of Münster in the hamlet of Handorf
USA Rep: Euro-Connection 800-645-3876

From the moment you step through the front door of the Spielweg Romantik Hotel you are surrounded by the warmth of a wonderful old farmhouse, lovingly converted into a small luxury hotel. To the left of the reception is a comfortable sitting area with chairs set about small tables for afternoon tea. An added bonus is an open fire place to add warmth on a chilly day. To the right of the lobby are a series of dining rooms, each a masterpiece of country-cozy with antique paneling covering the walls and low ceilings, ceramic plates and pictures, hunting trophies, tile stove, pretty hanging lamps. All the dining rooms look like settings for *Gourmet Magazine*. As the hotel has grown, the bedrooms have expanded from the original home to two additional wings. The rooms in the older part are smaller and more old fashioned in decor, but very good value for the money. The rooms in the newer wings are larger and have more modern furnishings, but are more costly. None of the bedrooms have the same antique country ambiance of the public rooms. If you are traveling with children, there is an enormous playroom for your little ones with all kinds of toys to keep them happy on a rainy day. Connected to the hotel by an underground passage is an indoor swimming pool, and just beyond in the garden, is an outdoor pool.

SPIELWEG ROMANTIK HOTEL
Owner: Hansjörg Fuchs
Spielweg 61
79244 Münstertal, Germany
tel: (07636) 70.90, fax: (07636) 70.966
76 rooms, Double: 190-380 DM
Suites to 540 DM
Open all year
Credit cards: all major
Restaurant-open daily, indoor & outdoor pools
Located 65 km N of Basel, 27 km S of Freiburg
USA Rep: Euro-Connection 800-645-3876

Most of the hotels in Oberammergau are irresistible outside with intricately painted facades and window boxes overflowing with brightly colored geraniums, but unfortunately, once inside most of the cozy ambiance usually evaporates. An exception to this saga is the Hotel Turmwirt where from the moment you enter, a rustic mood is established by the use of rustic pine paneling, antique trunks, oriental carpets, colorful draperies and carefully selected fabrics on comfortable chairs. There are two dining rooms, both very attractive. Especially cozy is one with 200-year-old paneled ceiling and walls. The Glas family has owned and operated the Hotel Turmwirt for over 60 years. Georg Glas now manages the hotel, but his mother continues to do the baking—when you see the mouth-watering display of cakes and marvelous pastries that she prepares each morning, you are certain to be most impressed. Some of the guest rooms are located in the original house, others in a newer wing. The bedroom decor is hotel-like with built-in beds and modern, Danish-style chairs. All have every amenity: mini-bar, television, telephone, and radio. The rooms with the best views are those in the new wing, with balconies that look out to the mountains. I think though, that perhaps my favorite is number 11, a front facing room that instead of a modern decor, has lovely hand-painted Bavarian-style furniture that dates back to the turn of the Century.

HOTEL TURMWIRT
Owner: Georg Glas
Ettaler Strasse 2
82483 Oberammergau, Germany
tel:(08822) 30.91, fax: (08822) 14.37
22 rooms, Double: 140-180 DM
Closed in November
Credit cards: all major
Restaurant-open daily
92 km SW of Munich, 19 km N of Garmisch

A hallway full of family antiques leads to a reception desk brightened by a bouquet of fresh flowers at the charming Gasthof Zur Rose, well located on a quiet street one block from the central square. The friendly, exceptionally gracious Stückl family warmly welcome guests to their small hotel. All the family members are experts on local sights and history (their talented son, Christian, is currently the youngest-ever director of the famous Passion Play that takes place every 10th year in Oberammergau). Artistic touches are found throughout the Zur Rose, from colorful dried flower arrangements and strategically placed paintings, to pleasing combinations of fabrics. Formerly a farmer's stable, the gasthof is almost 200 years old, and has been in the Stückl's family for many years. The two dining rooms are bright and cheerful, filled with pretty fabrics, rustic furniture, and green plants. The kitchen is much appreciated by guests as it offers many Bavarian specialties. Roswitha loves collecting and some of the simple guest rooms have antique accent pieces that she has found. My favorite room, number 3, has an antique bed and chairs and more of an old world ambiance than some of the others. For longer rentals, the Stückl family owns three Bavarian houses, with apartments for up to six persons. For warmth of reception and super-caring hosts, the Gasthof Rose is a real winner.

Gasthof zur Rose
Owner: Roswitha & Peter Stückl
Dedlerstrasse 9
82487 Oberammergau, Germany
tel: (08822) 47.06, fax: (08822) 67.53
25 rooms, Double: 96-110 DM
Closed month of November
Credit cards: all major
Restaurant-closed Mondays
92 km SW of Munch
19 km N of Garmisch-Partenkirchen

If you enjoy visiting cathedrals, you must not miss the sensational one in Ulm. And, if you enjoy staying in small castles, you will love the Schlosshotel Oberstotzingen located an easy 20-minute drive northeast of Ulm. Surrounded by a grassy moat and entered through an arched gateway, this friendly and inviting hotel is a white, three-story castle with a mansard roof and dormer windows. The guest rooms are reached by a dramatic, wooden-banistered staircase and are somewhat ship-like, with built in beds and dressing tables. The compact rooms have color coordinated draperies, bed-skirts, and chairs, and are comfortably furnished with fine linens, luxurious down pillows and comforters, good reading lights, television, and mini-bar. The marble bathrooms are spotlessly clean and have excellent showers. Request one of the rooms in the back overlooking the park. In addition to the standard bedrooms, there are two very luxurious suites located in the gate houses. For dining, there is a gourmet restaurant, offering fine cuisine in the main castle and a cozy, less formal restaurant just a few steps from the main building where regional specialties are featured.

SCHLOSSHOTEL OBERSTOTZINGEN
Manager: Klaus Kranz
89168 Oberstotzingen-Niederstotzingen
Germany
tel: (07325) 10.30, fax: (07325) 10.370
14 rooms, 3 suites; Double: 250-390 DM
Closed in January
Credit cards: all major
Restaurant-open daily, sauna, tennis
117 km SE of Stuttgart,
38 km NE of Ulm, near Niederstotzingen
Gast im Schloss

The Auf Schönburg is the perfect castle hotel. High atop a rocky bluff, the facade is a fairytale picture of towers and battlements reached by crossing a narrow wooden bridge. Cobbles worn smooth by feet through the ages wind through the castle to the hotel at the summit. The terrace view is superb, dropping steeply to the Rhine below. The bedrooms are shaped by the unusual castle buildings—tower rooms sit atop steep winding staircases while other rooms are tucked neatly into a darling little black and white cottage leaning against the castle wall. Each bedroom is delightful in its own way: four have romantic four-poster beds, all are furnished with antiques. Through the tiny lead-paned windows you may be able to catch a glimpse of the River Rhine far below. However, some of the castle's most beautiful accommodations do not have river views. The romance extends to the intimate dining rooms where you dine by candlelight. The terrace restaurant has lovely views to the vineyards while the tower dining room with its displays of pewter and weapons has medieval charm. Come spin yourself a dream or two in this fairytale castle above the Rhine.

AUF SCHÖNBURG
Owner: Family Hüttl
55430 Oberwesel, Germany
tel: (06744) 70.27, fax: (06744) 16.13
20 rooms, 2 suites; Double: 205-320 DM
Closed January, February & March
Credit cards: all major
Restaurant-closed Mondays
95 km W of Frankfurt
Between Mainz & Koblenz
On the Rhine, 21 km NW of Bingen

The Hotel Schwan, with its gray tile roof and timbered facade, has been around since 1628 when it was a travelers' inn along the River Rhine. Today both the road and the river in front of the hotel are a lot busier than in the days of carriages and river barges. Fortunately the hotel is saved from being overwhelmed by the busy Rhineside road by a broad band of garden that separates it from the highway. The Wenckstern family has owned and managed the inn for many generations. They produce their own wine which you can sample with dinner in the dignified dining room or sip on the outdoor terrace while watching the river. From a small hostelry, the Schwan has grown to a substantial hotel, and the joy of staying here is that you can obtain a Rhine-facing room. The nicest bedroom is the tower room. Decked out in floral fabric, this circular room commands lovely river views from its seven windows. Incidentally, the Hotel Schwan is only about an hour's drive from the Frankfurt airport, a convenient distance after a tiring transatlantic flight. Its location on the Rheingau Reisling Road makes it especially appealing.

HOTEL SCHWAN
Owner: Family Wenckstern
Rheinallee 5-7
65375 Oestrich-Winkel, Germany
tel: (06723) 80.90, fax: (06723) 78.20
60 rooms, 3 suites; Double: 187-310 DM
Open all year
Credit cards: all major
Restaurant-open daily
55 km W of Frankfurt
21 km W of Wiesbaden
USA Rep: Euro-Connection 800-645-3876

The town of Passau has a dramatic position at the intersection of three rivers: the Inn, the Ilz and the Danube. The town is built on a rocky peninsula where the swirling waters merge. Small twisting streets weave from the water's edge into a maze of ancient buildings, frequently joined to each other by stone arches. Passau has a strategic position both because of its river traffic and because it is right on the Austrian border. Should you be driving from Austria, or taking the Danube steamer to Vienna, you might be looking for a place to stay. There are no deluxe hotels in Passau, but the Schloss Ort is splendidly located. Although the decor has no old world charm (plastics and modern furniture prevail), the building itself is very old and quite attractive. The Danube, Inn and Ilz rivers all meet and flow below a number of the bedroom windows and the terrace and indoor restaurants enjoy views of passing boat traffic. Tucked on a small side street, amid the stone walls of the original castle, the 30 bedrooms of the Schloss Ort are quiet and comfortable, although, like the public rooms, quite plain in their decor and furnishings. The management and service are efficient if not overly personal.

SCHLOSS ORT
Owner: Christian Detzer
Im Ort 11, am Dreiflusseck
94032 Passau, Germany
tel: (0851) 34.072, fax: (0851) 31.817
30 rooms, Double: 85-170 DM
Open all year
Credit cards: all major
Restaurant
118 km SE of Regensburg
192 km NE of Munich, on the Austrian border

A local woman directed me to the Bavaria Hotel by pointing across to a dominating mountain and stating that at its base I would find the Bavaria. She spoke with a heavy German accent and referred to the hotel as if it were a local tradition. I was therefore surprised to find a very modern facade and then glad to discover a traditional and warm interior. If you are lucky, Herr Haff might even be at the front desk, dressed in lederhosen, to greet you personally. The lobby is lovely with plants, beams and a big open fireplace. There is a small attractive restaurant for a la carte dining and a bar off the main lobby. An exceptionally lovely room, paneled in light wood, furnished with heart-carved wooden chairs and country prints, is reserved for pension guests. Located in a sport and health region, the hotel has both an outdoor and indoor pool, sauna, and a lounge area shaded by white umbrellas and greenery. The bedrooms are very handsome in furnishings and very modern in comfort. You have the choice of a bedroom with loft, a "galeria studio"—a room with sitting area, an apartment that has a separate living room and studio, or a basic double bedded room. Many of the rooms have cozy fireplaces, all have private bathrooms and most have their own balcony or terrace.

BAVARIA HOTEL
Owner: Georg Haff
Kienbergstrasse 62
87459 Pfronten-Dorf, Germany
tel: (08363) 50.04, fax: (08363) 68.15
50 Rooms, Double: 260-340 DM
Closed November to mid-December
Credit cards: AX
Restaurant-open daily except Nov, pool, sauna
131 km SW of Munich
30 km W of Garmisch-Partenkirchen

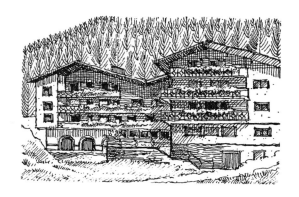

If you are arriving at or departing from Hamburg airport and have a car, the Jagdhaus Waldfrieden makes a splendid overnight for your first or last night in Germany. Although the hotel is peacefully set in a lovely, wooded park, the highway is conveniently close. During his career as the manager of large hotels, Siegmund Baierle formulated his plans for a small hotel with a first-rate restaurant—the result is the delightful Jagdhaus Waldfrieden. The latest renovation has added a glass enclosed, greenhouse-style restaurant where you dine elegantly, yet feel as if you are in the garden. Just beyond the intimate bar, there is a second high-ceilinged dining room with gleaming polished wood, Oriental carpets and groupings of tables laid with crisp white linen before a roaring log fire. Dinner is an event where guests linger at their tables after a splendid meal before retiring for a contented night's sleep. A few bedrooms are found in the main building. The remainder are across the courtyard in what were once the stables. All the rooms have been lovingly decorated with a traditional look of comfortable sophistication achieved through the use of beautiful, color-coordinated fabrics and fine furniture. My favorite, room 45, is especially fantastic—a corner room on the ground floor of the "stables" with French doors leading out to the garden, and just beyond to the forest.

ROMANTIK HOTEL JAGDHAUS WALDFRIEDEN
Owner: Siegmund Baierle
Kieler Strasse B4
25451 Quickborn, Germany
tel: (04106) 3771, fax: (04106) 69.196
25 rooms, Double: from 235 DM
Open all year
Credit cards: all major
Restaurant-closed for lunch on Mondays
23 km N of Hamburg
USA Rep: Euro-Connection 800-645-3876

From the moment you step from the cobbled streets of Rothenburg through the arched portal of the Hotel Bären, a romantic ambiance is created. Care has been taken to preserve the old world character of this inn that dates back to 1577. The attractive spacious lobby has paneled walls, beamed ceiling, two large crystal chandeliers, oriental carpets and lovely bouquets of fresh flowers. To the left of the reception there is a cozy paneled bar and breakfast room for the guests. Beyond, is the formal dining room where the mood changes from antique to trendy modern with metal and leather chairs setting the theme for a sleek sophisticated look. The hotel is well-known for its kitchen and the owner, Fritz Müller, is also the master chef. In addition to the regular menu, he prepares a special "Gourmet Menu of the Month" that is always accompanied by fine wines. From the reception area, a handsome wooden staircase leads up to the individually decorated guest rooms. Although the furnishings are unique in each, the rooms are consistently appealing and have a most attractive traditional look. All of the bedrooms have modern bathrooms. I particularly liked room 28 that looks out over a jumble of the ancient roof tops of Rothenburg. For guests who want to have a little exercise, there is an indoor swimming pool and sauna.

HOTEL BÄREN
Owners: Elisabeth & Fritz Müller
Hofbronnengasse 4-9
91541 Rothenburg ob der Tauber, Germany
tel: (09861) 60.31, fax: (09861) 48.75
32 rooms, Double: 280-350 DM
Open all year
Credit cards: MC, VS
Restaurant-closed Mondays and Tuesdays
62 km SE of Würzburg, 134 km NE of Stuttgart

The Hotel Eisenhut, Rothenburg's choice for a deluxe place to stay, is ideally set in the heart of Germany's most romantic town. The promise of a special experience is created as you walk into the spacious reception hall that has a hearty, hunting lodge look with beamed ceiling, oriental carpets, massive wrought iron chandeliers, and a sweeping wooden staircase. Beyond the stately entrance there are comfortable lounges and several dining rooms that open onto a garden terrace where delicious meals are served outside when the days are warm. Throughout the hotel there is a fascinating collection of large, mural-like oil paintings depicting scenes of the Thirty-Years-War. Because the Eisenhut was created out of four 15th to 16th-century patrician mansions, the guest rooms are intriguingly tucked along a maze of corridors. Each room has its own personality and is individual in decor. Most have homey touches that were chosen by the present owner's mother, Frau Pirner. The hotel has not changed hands since established four generations ago by the Eisenhut family. Throughout the years their tradition of hospitality has made the Eisenhut the choice of the rich and famous from around the world.

HOTEL EISENHUT
Owner: Dr Hans Pirner
Manager: Karl L. Prüsse
Herrngasse 3-7
91541 Rothenburg ob der Tauber, Germany
tel: (09861) 70.50, fax: (09861) 70.545
79 rooms, Double: 285-380 DM
Suites to 640 DM
Open Feb through Dec
Credit cards: all major
Restaurant-open daily
62 km SE of Würzburg, 134 km NE of Stuttgart
USA Rep: SRS 800-223-5652, Gast im Schloss

The Gasthof Hotel Kloster-Stüble is a perfect little inn, combining reasonable prices with history, charm, and a good location. Just two blocks from the central market square of Rothenburg ob der Tauber, the Kloster-Stuble is tucked away on a side street behind an old church. This tranquil location affords a restful night's sleep and pretty views of the surrounding countryside from most bedroom windows. Thirteen comfortable bedrooms are offered here, all with private shower and w.c. and furnished in beautiful country pine reproductions. Downstairs, the dining room and "stube" are cozily rustic. Murals depicting life in days gone by decorate the stube walls, while in the adjoining dining room pretty rose colored walls and tablecloths set a romantic tone. Tables are dressed with gleaming silver, china and glassware, topped off with pink candles and fresh flowers. French doors lead out onto two lovely terraces which enjoy a scenic view of church spires and distant hills. A sense of history prevails in this inn dating from 1300. Antique touches such as old duck decoys in a pretty pine hutch add a country ambiance throughout. Rudolf Hammel is the energetic host at the Kloster-Stuble who does an admirable job attending to guests' needs as well as chef's duties.

GASTHOF HOTEL KLOSTER-STÜBLE
Owners: Gutta & Rudolf Hammel
Heringsbronnengassechen 5
91541 Rothenburg ob der Tauber, Germany
tel: (09861) 67.74, fax: (09861) 64.74
13 rooms, 1 suite, Double: 126-156 DM
Open all year
Credit cards: visa
Restaurant-closed Tuesdays
62 km SE of Würzburg, 134 km NE of Stuttgart

Rothenburg is a fairytale town whose atmosphere is that of the Middle Ages. Completely enclosed by ramparts, walls and turrets, it is a popular destination of many and therefore, regardless of the season, it is often difficult to secure reservations. To overnight in the city, however, is to experience the best of its charm, as the early morning and evening light and quiet are gentle on the town's cobblestoned streets and timbered facades. The Markusturm reserves one of the town's best locations, on a main street, just a block or two from the main square and famous clock. Managed by the Berger family, the hotel was built in 1264 as a tollhouse, converted in 1488 to a brewery, and has been a hotel since 1902. The entry and restaurant are charmingly decorated with antiques. The decor in the hallways and public rooms is traditional but the rooms range from very modern to the favorite four-poster room. I was able to see only a few of the bedrooms as the hotel was fully occupied, but having acquainted myself with the Berger hospitality and the old world ambiance of the public rooms, I will recommend this hotel.

ROMANTIK HOTEL MARKUSTURM
Owners: Marianne & Stephan Berger
Rodergasse 1
91541 Rothenburg ob der Tauber, Germany
tel: (09861) 20.98, fax: (09861) 26.92
26 rooms, 2 suites; Double: 270-350 DM
Open all year
Credit cards: all major
140 km SE of Frankfurt,
Restaurant closed Jan to mid-Feb
62 km SE of Würzburg, 134 km NE of Stuttgart
USA Rep: Euro-Connection 800-645-3876

Rottweil, an attractive town perched on a plateau that is looped by the Neckar River, reflects its medieval past by streets lined with colorfully painted buildings, many with ornate oriel windows. One of the oldest of these buildings is a patrician house, "Zum Sternen," dating back to 1278. Rottweil has not been discovered by tourists and so there are no fancy boutiques or quaint pedestrian streets. Therefore it is a marvelous surprise to discover here such an outstanding small inn as the "Zum Sternen," which not only is an excellent place to stay, but also features an intimate gourmet restaurant on the ground level. Steps from the foyer lead up to the reception and another stunningly decorated dining room where breakfast is served each morning. More steps lead to the beautifully furnished guest rooms. My favorite rooms were 35, a bright and cheerful corner room with a handsome painted canopy bed, and room 37, a spacious room with antique brass bed, rich matching fabrics for the dust ruffle and draperies, and a small balcony. The view from the balcony is not perfect due to railroad tracks and some commercial buildings, but even so, the outlook over the river to the rolling green hills is very pretty. All the rooms are exceptionally well-decorated and antique furniture is used throughout.

ROMANTIK HOTEL "HAUS ZUM STERNEN"
Owner: Dorothee Ehrenberger
Manager: Manfred Lang
Hauptstrasse 60
78628 Rottweil, Germany
tel: (0741) 70.06, fax: (0741) 70.08
12 rooms, Double: 185-290 DM
Open all year
Credit cards: all major
Restaurant-open daily
98 km SW of Stuttgart
USA Rep: Euro-Connection 800-645-3876

This is it—Sleeping Beauty's Castle. Here, deep within the "enchanted" Reinhard forest, Jacob and Wilhelm Grimm set their famous fairytale. What was once a proud fortress is now largely a romantic ruin—a shell of towers and walls. Fortunately one wing has been restored as a hotel. The romance of staying in Sleeping Beauty's Castle cannot be denied, but be aware that the isolated location does not invite a long stay. There is no lounge or bar to gather in before or after dinner, so splurge and request a larger room. Tables in the dining room are assigned by management: the only way to ensure a lovely countryside view is to request a window table as you check in. The house specialty is mouthwatering venison. If you are familiar with Walt Disney's Sleeping Beauty Castle, be prepared for a disappointment, for this is not it. He chose the ethereal towers and turrets of Neuschwanstein Castle in Bavaria as his model. In honor of the Brothers Grimm and their world-famous tales, the German Tourist Office has outlined a fairytale route, the "Deutsche Marchen Strasse," signposted by a smiling good fairy and accompanied by a colorful picture map. The Burghotel Sababurg is included on this routing and as a consequence is a popular tourist attraction. Plan on arriving quite late in the afternoon after the coach loads of daytime visitors have left.

DORNRÖSCHENSCHLOSS SABABURG
Owner: Family Koseck
34369 Hofgeismar-Sababurg, Germany
tel: (05671) 80.80, fax: (05671) 80.82.00
19 rooms, Double: 185-310 DM
Closed mid-January to mid-February
Credit cards: all major
Restaurant-open daily, museum, garden
300 km S of Hamburg, 23 km N of Kassel
14 km NE of Hofgeismar
Gast im Schloss

The Romantik Hotel Josthof is located less than an hour's drive south of Hamburg in a lovely, peaceful region where spacious fields are dotted with handsome old thatched roof farmhouses. These large buildings are often constructed using exposed red brick between the wooden framework instead of the more commonplace stucco and half-timber combination. This unusual, and very attractive, architectural style is typified by the Romantik Hotel Josthof. Happily, the interior is as charming as the exterior. The first floor houses a gourmet restaurant which is well-known and frequented by diners from far and wide. Decorated in typical German country style, the several dining rooms of the restaurant are all very cozy; each with its own personality. Ceilings are laced with massive beams, candlelight reflects off mellow paneled walls, and beautiful tiled ceramic ovens and cheerful fireplaces warm the rooms on cold evenings. Antique galore —grandfather clocks, cradles, pewter plates, copper pans—enhance the old-fashioned ambiance. Upstairs and in an adjacent building, reflecting the same style of architecture, there are 16 rooms available for overnight guests. These bedrooms, although not decorated with antiques, are modern and pretty and each has a private bathroom.

ROMANTIK HOTEL JOSTHOF
Owners: Martina & Jörg Hansen
Am Lindenberg 1
21376 Salzhausen, Germany
tel: (04172) 90.980, fax: (04172) 62.25
16 rooms, Double: 145-227 DM
Open all year
Credit cards: all major
Restaurant-open daily in summer
45 km SE of Hamburg, 18 k SW of Lüneburg
USA Rep: Euro-Connection 800-645-3876

In the Black Forest, on a hillside in the town of Schluchsee, is a delightful, modern hotel. Constructed in 1969 with a new wing added in 1984, Heger's Parkhotel Flora is beautiful in its decor and in the views that it affords down to the Schluchsee. Each room is pleasant in decor with modern furniture, built-in headboards, and good lights for reading. Each also has a modern tiled bathroom. All the bedrooms overlook the lake: views can be enjoyed from either a private balcony or terrace. The hallways are beamed, spacious and airy, with floor to ceiling windows. The public rooms are attractive with colorful prints on the walls, wrought iron fixtures, plants, and pink and green fabrics. Herr Heger, dressed impeccably in chef's attire, is frequently found in the lobby to greet guests, and is as eager to make you comfortable as he is to please and tempt your palate. The "St Georgstube" and the cafe-terrace restaurant are delightful. It is especially romantic to eat outside when the weather permits. The entry hall with its open fireplace is a cozy place to settle in inclement weather. In warm summer weather the Schluchsee comes alive with the sails of gay colored sailing boats and wind surfers.

HEGER'S PARKHOTEL FLORA
Owner: Hugo Heger
Sonnhalde 22
79857 Schluchsee, Germany
tel: (07656) 452 or 521, fax: (07656) 14.33
34 rooms, Double: 148-195 DM
Closed November to Christmas
Credit cards: AX, DC
Restaurant-for guests only
172 km SW of Stuttgart
47 km SE of Freiberg

The Hotel Goldener Adler, an exceptionally attractive building facing the Markplatz in Schwäbisch Hall, was built in 1500 as the manor house of the Lords of Mückheim. Today the colorful timbered Goldener Adler is owned by the gracious Rapp family (Peter Rapp is the chef and his wife, Marion, is in charge of the day-to-day operation of the hotel). The entrance is through a gigantic archway, a reminder of the colorful past when horse-drawn coaches would come clomping through the portals. Inside, the hotel has been recently redone and the decor, which was quite dated, is improved. Schwäbisch Hall is special—a well-preserved, medieval town built on a steep hillside that slopes down to the Kocher River. The Markplatz is one of the prettiest in Germany, and always teeming with activity—a "real town" with women carefully selecting their produce for the evening meal from small stalls in the square and children neatly dressed in uniforms gaily chatting on their way to school. Dominating the square (impressively set at the top of a wide flight of 53 steps) is St Michael's Church. The prime objective in coming to Schwäbisch Hall should be to soak in the wonderful ambiance of this lovely old city—and for this, the Hotel Goldener Adler could not be more ideally located.

ROMANTIK HOTEL GOLDENER ADLER
Owners: Marion & Peter Rapp
Am Marktplatz 11
74523 Schwäbisch Hall, Germany
tel: (0791) 61.68, (0791) 73.15
21 rooms, Double: 140-200 DM
Open all year
Credit cards: all major
Restaurant-closed Wednesdays
68 km NE of Stuttgart
USA Rep: Euro-Connection 800-645-3876

The friendly Heim family has been welcoming guests into their home since 1959 and Herr Heim keeps all his old guest books filled with entries and artwork by former guests. Some of the original guests still visit the Pension Heim, but now they are accompanied by children and even grandchildren. It is easy to see why the Pension Heim is such a success: the entire family is warm and genuine and the house spotless and homey. Cheerful house plants brighten all the rooms and hallways and a rustic feeling pervades the dining rooms and "stube." Home-cooked meals are offered if guests so desire, and the ambiance is very convivial, fostering many new friendships. There are no a la carte dishes: only one meal is offered (hot or cold). Guests need to advise Herr Heim in the morning if they want to dine so that enough food can be purchased. Upstairs, most of the comfortable bedrooms have balconies that overlook spectacularly unspoilt mountain scenery, even offering a glimpse of the famous Zugspitze on a clear day. The rolling hills and pastures of this region make it ideal for relaxed hiking in the summer and cross country skiing in the winter. Pension Heim offers comforts such as private bath or shower in each room, direct dial phones, and even a sauna. Just the right ending to a day of enjoying all the activities that this scenic area has to offer.

PENSION HEIM
Owner: Josef Heim
Aufmberg 8
87637 Seeg/Ostallgau, Germany
tel: (08364) 258
16 rooms, Double: 108-120 DM
Closed November to December 20
Credit cards: none accepted
Restaurant-open daily, sauna, ping-pong
120 km SW of Munich,
10 km N of Füssen

The Schloss Sommersdorf, conveniently located near the "Romantic Road," is a sensational small castle, with all the ingredients of a proper fairytale keep: turrets, tall towers, spiral staircases, stone bridges, ramparts and even a moat. This is a special place, not a standard hotel at all, but rather the elegant and historical home of Dr Manfred von Crailsheim, who welcomes guests on a "Bed & Breakfast" basis. Guests enter the castle through an outer gate (a pink house topped by a whimsical clock), over the moat, into the rose-filled courtyard, through a massive door and up a spiral staircase. Each of the guest rooms and apartments varies in decor and size, but all have an "old world" feel. Especially dramatic is the Gothic Room; an enormous corner bedroom with a canopied bed, oriental carpets, an antique armoire and an incredible carved wooden column in the center of the room that supports massive ceiling beams. The Schloss Sommersdorf is an ideal base for exploring the Romantic road and the surrounding region, and would thus be a marvelous find simply on the merit of its location and accommodations, but the presence of host Manfred von Crailsheim makes this a very special place to stay. He lived in the castle as a boy, loves to share his home with guests, is a natural host and an absolute delight. Note: Sommersdorf is not on most maps, ask for directions when making reservations.

SCHLOSS SOMMERSDORF
Owner: Dr Manfred von Crailsheim
91595 Sommersdorf, Germany
tel: (09805) 647
6 rooms, 2 apartments; Double 120-180 DM
one week minimum stay
Open all year
*No restaurant-breakfast only, pool
*dinner can be arranged by special request
50 km SW of Nürnberg, E of Dinkelsbühl

Hotel Descriptions

Come dream a romantic dream or two at one of our favorite castles, the idyllic Schloss Spangenberg. High atop a hill with the town of Spangenberg spread at its feet far below, this once proud fortress is now a gem of a castle hotel. All the romantic castle ingredients are here—a deep grassy moat, a tower keep and thick fortified walls. After surviving a seven-century-history of battles, this fortification was badly damaged by British bombers in the closing days of World War II. The exterior has been painstakingly reconstructed and the interior converted into an inviting hotel. A few steps away, where soldiers once guarded the ramparts, gay tables and chairs now provide a perfect place for afternoon coffee and cake. Gleaming polished floors lead you down the long hallways to extremely attractive, individually furnished guest rooms. Everything is meticulously maintained and the decor throughout is comfortable and welcoming—not in the least stiffly formal or hotel-like. Many of the guest rooms have a fabulous bird's eye view over the dense forest to the charming town of Spangenberg nestled at the foot of the hill. My favorite room (number 16) has a romantic bay window—a perfect niche to sit and dream of knights and their ladies while gazing out over the castle walls. If you are traveling with your family, just at the castle entrance, is a dear little gatekeeper's house comprising a doll-sized living room, sleeping loft, tiny bedroom and two bathrooms.

SCHLOSS SPANGENBERG
Owner: Family Wichmann
34286 Spangenberg, Germany
tel: (05663) 866, fax: (05663) 75.67
24 rooms, 1 suite; Double: 150-280 DM
Closed in January
Credit cards: all major
Restaurant-closed Sunday evenings
210 km S of Hamburg, 36 km SE of Kassel
Gast im Schloss

The Hotel Traube, conveniently located across the expressway from the Stuttgart airport, is a beguiling little inn. Should you be flying into Stuttgart to visit the Mercedes factory and perhaps pick up a car, the Hotel Traube would be an excellent choice for a place to spend the night since the factory is only a short drive from the hotel. The contrast between this small inn and the modern industrial city of Stuttgart, located only about a half hour's drive away, is dramatic. Located on a small cobblestoned square, contained in a cluster of three timbered buildings, the Hotel Traube would stand out as a perfect inn regardless of its location. The most famous feature of the hotel is its restaurant. The food is exceptional and the decor worthy of multiple stars. Tables laid with soft pink cloths, flowers and candles are tucked under beams into cozy corners paneled in rich wood. If you'd prefer less formal dining, consider the neighboring rotisserie, managed by the gracious son and daughter who maintain the same high standards set by their parents. The rotisserie has a welcoming bar and a lighter fare on the menu, letting you select from different cuts of meat grilled on the open barbecue. The guest rooms, located far enough away from the street to be quiet, are most attractive with traditional decor and comfortable beds topped with fluffy down comforters.

HOTEL TRAUBE
Owner: Family Recknagel
Brabandgasse 2
70599 Stuttgart-Plieningen, Germany
tel: (0711) 45.89.20, fax: (0711) 45.89.220
22 rooms, Double: 185-285 DM
Closed Christmas & New Year
Credit cards: EC, MC
Restaurant-closed Saturdays & Sundays
Near the Stuttgart airport

Sylt, a sand-dune island located in the northernmost tip of Germany, is reached by taking the car-train across the narrow causeway linking the island to the mainland—a 45-minute ride. The Benen Diken Hof is one of the island's loveliest hotels. The hotel is several squat Friesian farmhouses joined into a complex by means of glass corridors that appear to bring the outdoors indoors. Decorated throughout in white and cream with accents of pale pink and blue, the hotel is "decorator perfect," warm and welcoming. After a walk along the sand dunes in the bracing sea air, you return to the hotel to pamper yourself with a sauna and a massage or a relaxing swim. The hotel's greatest asset is its owner, Claas Johannsen. In the evening he can be found, surrounded by his collection of old model fire engines, hosting the hotel's cozy bar. His warmth and graciousness transcend the language barrier and make you feel at home. The restaurant serves only breakfast: but do not worry: the small island abounds with restaurants. A particular recommendation goes to the restaurant Landhaus Stricker in the adjacent village of Tinnum, offering elegant gourmet dining in a Friesian farmhouse.

ROMANTIK HOTEL BENEN DIKEN HOF
Owner: Claas Johannsen
Süderstrasse
25985 Keitum-Sylt, Germany
tel: (04651) 31.038, fax: (04651) 35.835
38 rooms, Double: 225-410 DM
Open all year
Credit cards: all major
230 km NW of Hamburg, 70 km
NoRestaurant-open sauna, pool
Island of Sylt, 160 km NW of Hamburg
USA Rep: Euro-Connection 800-645-3876

There are many restaurants on Germany's lovely Isle of Sylt. One of the finest is the Restaurant Jorg-Müller, justifiably well-known for its cuisine that has earned a coveted Michelin star. Luckily for the gourmet traveler, there are also three pretty guest rooms upstairs for overnight guests. The restaurant is situated on one of the main roads into Westerland, the largest town on the magical island of Sylt. In keeping with the fairytale quality of most of the houses on the island, the Restaurant Jörg Müller is brimming with charm. The pretty red brick house with thick thatched roof is given even further romantic appeal by a lacing of climbing roses. A small lawn and garden in front complete the attractive picture. Inside, there is a sitting area for guests waiting for dinner. On the left are two subdued, pastel-colored dining rooms where French cuisine is served. To the right of the reception is, in my opinion, the most enchanting dining room. It is decorated entirely in white, blue, and light-toned woods. The walls are covered in white tiles whose blandness is relieved by interspersing some tiles that have blue designs that seem Dutch in origin. The ceiling is paneled in a light wood, and the chairs and floor are also of light wood. The cushions on the chairs and the draperies repeat the blue accents on the tiles. In this extraordinarily fresh and pretty room, regional specialties are served. Jörg Müller, the owner, is also the chef and dining at his restaurant is a memorable occasion.

RESTAURANT JÖRG MÜLLER
Owner: Jörg Müller
Süderstrasse 8
25980 Westerland-Sylt, Germany
tel: (04651) 27.788, fax: (04651) 20.14.71
3 rooms, Double: 230-280 DM
Restaurant-closed Tuesdays
Closed November 21 to December 25
Credit cards: all major
Island of Sylt, 160 km NW of Hamburg

Sylt, a tiny island in the north of Germany, is connected to the mainland by a narrow thread of land that is only negotiable by train. Although most of the island embraces a tranquil scene of wind swept sand dunes, long stretches of beach and picture-perfect thatched cottages, the principal town of Westerland, with its large hotels, designer boutiques, souvenir shops, ice cream parlors and pizzerias, bustles with activity. In the midst of this touristy town, the Hotel Stadt Hamburg is an absolute oasis of charm and tranquillity. The hotel, in the Hentzchel family for three generations, dates back to 1869 when the only means of transportation to the island was by boat. You will be enchanted by the Stadt Hamburg from the moment you walk into the exquisite lounge where rich-red walls create the perfect background for comfortable sofas and chairs grouped in intimate settings. Fine English antiques abound including many grandfather clocks (twenty throughout the hotel I am told), gorgeous tables, and chests whose woods gleam with the patina of age. The lounge is so home-like, so inviting, that guests must almost welcome dreary weather for an excuse to settle into a cozy corner with a good book. The guest rooms, some located in the original hotel and others in a new wing, are exquisitely furnished and resemble rooms in an English country estate. Although the Stadt Hamburg is an elegant, Relais & Chateaux hotel, it happily maintains the exceptional warmth and sincere hospitality of a small inn.

HOTEL STADT HAMBURG
Owner: Harald Hentzschel
2, Strandstrasse
25980 Westerland-Sylt, Germany
tel: (04651) 85.80, fax: (04651) 85.82.20
72 rooms, Double: 348-450 DM
Open: all year
Credit cards: all major
Restaurant-open daily
Island of Sylt, 160 km NW of Hamburg

Cuckoo clocks and fabulous Black Forest trails are the initial draw to the popular town of Triberg. The Parkhotel Wehrle is the reason for one's return. This appealing, ivy-covered yellow stone inn occupies a prime corner position on the main street of Triberg. From the moment you enter, you will experience the outstanding warmth of welcome that makes this inn so very special. This is one of the friendliest, best-run small hotels in Germany. It has the incredible record of being owned by the same family every since it was built was in 1707. There are several parts to the hotel. The reception counter, beautifully decorated dining rooms, and antique-filled lounges are in the original inn, as are some of the guest rooms. This main house is my first choice of where to stay because the rooms have such a comfortable, homey ambiance and old world charm. One of my favorites (number 3) is a spacious room with fine antique furniture. There is also a romantic little house nestled in the garden, with excellent accommodations. (The least characterful rooms are those located in the modern annex.) The Parkhotel Wehrle, in conjunction with neighboring hotels, has a plan whereby you can walk between hotels. You need only carry your picnic lunch—your luggage is magically transferred to your next destination.

Romantik Hotel Parkhotel Wehrle
Owner: Family Blum-Wehrle
Gartenstrasse 24
78094 Triberg, Germany
tel: (07722) 86.020, fax: (07722) 86.02.90
56 rooms, 2 suites; Double: 186-296 DM
Open all year
Credit cards: all major
Restaurant-open daily, pool, sauna
130 km SW of Stuttgart, 51 km NE of Freiburg
USA Rep: Euro-Connection 800-645-3876

The exterior of the Romantik Hotel Menzhausen is a 16th-century dazzler: its facade half timbered, with painted decorations. Found on the main street of this attractive town, the Hotel Menzhausen has been offering travelers lodging for over 400 years. Like so many tiny town hostelries, the hotel has needed to expand and has done so by adding a modern extension of 20 bedrooms at the rear of the building. Decorated in a modern style, these rooms are rather bland. I was unable to see any of the older rooms as they were all occupied, but Fritz Körber, the owner, assured me that they are decorated in keeping with the historic core of the hotel. Herr Körber's special pride is his wine cellar and he will be happy to show you around. It is great fun to follow him down the low, narrow, dark, brick passage into the cellars lined with neat rows of bottles. The dining room is delightful: roughhewn beams and country charm or polished light pine contrasting with gay red and white checked tablecloths. Uslar features on the "Deutsche Marchen Strasse," or "Fairytale Route," signposted by a smiling fairy inviting you to follow her down the fairytale road.

ROMANTIK HOTEL MENZHAUSEN
Owner: Fritz Körber
Lange Strasse 12
37170 Uslar, Germany
tel: (05571) 20.51, fax: (05571) 58.20
28 rooms, 6 suites, Double: 165-315 DM
Open all year
Credit cards: all major
Restaurant-open daily, pool
133 km S of Hannover
62 km N of Kassel
USA Rep: Euro-Connection 800-645-3876

Schlosshotel Waldeck has a stunning, hilltop location overlooking the Eder-See. If you arrive mid-day, you might be surprised to see so many cars, but most of these belong to the day-tourists who have come to visit the museum located in one wing of the castle. (Be sure to go through the museum—it is well worth a visit, especially the foyer where life-size figures depict what peasant life must have been like 1,000 years ago.) As you enter the hotel, you find a large room with stone walls. The reception counter is to the left and sitting areas are tucked beneath into cozy niches formed by the vaulted ceiling. Look carefully and you will see above the reception desk the chimney for the giant fireplace that warmed the room in days-gone-by. Although the "castle-look" is dominant, the hotel exudes a sleek, sophisticated ambiance and offers all the amenities of a modern day hotel with three dining rooms, various conference rooms, banquet facilities, outdoor terraces for dining and even an indoor swimming pool nestled within stone walls with a skylight overhead. Some of the guest rooms are in the castle, others are in an impressive new wing. The rooms, which have a modern hotel decor, look similar whatever section you are in, but my preference is for staying in the old castle. I especially like number 407, a spacious room with large windows that give you a bird's eye view of the evening sun setting over the lake.

SCHLOSSHOTEL WALDECK
Manager: K.F. Isenberg
34513 Waldeck am Edersee, Germany
tel: (05623) 58.90 , fax: (05623) 58.92.89
41 rooms, Double: 250-350 DM
Closed January
Credit cards: all major
Restaurant-open daily, indoor pool
200 km N of Frankfurt, 57 km SW of Kassel
Gast im Schloss

The main claim to fame of the Hotel Alte Post is its location in the very heart of Wangen, one of Germany's colorful medieval villages. The Alte Post was built in 1409 as a posting station and is now one of the oldest hotels in Germany. In days-gone-by horses were stabled below the existing building and exchanged for the next postal journey. You can easily spot the hotel (a boxy, three story building with small gabled windows peaking out from a steeply pitched gray roof) as it sits in the center of town, opening onto a cobblestoned, pedestrian-only-square. Rooms on the first level are devoted to the restaurants of the hotel. As in many German hotels, the dining rooms have more personality than the guest rooms. As you climb the stairs to the various bedrooms, the carpets appear a bit worn but everything is spotlessly clean, and polished and scrubbed daily. The decor varies from comfortable contemporary to traditional. From the third floor guest rooms (tucked under beamed ceilings) you can hear the peal of the nearby church bells. The Veile family also owns the Romantik Hotel "Postvilla" that is located on the outskirts of Wangen.

ROMANTIK HOTEL "ALTE POST"
Owners: Gisela and Thomas Veile
Postplatz 2
88239 Wangen im Allgau, Germany
tel: (07522) 40.14, fax: (07522) 22.604
19 rooms, Double: 180-280 DM
Open all year
Credit cards: all major
Restaurant-closed on Sundays
194 km S of Stuttgart, 27 km N of Bregenz
23 km SE of Ravensburg
USA Rep: Euro-Connection 800-645-3876

Weimar is a magical city where you can still hear the haunting melodies of Bach and Liszt, who long ago called Weimar home. As renovations continue (following its long slumber under socialist rule), Weimar will undoubtedly evolve as one of Germany's most coveted destinations—and a "must" for lovers of classical music. As for location, the Hotel Elephant wins hands down. The hotel faces a large market square, enclosed by beautifully preserved medieval buildings, including a stunning timbered, 16th-century Rathaus—one of Germany's finest. Although the Hotel Elephant has been reconstructed, its history dates back hundreds of years. The hotel lists many famous guests such as Johann Sebastian Bach, Franz Liszt, Richard Wagner, and Lilly Palmer. The lobby has a modern-hotel-look with gray marble floor, black leather sofas, and black accent tables. There are three restaurants—my favorite is the "Elephantenkeller," a pub-like restaurant (serving regional specialties) located on the lower level. On weekends there is live music played by students from Weimar's music school. A curved stairway with polished brass handrails leads to the floors above. The guest rooms have been completely renovated and now all have private bathrooms, minibars and television. Instead of an old world ambiance, the mood is modern and sophisticated. Room 308, decorated in rich tones of deep blues and wines, is very pleasant in a masculine sort of way.

HOTEL ELEPHANT
Manager: Dr Soller
Markt 19
99423 Weimar, Germany
tel: (03643) 61.471, fax: (03643) 65.310
116 rooms, Double: 230-400 DM
(rate quoted without breakfast)
Open all year
Credit cards: all major
Restaurant-open daily
22 km E of Erfurt, in city center

If you cannot secure a room at the Elephant Hotel (where space is often unavailable), the Hilton is certainly a good alternate choice for a place to stay in the lovely town of Weimar. Hiltons are a far cry from the small, intimate hotels we usually recommend, but the one in Weimar, although large and commercial, is very pleasant and not a concrete high-rise. The six-story hotel has a lovely setting overlooking Weimar's beautiful Goethe Park. The entry is glass enclosed, like a green house, creating a bright cheerful ambiance. A modern brass-railed, double stair-case spirals up from the lobby to the mezzanine where there are two restaurants, the "Esplande" serving international cuisine and the "Trattoria Esplanade" with Italian specialties. On the same floor as the restaurants is a superb health club that features a stunning indoor pool—completely tiled in white with a domed sky-light above. The guest rooms (60 designated non-smoking) are all similar in decor: modern built in furniture, top notch mattresses, good lighting, pastel color scheme, mini-bars, international TV stations, and of course, tiled bathrooms. The location of the Hilton is not as perfect as that of the Elephant, however, it is only a 20-minute walk along the lovely tree-lined paths of Goethe Park to the center of town.

WEIMAR HILTON
Manager: Alfons J. Walsch
Belvederer Allee 25
99425 Weimar, Germany
tel: (03643) 72.20, fax: (03643) 72.27.41
294 rooms, Double: 260-310 DM
(weekend specials from 219 DM)
Open all year
Credit cards: all major
Restaurant-open daily
25 km E of Erfurt, 260 km SW of Berlin
USA Rep: Hilton 800-445-8667

Although built in 1993, the Hotel Schwartze has a traditional ambiance. Its exterior is reminiscent of a simple country home—very pretty, very appealing. The simple, two-story hotel is painted a crisp white and has arched windows enhanced by boxes of colorful red geraniums. A traditional red-tiled roof accented by gabled windows completes the picture. Inside everything is new and sparkling fresh and clean. There is no antique decor, but for a relatively inexpensive place to stay, the accommodations are an excellent value. You enter into a reception-lobby with white marble floor. A doorway on the left leads to the cheerful breakfast room where a bountiful buffet is served each morning. Attractive water colors decorate the white walls of the staircase that leads up to the bedrooms, which although small, are sweet and attractive and have colored television and modern white-tiled bathrooms. It is fun to stay in the center of the old town of Weimar, but the Hotel Schwartze is certainly a most acceptable option if the Hotel Elephant is over your budget or booked to capacity. It is only about a 15-minute drive into the heart of the city, where you can park your car and delve into sightseeing. Note: The Hotel Schwartze is very easy to find. Take the Weimar exit from expressway 6, and in less than half a kilometer, you will see the hotel on your left. It is not actually on the main road into Weimar, but if you are looking closely, you can see it.

HOTEL SCHWARTZE
Owner: Gerhard Schwartze
99428 Gelmeroda bei Weimar, Germany
tel: (03643) 59.950
30 rooms, Double: 160 DM
Open all year
Credit cards: all major
No restaurant-breakfast only
Just off freeway exit, 6 km S of Weimar

The Schloss Weitenburg, dating back to the 11th Century, is superbly positioned in the rolling wooded hills south of Stuttgart. The castle has been in the von Rassler family since 1720, and the present Baron of Rassler still lives in a wing that encloses one side of the entry courtyard. Once within the castle, you are thrust back to days-gone-by: small windows looking out through four-foot-thick walls, massive stone floors, beamed ceilings, hunting trophies, and ancestors watching your every move from portraits on the walls. The dining room was in olden days the kitchen as evidenced by the enormous metal flue in the ceiling where the smoke from the stove escaped. The bedrooms are scattered throughout the maze of hallways. Some are quite mediocre in decor with modern furnishings, but others have a marvelous antique flair. I especially like number 4, a paneled corner room with antique furniture and an exquisite panorama of rolling forest and the meandering Neckar River. Another favorite, number 7, is a bright and cheerful room overlooking the front courtyard. For exercise, an old-fashioned enclosed swimming pool is just over a covered foot-bridge from the castle. Note: Weitenburg is not on most maps, but is easy to find. Driving south from Stuttgart on expressway 81, take the Rottenburg exit. Turn right to Ergenzingen and follow the white Schloss Weitenburg signs that will guide you back over the highway to the castle.

HOTEL SCHLOSS WEITENBURG
Owner: Freiherr von Rassler
72181 Weitenburg, Germany
tel: (07457) 80.51, fax: (07457) 80.54
34 rooms, Double: 190-265 DM
Closed Dec 20-24
Credit cards: all major
Restaurant-open daily
40 km S of Stuttgart
Gast im Schloss

Wirsberg is a village just off the autobahn north of Bayreuth. The Romantik Posthotel, found on the village's main square, was once a posting station. Although part of the hotel appears modern, the reception area and hallway are set under heavy beams and there is a cozy little room tucked back into a corner with leaded glass windows where breakfast is served. For lunch or evening meals the hotel's "Patrizier salon" is an elegantly set restaurant, while the "Jagerstube" affords an environment for a more casual rendezvous, beer or supper. For overnight guests, the Herrmann family's wish is to see to all their comforts and create an atmosphere that will tempt them to linger: "Gastlichkeitmit Herz," "hospitality with heart." The bedrooms range in decor from comfortable modern to an attractive traditional, but all are with private bath, superb in facilities and comfort. Also available to hotel guests is the use of a pool styled after a Roman bath, sauna, fitness room, solarium and massage. Werner and Herta Herrmann are the fifth generation of the Herrmann family to offer a warm welcome to guests at the Romantik Posthotel.

ROMANTIK POSTHOTEL
Owner: Herta & Werner Herrmann
Marktplatz 11
95339 Wirsberg, Germany
tel: (09227) 20.80, fax: (09227) 58.60
42 rooms, Double: 188-298 DM
6 suites: 240-550 DM
Open all year
Credit cards: all major
Restaurant-open daily, pool
250 km N of Munich, 21 km N of Bayreuth
USA Rep: Euro-Connection 800-645-3876

Hotel Descriptions

It is difficult to pinpoint the best feature of the Gasthof Hecht because one must choose between its country charm, wonderfully gracious, friendly hosts, and extremely reasonable rates. The 300-year-old gasthof is located on the picturesque main street and square of Wolfach where its half-timbered facade, overflowing with vari-colored geraniums, has long been a welcome sight for travelers. The ground floor contains two atmospheric dining rooms with pewter and pottery collections, beamed ceilings, wood paneled walls and fresh flower bouquets. A friendly neighborhood gathering was in progress when we arrived, adding to the convivial ambiance. Leave your diet at home, as traditional, home-style meals are served here including pork and veal dishes, plenty of vegetables and mouthwatering tortes for dessert. On our last visit, process was underway to redo all of the guest rooms. The furnishings will be improved and worn carpeting replaced (some of the rooms will be closed during this process). Even when the renovation is complete, the Hasthof Hecht will remain a simple hotel, not for those seeking sleek perfection, but a great choice for those seeking an inexpensive place to stay with heart. A guest at the Gasthof Hecht truly has the feeling of visiting a private home rather than a hotel.

GASTHOF HECHT
Owner: Family Sattler
Hauptstrasse 51
77709 Wolfach, Germany
tel: (07834) 538, fax: (07834) 47.223
17 rooms, Double: from 85 DM
Closed January 8 to February 8
Restaurant-closed Mondays & Tuesdays
Credit cards: all major
40 km NE of Freiburg

A picturesque drive past green meadows and flower bedecked chalets leads to the Gasthof Hirschen, located about 6 kilometers beyond Oberwolfach in the tiny hamlet of Oberwolfach-Walke. Colorful geraniums adorn the Hirschen's many window boxes, and a small stream flows by across the street. This inn is one of the oldest in the Black Forest, dating from 1609. Its dining room is filled with antique items, fresh flowers and waitresses wearing traditional dirndls. The menu is enticing, offering a delicious variety of local dishes. Follow the Oriental rug runners up the old staircase to a small lobby area that displays an antique clock and a cabinet filled with antique dolls. There are 17 guest rooms in the main building, all with private bathes. These bedrooms are not overly large, but are pleasantly furnished and very clean. Additional rooms and suites are available in a new wing. These rooms, many with balconies overlooking the garden, are freshly modern in decor. Sunny days are enjoyed on the flower filled terrace or in the tranquil garden, the only audible sound the birds in surrounding trees. In winter cross country skiing is a popular sport in this region of forests and rolling hills. The quiet rural location and warm welcome of the Junghanns family, make it easy to see why the Gasthof Hirschen is a popular country inn for travelers "in the know."

GASTHOF HIRSCHEN
Owner: Family Junghanns
Schwarzwaldstrasse 2
77709 Oberwolfach-Walke, Germany
tel: (07834) 366, fax: (07834) 67.75
42 rooms, 15 suites; Double: 104-150 DM
Closed January
Credit cards: all major
Restaurant-open daily for guests
5 km N of Wolfach
40 km NE of Freiburg

Germany is chock full of appealing walled villages: many are well-known tourist destinations; others, like the ever-so-tiny village of Wolframs-Eschenbach (in the "Romantic Road" region, are tucked away off the beaten path, seldom discovered by the tourist. There are only two entrances to this medieval jewel, both through old watchtowers. The village's perimeter is formed by old stone walls, and the main street is lined with colorful half-timbered houses. One of the prettiest of these houses is the Gasthof Alte Vogtei, which was welcoming guests 100 years before Christopher Columbus discovered America. Its picturesque facade features an intricate pattern of timbered wood, white stucco, green shutters and bountiful geraniums spilling from the window boxes. The main claim to fame of this small hotel is its restaurant, attracting guests from near and far. There are several intimate dining rooms, each brimming with antique charm. The food is excellent and reasonably price. Upstairs in the old section of the inn is the best room, the "Bridal Suite" with pretty painted furniture and a canopy bed. A corridor leads to the newer section of the hotel where the bedrooms are more "motel-like" and less charming. If the bridal suite is not available, ask for number 30–a large room decorated in a pleasant, contemporary style.

ALTE VOGTEI
Owners: Monika & Georg Dörr
Hauptstrasse 21
91639 Wolframs-Eschenbach, Germany
tel: (09875) 270, fax: (09875) 705
18 rooms, 1 suite, Double: 98-110 DM
Open all year except Christmas
Credit cards: EC, MC, VS
Restaurant-closed Mondays
177 km NW of Munich, 48 km SW of Nürnberg
16 km SE of Ansbach

Key Map of Germany

Map 1

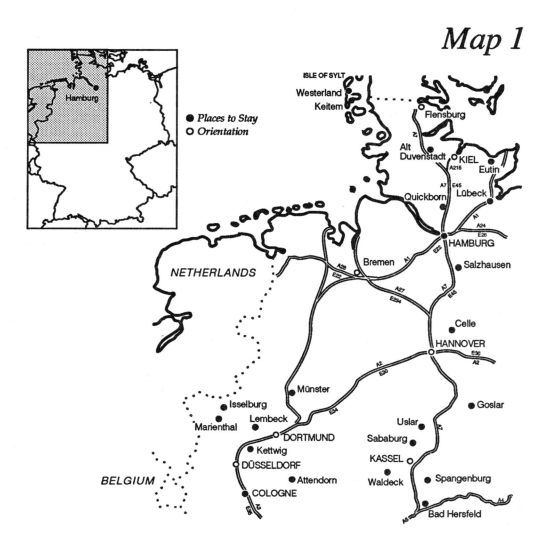

ISLE OF SYLT
Westerland
Keitem

Flensburg

Alt Duvenstadt

KIEL

Eutin

Lübeck

Quickborn

HAMBURG

Salzhausen

Bremen

NETHERLANDS

Celle

HANNOVER

Münster

Goslar

Isselburg

Uslar

Lembeck

DORTMUND

Sababurg

Marienthal

Kettwig

KASSEL

DÜSSELDORF

Attendorn

Waldeck

Spangenburg

BELGIUM

COLOGNE

Bad Hersfeld

● Places to Stay
○ Orientation

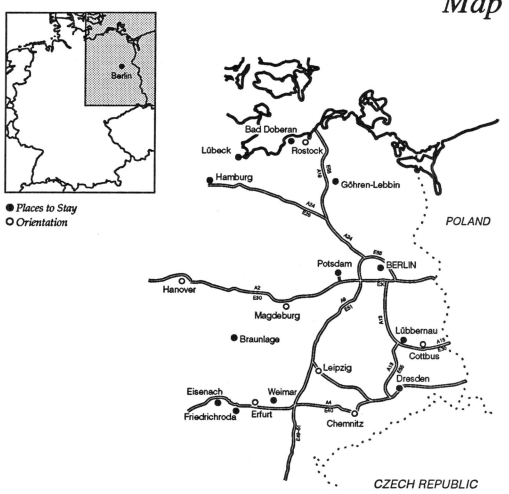

Map 2

Map 3

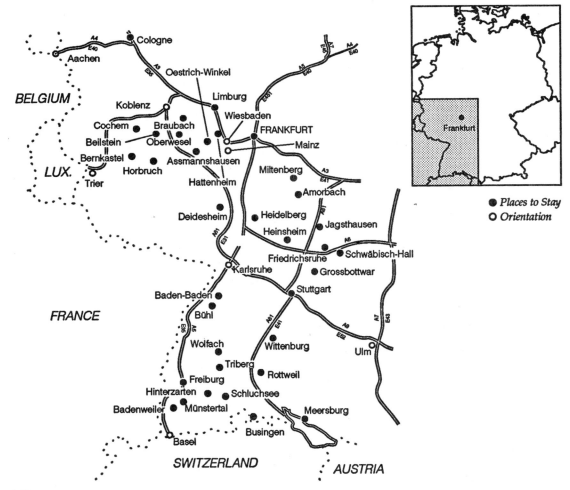

BELGIUM

LUX.

FRANCE

SWITZERLAND

AUSTRIA

Cologne
Aachen
Oestrich-Winkel
Limburg
Koblenz
Wiesbaden
Cochem
Braubach
FRANKFURT
Beilstein
Oberwesel
Mainz
Bernkastel
Assmannshausen
Horbruch
Miltenberg
Trier
Hattenheim
Amorbach
Deidesheim
Heidelberg
Jagsthausen
Heinsheim
Friedrichsruhe
Schwäbisch-Hall
Karlsruhe
Grossbottwar
Baden-Baden
Stuttgart
Bühl
Wolfach
Wittenburg
Ulm
Triberg
Freiburg
Rottweil
Hinterzarten
Schluchsee
Badenweiler
Münstertal
Meersburg
Basel
Busingen

Frankfurt

● *Places to Stay*
○ *Orientation*

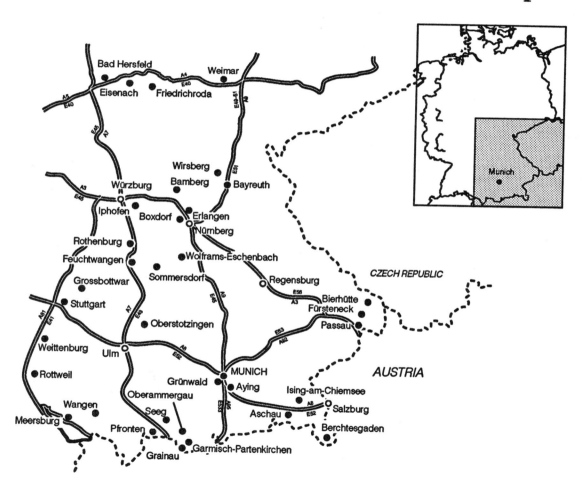

Map 4

Bad Hersfeld
Weimar
Eisenach   Friedrichroda

Wirsberg
Bamberg
Würzburg   Bayreuth
Iphofen
Boxdorf   Erlangen
Nürnberg
Rothenburg
Feuchtwangen   Wolframs-Eschenbach
Grossbottwar   Sommersdorf   Regensburg
Stuttgart   Bierhütte
Fürsteneck
Oberstotzingen
Weittenburg   Passau
Ulm
Rottweil   MUNICH
Grünwald
Aying
Wangen   Oberammergau   Ising-am-Chiemsee
Meersburg   Seeg   Aschau   Salzburg
Pfronten   Berchtesgaden
Grainau   Garmisch-Partenkirchen

CZECH REPUBLIC

AUSTRIA

Munich

RESERVATION REQUEST LETTER IN GERMAN & ENGLISH

HOTEL NAME & ADDRESS—clearly printed or typed

Ich mochte anfragen: I would like to request:

Number of rooms with private bath/shower
Wieviele zimmer mit bad oder douche _____

Number of rooms without private bath/shower
Wieviele zimmer ohne bad oder douche _____

Number of persons in our party
Die anzahl der person unsere groupe _____

Arrival date (spell out month)   Departure date (spell out month)
Wir kommen an _____   *Wir fahren ab* _____

Please let me know as soon as possible the following:
Bitte lassen sie mich bald wie moglich:

Can you reserve the space requested?   Yes   No
Ob sie die angefragten zimmer haben?   Ja _____   Nein _____

Rate per night?
Der preis per nacht? _____

Are meals included in your rate?   Yes   No
Sind die mahlzeit in diesem preis einschliesslich?   Ja _____   Nein _____

Do you need a deposit?   Yes   No
Benotigen sie eine anzahlung?   Ja _____   Nein _____

How much deposit do you need?
Wenn ja, wie hoch? _____

Thanking you in advance, and Best Regards,
In voraus, herzlichen dank, mit Freundlichen Grussen,

YOUR NAME & ADDRESS (and fax number if applicable)—clearly printed or typed

262

Index

Index   267

Index   273

Index

DISCOVERIES FROM OUR READERS

If you have a favorite hideaway that you would be willing to share with other readers, we would love to hear from you. The type of accommodations we feature are those with old-world ambiance, special charm, historical interest, attractive setting, and, above all, warmth of welcome. Please send the following information:

Your name, address, and telephone number.

Name, address, and telephone number of your discovery.

Rate for a double room including tax, service, and breakfast

Brochure or picture (we cannot return material).

Permission to use an edited version of your description.

Would you want your name, city, and state included in the book?

Please send information to:

KAREN BROWN'S GUIDES
Post Office Box 70, San Mateo, CA 94401, USA
Telephone: (415) 342-9117 Fax: (415) 342-9153

Karen Brown's Country Inn Guides

The Most Reliable & Informative Series on Country Inns

Detailed itineraries guide you through the countryside. Every recommendation, from the most deluxe hotel to a simple B&B, is personally inspected, approved and chosen for its romantic ambiance and warmth of welcome. Our charming accommodations reflect every price range, from budget hideaways to the most luxurious palaces.

KAREN BROWN'S
IRISH
Country Inns & Itineraries
UPDATED AND REVISED

KAREN BROWN'S
SWISS
Country Inns & Itineraries
D AND REVISED • FOURTH

KAREN BROWN'S
ITALIAN
Country Inns & Itineraries

KAREN BROWN'S
FRENCH
Country Bed & Breakfasts

KAREN BROWN'S
ENGLISH
Country Bed & Breakfasts
VISED • FIFTH EDITION

KAREN BROWN'S
FRENCH
Country Inns & Itineraries
• THIRD ED

KAREN BROWN'S
GERMAN
Country Inns & Itineraries
D AND REVISED

KAREN BROWN'S
ITALIAN
Country Bed & Breakfasts

KAREN BROWN'S
CALIFORNIA
Country Inns & Itineraries
UPDATED AND REVISED • THIRD EDITION
Charming Places to Stay & Easy to Follow Itineraries

KAREN BROWN'S
SPANISH
Country Inns & Itineraries
UPDATED AND REVISED • FOURTH EDITION
Charming Places to Stay & Easy to Follow Itineraries

KAREN BROWN'S
English, Welsh & Scottish
Country Hotels & Itineraries
UPDATED AND REVISED • SEVENTH EDITION
Charming Places to Stay & Easy to Follow Itineraries

Order Form for Shipments within the U.S.A.

Please ask in your local bookstore for KAREN BROWN'S GUIDES. If the books you want are unavailable, you may order directly from the publisher.

California Country Inns & Itineraries $14.95

English Country Bed & Breakfasts $13.95

English, Welsh & Scottish Country Hotels & Itineraries $14.95

French Country Bed & Breakfasts $13.95

French Country Inns & Itineraries $14.95

German Country Inns & Itineraries $14.95

Irish Country Inns & Itineraries $14.95

Italian Country Bed & Breakfasts $14.95

Italian Country Inns & Itineraries $14.95

Portuguese Country Inns & Pousadas (1990 edition) $6.00

Spanish Country Inns & Itineraries $14.95

Swiss Country Inns & Itineraries $14.95

Name _____ Street _____

City _____ State ____ Zip _____ Tel: _____

Credit Card (MasterCard or Visa) _____ Exp: _____

Add $3.50 for the first book and .50 cents for each additional book for postage & packing. California residents add 8.25% sales tax. *Order form only for shipments within the U.S.A.* Indicate number of copies of each title; send form with check or credit card information to:

KAREN BROWN'S GUIDES
Post Office Box 70, San Mateo, California, 94401, U.S.A.
Tel: (415) 342-9117   Fax: (415) 342-9153

KAREN BROWN wrote her first travel guide, *French Country Inns & Chateaux*, in 1979, now in its seventh edition. Thirteen other books have been added to the series which has become known as the most personalized, reliable reference library for the discriminating traveller. Although Karen's staff has expanded, she is still involved in the publication of her guide books. Karen, her husband, Rick, their daughter, Alexandra, and son, Richard, live on the coast south of San Francisco at their own country inn, Seal Cove Inn, in Moss Beach.

CLARE BROWN, CTC, has many years experience in the travel field, dating back to 1969 when she began her career as a travel consultant, where her specialty was planning countryside itineraries to Europe using charming small hotels. The focus of her job remains unchanged, but now her expertise is available to a larger audience— the readers of her daughter Karen's Country Inn Guides. Clare lives in the San Francisco Bay area with her husband, Bill.

JUNE BROWN, CTC, born in Sheffield, England, has an extensive background in travel, dating back to her school-girl days when she "youth hosteled" throughout Europe. When June moved to California, she worked as a travel consultant for several years before joining her friend Karen to research, write, and produce travel guides. June lives San Mateo with her husband, Tony, their son, Simon, and daughter, Clare.

BARBARA TAPP, the talented artist responsible for all of the hotel sketches and delightful illustrations in this guide, was raised in Australia where she studied in Sydney at the School of Interior Design. Although Barbara continues with freelance projects, she devotes much of her time to illustrating the Karen Brown guides. Barbara lives in the San Francisco Bay area with her husband, Richard, their two sons, Jonothan, Alexander, and daughter, Georgia.

JANN POLLARD, the artist responsible for the beautiful painting on the cover of this guide, has studied art since childhood, and is well-known for her outstanding impressionistic-style water colors which she has exhibited in numerous juried shows, winning many awards. Jann travels frequently to Europe (using Karen Brown's guides) where she loves to paint historical buildings. Jann lives in the San Francisco Bay area with her husband, Gene, and their two daughters.

SEAL COVE INN—LOCATED IN THE SAN FRANCISCO AREA

Karen Brown Herbert (best known as author of the Karen Brown's Guides) and her husband, Rick, have put seventeen years of experience into reality and opened their own superb hideaway, Seal Cove Inn. Spectacularly set amongst wild flowers and bordered by towering cypress trees, Seal Cove Inn looks out to the ocean over acres of county park: an oasis where you can enjoy secluded beaches, explore tide-pools, watch frolicking seals, and follow the tree-lined path that traces the windswept ocean bluffs. Country antiques, original-watercolors, flower-laden cradles, rich fabrics, and the gentle ticking of grandfather clocks create the perfect ambiance for a foggy day in front of the crackling log fire. Each bedroom is its own haven with a cozy sitting area before a wood-burning fireplace and doors opening onto a private balcony or patio with views to the distant ocean. Moss Beach is a 35-minute drive south of San Francisco, 6 miles north of the picturesque town of Half Moon Bay, and a few minutes from Princeton harbor with its colorful fishing boats and restaurants. Seal Cove Inn makes a perfect base for whale-watching, salmon-fishing excursions, day trips to San Francisco, exploring the coast, or, best of all, just a romantic interlude by the sea, time to relax and be pampered. Karen and Rick look forward to the pleasure of welcoming you to their hide-away by the sea.

Seal Cove Inn, 221 Cypress Avenue, Moss Beach, California, 94038, U.S.A.
telephone: (415) 728-7325   fax: (415) 728-4116